Medieval
Clothing and Textiles

Volume 2

Medieval
Clothing and Textiles

ISSN 1744-5787

Medieval
Clothing and Textiles

Volume 2

edited by

ROBIN NETHERTON

GALE R. OWEN-CROCKER

THE BOYDELL PRESS

First published 2006
The Boydell Press, Woodbridge

ISBN 1 84383 203 8

The Boydell Press is an imprint of Boydell & Brewer Ltd
PO Box 9, Woodbridge, Suffolk IP12 3DF, UK
and of Boydell & Brewer Inc.
668 Mt Hope Avenue, Rochester, NY 14620, USA
website: www.boydellandbrewer.com

A CIP catalogue record for this book is available
from the British Library

This publication is printed on acid-free paper
Typeset by Frances Hackeson Freelance Publishing Services, Brinscall, Lancs
Printed in Great Britain by
Cromwell Press, Trowbridge, Wiltshire

Contents

Illustrations

Tables

Contributors

ROBIN NETHERTON (Editor) is a costume historian specializing in Western European clothing in the twelfth through fifteenth centuries. Since 1982, she has given lectures and workshops on practical aspects of medieval costume and on costume as an approach to social history, art history, and literature. A journalist by training, she also works as a professional editor.

GALE R. OWEN-CROCKER (Editor) is Reader in Anglo-Saxon Culture at the University of Manchester and Deputy Director of the Manchester Centre for Anglo-Saxon Studies. Her most recent books are *The Four Funerals in Beowulf* (2000), *Dress in Anglo-Saxon England: Revised and Enlarged Edition* (2004), and *King Harold II and the Bayeux Tapestry* (2005).

SHARON FARMER is Professor of History at the University of California, Santa Barbara. She is currently at work on a book titled *From Saracen Work to Oeuvre de Paris: Oriental Goods, Parisian Crafts, and the Making of Europe's Fashion Capital (1250–1350)*, for which she has received 2005–2006 fellowships from the National Endowment for the Humanities and the Guggenheim Foundation.

MARGARET ROSE JASTER is Associate Professor of Humanities and English at the Pennsylvania State University at Harrisburg. She has published essays on clothing and conduct in early modern English society, the relations between the English and the Irish in early modern England, and Shakespeare in popular culture.

DREA LEED is a costume historian focusing on the clothing and textile trades of the fifteenth through seventeenth centuries. She has given lectures and published works on such topics as masque costume, dress in Flemish genre art, and the tailoring trade in Elizabethan England. Her current projects include transcribing Elizabeth I's wardrobe accounts and experimenting with Renaissance dyeing techniques.

DANIELLE NUNN-WEINBERG earned her master's degree in Art History from the University of St. Thomas in St. Paul, Minnesota, and is working on her doctorate at the University of Manchester. Her research interests include sixteenth-century material culture, particularly the areas of clothing and textiles.

TAWNY SHERRILL is a lecturer in costume history and the coordinator of the Costume and Textiles Collections Management Program at California State University, Long Beach. Her particular area of interest is sixteenth-century Italian women's dress. Her current research focuses on the career of Cesare Vecellio.

NIAMH WHITFIELD has a background in both archaeology and art history. She received her initial training in Dublin, including a master's degree at University College, Dublin, and went on to complete a master's degree at the Courtauld Institute of Art and a doctorate at University College, London. She teaches part-time at Morley College, London. She specializes in early medieval metalwork, particularly from Ireland.

MONICA L. WRIGHT is Assistant Professor of French at Middle Tennessee State University. Her research focuses on the narrative use of clothing in Old French romance, and she is especially interested in the interrelation of romance composition and textiles. She has published articles on clothing in twelfth-century romance and is currently preparing a monograph on the topic.

Preface

Since the launch of *Medieval Clothing and Textiles* in May 2005 at the International Congress on Medieval Studies at Kalamazoo, response to the journal has been uniformly enthusiastic, as measured by sales figures, reader feedback, and interest from potential authors. We are gratified at this warm reception, which confirms that the journal is fulfilling a distinct need in the growing field of medieval textile and clothing study.

Volume 2 maintains *MC&T*'s emphasis on an international, interdisciplinary approach. The papers range chronologically from the seventh to the seventeenth centuries. Their geographic scope includes England, France, Germany, Ireland, and Italy. They consider evidence of texts in the vernacular languages of all these countries and in Latin, as well as art and artifacts. Subjects include cloth production in the commercial, artistic, and metaphorical senses; fashionable garments and accessories as diverse as Renaissance furs, Hiberno-Viking jewelry, and Elizabethan jackets; the financial implications of extravagant dress; and the practical matter of keeping clothing clean.

The editors are grateful to the members of the editorial board for their prompt and scholarly advice, and to the many other anonymous referees whose generous contributions of time and knowledge are essential to a peer-reviewed journal such as this. Their enthusiastic response to unexpected queries and their wholehearted pursuit of solutions to other people's research problems is greatly appreciated. It has also been encouraging to find contributors to the first volume willingly giving references and advice to contributors to the second. Their interaction has demonstrated the presence of a productive network of truly dedicated scholars.

The editors welcome submissions for future volumes from both experienced scholars and new writers. Potential contributors should initially send a 300-word synopsis to Gale Owen-Crocker at groc@manchester.ac.uk. Submissions should be in English and must conform to *MC&T*'s guidelines for authors, available from Robin Netherton at robin@netherton.net. All papers will be peer-reviewed and subject to editing.

Papers read at sessions sponsored by DISTAFF (Discussion, Interpretation, and Study of Textile Arts, Fabrics, and Fashion) at the medieval congresses at Kalamazoo, Michigan, and Leeds, England, are automatically considered for publication. Scholars interested in reading a 20-minute paper at one of these sessions should contact Robin Netherton (for the Kalamazoo congress) or Gale Owen-Crocker (for the Leeds congress). Scholars presenting papers on medieval dress and textile topics in other sessions at these conferences, or in other academic venues, are most welcome to contact us to discuss publication possibilities.

Dress and Accessories in the Early Irish Tale "The Wooing Of Becfhola"

Niamh Whitfield

Ireland possesses one of the most extensive vernacular literatures in Europe, some stories going back at least to the seventh century. Heroic tales, especially, contain many descriptions of the dress and equipment of their aristocratic protagonists. The question of how seriously these should be taken as accurate depictions of ancient artefacts has been discussed by J. P. Mallory, in a study of the Ulster Cycle of Tales.[1] The stories in this cycle purport to describe a distant past, and it has been famously claimed that they provide a "window on the Iron Age."[2] However, when the objects described in the sagas are compared with actual items which survive from the Irish Iron Age, they do not make a good fit. On the other hand, they often match finds dating to the early Middle Ages, either to the period immediately preceding the Viking settlement (sixth to ninth centuries) or to time when the Viking taste for silver strongly affected the Irish (mid-ninth to mid-tenth centuries). Mallory concluded that the material culture employed to flesh out the stories was more or less contemporary with the language in which the text was composed, rather than with the period in which the drama purports to take place.

In addition to those who are acknowledged elsewhere in this paper, I am grateful for generous help from the following: Breandán Ó Cíobháin, Edel Bhreathnach, Anne Connon, Barbara Hillers, Cormac Bourke, Dáibhí Ó Cróinín, Paul Mullarkey, and Raghnall Ó Floinn. I also thank the staff of the libraries of the Royal Irish Academy and of the Society of Antiquaries of London for producing many texts at short notice. Finally I thank Siobhán Cuffe and David Bennett for the skill and patience with which they drew the accompanying illustrations. A spoken version of this paper was presented in May 2004 at the International Congress on Medieval Studies at Kalamazoo, Michigan. I am grateful to the British Academy for funding my travel there. An article on the wider context of "The Wooing of Becfhola," provisionally titled "Finery in Fact and Fiction," will appear in a future volume of *Peritia: Journal of the Medieval Academy of Ireland.*

1 J. P. Mallory, "Silver in the Ulster Cycle of Tales," in *Proceedings of the Seventh International Congress of Celtic Studies held at Oxford from 10th to 15th July, 1983*, ed. D. Ellis Evans, John G. Griffith, and E. M. Jope (Oxford: D. Ellis Evans, distributed by Oxbow Books, 1986), 31–65.

2 Kenneth Hurlstone Jackson, *The Oldest Irish Tradition: A Window on the Iron Age*, Rede Lecture (Cambridge: Cambridge University Press, 1964).

This paper examines references to clothing and accessories in a tale from the Cycle of the Kings, "The Wooing of Becfhola" (*Tochmarc Becfhola*), with a view to seeing if Mallory's findings hold good in this instance. Two versions are each found in two different manuscripts; both versions have been edited and translated by Máire Bhreathnach.[3] Only the earlier version contains detailed description of aristocratic dress. The most accurate and consistent text of this version is found in the fourteenth-century *Yellow Book of Lecan*. It is composed in early Middle Irish, dated on linguistic grounds to before the year 1000, though the tale may have originated in the late ninth or early tenth century.[4]

It will be suggested that the bulk of the objects mentioned fit best into the native Irish tradition of the late seventh to ninth centuries or, alternatively, into the Hiberno-Viking tradition of the mid-ninth to tenth centuries. There was a strong Viking presence in Ireland at this time, so some Hiberno-Viking influence on the text is not surprising.

"The Wooing of Becfhola" purportedly describes events which took place in the kingdom of Brega in the reign of Díarmait mac Áeda Sláine, king of Tara from 642 to 664.[5] The saga tells how he married a fictitious character, a beautiful stranger who soon became bored with him and sought fulfilment with first one and then another younger man.

The early medieval Irish imagined Sovereignty as a goddess whom the king must wed to ensure the fertility of the land and the prosperity of his people. This marriage was symbolically enacted in inauguration rituals[6] and is a common motif in sagas, where the figure of Sovereignty appears as a woman who enters the everyday world and plays a role in the plot. The beautiful stranger in "The Wooing of Becfhola" probably represents Sovereignty, but in her malign, rather than benevolent, personification.[7]

The tale begins when Díarmait is travelling to the ford at Trim (*Áth Truim*) accompanied by only one attendant and his foster-son Crimthann, also a historically attested figure.[8] The group encounters a magnificently dressed woman crossing the ford in a chariot. She has all the trappings of Sovereignty, and tells Díarmait that she is seeking seed wheat for her good arable land, a remark he appears to interpret as a reference to the need for a legitimate king to mate with Sovereignty to ensure the fertility of the land in his kingdom. He immediately offers his hand and she accepts, but demands the bride-price, whereupon he gives her his "little brooch" (*delg bec*). They return to Tara where everyone is curious about the stranger. Since Díarmait has to admit that he does not know her name and that the bride-price was just his small

---

3 Máire Bhreathnach, "A New Edition of *Tochmarc Becfhola*," *Ériu* 35 (1984): 59–91.
4 Ibid., 70.
5 Ibid., 60–61.
6 Francis John Byrne, *Irish Kings and High-Kings* (London: B. T. Batsford, 1973), 16–22.
7 Anne Connon, "Prosopography II: A Prosopography of the Early Queens of Tara, Fourth to Seventh Centuries," in *The Kingship and Landscape of Tara*, ed. Edel Bhreathnach (Dublin: The Discovery Programme, forthcoming).
8 M. Bhreathnach, "*Tochmarc Becfhola*," 61.

brooch, the druid names her "Becfhola," meaning "small worth." True to her name, Becfhola next tries to seduce Díarmait's foster-son, Crimthann. She lies to her husband about her need to retrieve various items from her wardrobe, which she claims to have left behind on her travels, and arranges a tryst with Crimthann. He is persuaded by his relatives not to go, but meanwhile Becfhola sets off. En route she spies another young warrior, Flann, who, like Becfhola herself, appears to be fictitious.[9] He resists her advances, saying he cannot woo her until he has succeeded in securing an island to which his cousins are also laying claim. A year later, when Flann has won the island, he arrives at Tara to take Becfhola away. Díarmait renounces his claim on her and lets her go.

In order to interpret the evidence concerning clothing and accessories in such a tale, one needs to check the descriptions of the various items against the archaeological record. Some confirmation may also be obtained from the Old Irish laws, many of which originated in the seventh or eighth century and are thus a very reliable source.[10] But there are many pitfalls to avoid. An obvious problem with any text of this sort is that the surviving versions are not necessarily the earliest which existed. Moreover, given the late date of the manuscripts in which the various versions of the tale are recorded, the text may have passed through several hands, leaving us, as David Greene said, "at the mercy of scribes who might be careless, or given to archaisms, or to wholesale re-editing of their material."[11] It is also important to recognise that a story is, by its very nature, a work of the imagination. Descriptions follow established formulae, the splendour of the protagonists may be exaggerated, and literary models may have provided inspiration. Furthermore, the text cannot be studied solely in translation, and a proper understanding of the language of the original text is essential. This is because the linguists who make the published translations generally lack specialist knowledge of ancient artefacts. Some modifications to Máire Bhreathnach's translation will therefore be suggested.

We will first consider the description of Becfhola's finery (fig. 1.1, left) and then move on to that of the young hero, Flann (fig. 1.1, right). Early Irish society was extremely hierarchical, and the set-piece descriptions of Becfhola and Flann are designed to show that they are individuals of the highest rank. In the first version of "The Wooing of Becfhola," the beauty of the lovers is conveyed solely by reference to their dress and equipment. Both are introduced like actors dressed for the part. Their clothing, jewellery, and equipment act as lavish stage props, which convey a clear message about their wealth and status. These props are drawn from a standard repertory, and recur in many early medieval Irish tales.

9 Ibid., 61–62.

10 Fergus Kelly, *A Guide to Early Irish Law*, Early Irish Law Series 3 (Dublin: Dublin Institute for Advanced Studies, 1988); Colmán Etchingham and Catherine Swift, "English and Pictish Terms for Brooch in an 8th-century Irish Law-Text," *Medieval Archaeology* 48 (2004): 31–49.

11 David Greene, "Early Irish Literature," in *Early Irish Society*, ed. Myles Dillon (Dublin: Colm O Lochlann at the Sign of the Three Candles, 1954), 26.

DESCRIPTION OF BECFHOLA

Following is the description of Becfhola, together with Máire Bhreathnach's translation:

> Co n-acatar in mnái darsin n-áth aníar hi carput. Dá máelassa fhindruine impe; dá gem do lic lóghmar eistib; léne fo dergindlaith óir impe; brat corcra lé; delg óir láinegair co mbrechdrad ngem n-illdathach isin brut osa bruinne; munci di ór forlosce ima brágait; mind n-óir fora cind; dá each dubglasa fona carput; dá n-all óir friu; cungi co túagmílaib argdidib foraib.[12]

> [They beheld a woman coming from the west across the ford in a chariot. She wore rounded sandals of white bronze, inset with two jewels of precious stone; a tunic

Fig. 1.1: Speculative reconstructions of the appearance of Becfhola and Flann. Drawing: Siobhán Cuffe, by permission.

12 M. Bhreathnach, *"Tochmarc Becfhola,"* 72, §1.

covered with red-gold embroidery about her; a purple cloak on her; a brooch in fully-wrought gold with shimmering gems of many hues fastening the cloak over her breast; necklets of refined gold around her neck; a golden circlet upon her head; two dark-grey horses drew her chariot {harnessed} with a pair of golden bridles, yokes with animal designs worked in silver upon them.][13]

Becfhola (fig. 1.1, left) wears the costume of kings, queens, and nobles in early medieval Ireland. This consisted of a tunic (*léne* or *léine*) probably made of linen,[14] over which was worn a cloak (*brat*) probably made of wool, held in place by a precious brooch, together with shoes and jewellery.[15] Perishable objects such as garments are seldom retrieved intact in excavations, and in Ireland only fragments survive to date,[16] but there is plenty of evidence from sagas, law texts,[17] stone sculpture, and illuminated manuscripts to show that the *léine* and *brat* existed. Metal and leather are more durable, and a number of items described in the tale may be compared with surviving artefacts.

Becfhola's shoes

Becfhola wears *dá máelassa fhindruine*, two "rounded sandals of white bronze" in Máire Bhreathnach's translation, which are inset with *dá gem do lic lóghmar*, "two jewels of precious stone."

Various points arise from this translation. The word *máelassa* is open to different interpretations. *Assa* is the element which means sandals or slippers.[18] Máire

---

13 Ibid., 77, §1.

14 This is the implication of the written sources. Flax seeds are well represented in the archaeobotanical samples from excavations. Cellulose vegetable fibres do not survive well in Ireland, but occasional pieces of vegetable fibre cloth, most probably linen, have been recovered through excavation. Fergus Kelly, *Early Irish Farming: A Study Based Mainly on the Law-texts of the 7th and 8th Centuries AD* (Dublin: Dublin Institute for Advanced Studies, 1997), 269; Elizabeth Wincott Heckett, "Textiles, Cordage, Basketry, and Raw Fibre," in *Late Viking Age and Medieval Waterford: Excavations 1986–1992*, ed. Maurice F. Hurley, Orla M. B. Scully, and Sarah W. J. McCutcheon (Waterford, Ireland: Waterford Corp.), 753–54.

15 For previous discussions of early medieval Irish dress, see the following: Barbara L. Hillers, "Topos in Early Irish Literature" (M.Phil. thesis, University College Dublin, October 1989), 21–35; Mairead Dunlevy, *Dress in Ireland: A History* (Cork: Collins Press, 1989), 17–22; M. A. FitzGerald, "Insular Dress in Early Medieval Ireland," in *Anglo-Saxon Texts and Contexts*, ed. Gale. R. Owen-Crocker, *Bulletin of the John Rylands University Library of Manchester* 79, no. 3 (Autumn 1997): 251–61; Maggie McEnchroe Williams, "Dressing the Part: the Depiction of Noble Costume in Irish High Crosses," in *Encountering Medieval Textiles and Dress: Objects, Texts, Images*, ed. Désirée G. Koslin and Janet E. Snyder (New York and Basingstoke: Palgrave Macmillan, 2002), 45–63.

16 For the most up-to-date discussion of the archaeological remains of clothing from Ireland, see Elizabeth Wincott Heckett, "The Textiles and a Leather Tablet," in *Deer Park Farms: Excavation of an Early Christian Settlement in Glenarm, Co. Antrim*, as of April 2005 available in draft form online at http://www.ehsni.gov.uk/built/monuments/Chapter15.shtml (accessed April 25, 2005).

17 Kelly, *Early Irish Farming*, 598–89.

18 Royal Irish Academy, *Dictionary of the Irish Language: Compact Edition* (Dublin: Royal Irish Academy, 1913–76; compact edition 1998), "A," 437.14. Henceforth this source will be abbreviated *DIL*.

Bhreathnach's view that they were "rounded" derives from the word *máel*, one of whose meanings is "rounded."[19] "Blunt" conveys the same idea, and "blunt sandals" is another common translation of *máelassa*. However, there are alternative meanings. *Máel* may be used here in its primary sense of "shorn,"[20] which in this context could mean low-cut. Interestingly, archaeology confirms that low-cut shoes were in fashion in Ireland in the Hiberno-Viking period.[21] On the other hand, *máel* can also be translated as "bald,"[22] and our heroine's sandals may have been made of "bald" leather, i.e., leather with the skin side (rather than hair side) facing outward.[23]

However, Becfhola's sandals are said to be of *findruine* (in the nominative), a metal whose nature has been much discussed.[24] Is this a reference to shoes of solid metal, never worn in real life, perhaps inspired by shoe-like relics made of metal like the sixteenth-century brass Shrine of St. Brigid's Shoe,[25] which seems to have had early medieval antecedents?[26] Alternatively, does the phrase refer to leather shoes like the many examples found in waterlogged sites in Ireland,[27] but with the difference that they had decorative straps with metal fastenings or strap-ends (as in figure 1.2) or, alternatively, mounts inset with gems (as in figure 1.1)? And if such fashionable footwear were not worn within Ireland itself, could the fictional examples have been modelled on aristocratic shoes from parts of the world known to the Irish in the early Middle Ages? We can only speculate.

The final piece of information given about Becfhola's shoes is that they are decorated with "two jewels of precious stone" (*dá gem do lic lóghmar*). This is the first of three references in the tale to gems of different types. In this case the word used to describe the jewel, nominative singular *lía*,[28] denotes a precious stone found in nature and not one manufactured by man. Therefore it is unlikely to have been used by the ancient storyteller to refer to one made of a synthetic material, such as glass, often found in early medieval Irish metalwork.

---

19 *DIL* "M," 18.49.

20 Breandán Ó Cíobháin, pers. comm.

21 Quita Mould, Ian Carlisle, and Esther Cameron, *Craft, Industry and Everyday Life: Leather and Leatherworking in Anglo-Scandinavian and Medieval York*, The Archaeology of York: The Small Finds 17/16 (York: Council for British Archaeology for the York Archaeological Trust, 2003), 3281–88.

22 *DIL* "M," 18.23.

23 Máire Herbert, pers. comm.

24 *Findruine* may have referred to tinned bronze; an argument for this translation will appear in Whitfield, "Finery in Fact and Fiction."

25 Raghnall Ó Floinn, *Irish Shrine & Reliquaries* (Dublin: National Museum of Ireland in association with Country House, 1994), photo 27.

26 Cormac Bourke, pers. comm.; Whitley Stokes, ed., *Félire Óengusso Céli Dé: The Martyrology of Oengus the Culdee* (1905; repr., Dublin: Dublin Institute for Advanced Studies, 1984), 112–15.

27 A. T. Lucas, "Footwear in Ireland," *Journal of the County Louth Archaeological Society* 13, no. 4 (1956): 309–94; John Barber, "Some Observations on Early Christian Footwear," *Journal of the Cork Historical and Archaeological Society* 86, no. 244 (1981), 103–6; Daire O'Rourke, "Leather Artefacts," in Hurley, Scully, and McCutcheon, *Late Viking Age and Medieval Waterford*, 702–22.

28 1 *lía*, [precious] stone, *DIL* "L," 143.37–38. I am grateful to Thomas Charles-Edwards for this information.

Fig. 1.2: Reconstruction of dress of seventh-century aristocratic Roman woman and man.
Drawing: David Bennett, after *Museo Nazionale Romano: Crypta Balbi*, ed. Francesca Consoli
(Rome: Electa, per la Soprintendenza Archaeologica di Roma, 2000), 68–69.

Garnet, a natural gemstone common on Anglo-Saxon and other Germanic
jewellery, was barely available to the early medieval Irish and can be discounted.
Crystal is a possibility, but was very rare. To my knowledge, the only other natural
gem found on the jewellery in question is amber. This "stone," which can be picked
up on the shores around the North Sea, ranges in colour from yellow to orange, and
plays a very important role in the decoration of objects dated from c. 700 to the
Hiberno-Viking period. Major pieces profusely decorated with amber include the
late-seventh- to early-eighth-century Hunterston and "Tara" brooches and the ninth-
century Derrynaflan chalice.[29] Moreover, a succession of amber workshops were

29 Susan Youngs, ed. *"The Work of Angels": Masterpieces of Celtic Metalwork, 6th–9th Centuries*
(London: British Museum Publications, 1989), 75, 77, 160–61.

discovered during excavations at Fishamble Street, Dublin, dating to the approximate period of the language of the tale.[30]

Becfhola's tunic

We are not told the colour of Becfhola's tunic (*léne* or *léine*), but *gel*, "bright," is the typical adjective applied to such garments in the sagas, though other colours are occasionally mentioned.[31] We are told, however, that her tunic is decorated with *dergindlaith óir*, "red-gold embroidery" in Máire Bhreathnach's translation. Red gold was the most valuable form of gold,[32] so Becfhola's tunic was evidently very costly.

It is not clear if the term *dergindlaith óir*[33] in fact refers to gold interwoven in the fabric (brocading) or to true embroidery added later. Both techniques were used in the early Middle Ages.

Illustrations suggest that, like the seventh-century Roman tunic illustrated in figure 1.2, the *léine* could be decorated at the neck, the cuffs, and particularly the hem. This suggests that these garments were edged by brocaded woven bands, which may have been tablet-woven. Gold was widely used in tablet weaving throughout the early Middle Ages to create geometric patterns, such as lozenges, rectangles, crosses, zig-zags, and fretwork. Various types of gold thread were used. The most flexible was "spun gold," sometimes referred to as "spirally spun ribbon," which consisted of a thin strip of gold foil wound spirally around a fibre core. This type of gold thread was in use in Europe certainly since Roman times until at least the Middle Ages. Alternatively, flat gold strips were used, for example, on Anglo-Saxon gold bands of the sixth to seventh centuries. A third type of thread, found on Viking bands, consisted simply of gold and silver wires.[34]

Tablet-woven bands brocaded with gold, many used as borders of garments, occur over a wide area. They are often found in Germanic graves from across Europe dating from the fifth to eighth centuries[35] and continued to be used in later centuries,

30 Patrick F. Wallace, "The Economy and Commerce of Viking Age Dublin," in *Der Handel der Karolinger- und Wikingerzeit: Bericht über die Kolloquien der Kommission für die Altertumskunde Mittel- und Nordeuropas in den Jahren 1980 bis 1983*, ed. Klaus Düwel et al., Untersuchungen zu Handel und Verkehr der Vor- und Frühgeschichtlichen Zeit in Mittel- und Nordeuropa 4 (Göttingen/Zürich: Vandenhoech & Ruprecht, 1987), 215–16. I am grateful to Dr. Wallace for giving me a copy of this article and for helpful discussion.

31 Hillers, "Topos," 30. I am grateful to Barbara Hillers for generously allowing me to quote from her unpublished thesis.

32 Mallory, "Silver in the Ulster Cycle," 36. Red gold was probably gold with a relatively high copper content. B. G. Scott, "Goldworking Terms in Early Irish Writings," *Zeitschrift für Celtische Philologie* 38 (1981): 243.

33 3 indled, DIL "I," 233.42–46, 52. The term *dergindlaith* is usually followed (as here) by *óir* (gold) or *órsnath* (gold thread).

34 Elisabeth Crowfoot, "Textiles," in *Object and Economy in Medieval Winchester: Artefacts from Medieval Winchester*, ed. Martin Biddle, Winchester Studies 7.ii (Oxford: Clarendon Press, 1990), 468.

35 Elisabeth Crowfoot and Sonia Chadwick Hawkes, "Early Anglo-Saxon Gold Braids," *Medieval Archaeology* 11 (1967): 42–86; Elisabeth Crowfoot, "Early Anglo-Saxon Gold Braids: Addenda and Corrigenda," *Medieval Archaeology* 13 (1969): 209–10.

particularly fine examples being found in Viking-age graves at Birka, Sweden.[36] There is some archaeological evidence that such bands were known in Ireland. Tablets have been found at a number of sites,[37] and two fragments of woven woollen trims without metal embellishments were found at Lagore.[38] Moreover, silken tablet-woven bands with gold and silver threads, perhaps imports from Germany, have been discovered in Hiberno-Viking contexts in Dublin; some of these were probably used to edge garments.[39]

Alternatively, the gold decoration on Becfhola's tunic may have been stitched. Embroidery is very fragile and disintegrates above and below ground,[40] and none seems to have been recovered from early medieval Ireland to date. However, an embroideress's needle is referred to in the eighth-century law tract "Judgements about Pledge-Interests" (*Bretha im Fuillema Gell*)[41] suggesting that the art of embroidery was widely known.[42] The Old Irish Laws also suggest that this craft was the prerogative of high-ranking women.[43] The description of the heroine of the early Irish tale "The Wooing of Étaín" demonstrates that skill at embroidery was highly valued: "She surpassed all women at embroidery. Her eyes saw nothing that her hands could not embroider."[44] Embroidering was also clearly a lucrative activity; the "Judgements about Pledge-Interests" states that "the woman who embroiders earns more profit even than queens."[45]

---

36 Agnes Geijer, *Birka III: Die Texilfunde aus den Gräbern* (Uppsala: Almqvist and Wiksell, 1938); Agnes Geijer, "The Textile Finds from Birka," in *Cloth and Clothing in Medieval Europe: Essays in Memory of Professor E. M. Carus-*Wilson, ed. N. B. Harte and K. G. Ponting (London: Heinemann Educational Books, 1983), 93–96.

37 Wincott Heckett, "Textiles and a Leather Tablet," 5–7.

38 L. Start, in "Lagore Crannog, an Irish Royal Residence of the 7th to 10th Centuries A.D.," *Proceedings of the Royal Irish Academy* 53C (1950): 214–17.

39 Frances Pritchard, "Silk Braids and Textiles of the Viking Age from Dublin," in *Archaeological Textiles: Report from the 2nd NESAT Symposium 1.–4.V.1984*, ed. Lise Bender Jørgensen, Bente Magnus, and Elizabeth Munksgaard, North European Symposium on Archaeological Textiles (henceforth NESAT) 2 (Copenhagen: Arkaeologisk Institut, Copenhagen University, 1988), 151–56; Wallace, "Economy and Commerce," 219–20.

40 Elizabeth Coatsworth, "Stitches in Time: Establishing a History of Anglo-Saxon Embroidery," *Medieval Clothing and Textiles* 1 (2005): 2.

41 Kelly, *Guide to Early Irish Law*, appendix 1, no. 60, p. 278.

42 Daniel A. Binchy, ed., *Corpus Iuris Hibernici* [henceforth *CIH*], 6 vols. (Dublin: Dublin Institute for Advanced Studies, 1978), 2:464.1; W. Neilson Hancock et al., eds., *Ancient Laws of Ireland* [henceforth *AL*], 6 vols. (Dublin: Commissioners for Publishing the Ancient Laws and Institutes of Ireland, 1865–1901), 5:282.3–4. There, embroidery done with a needle is referred to as *imdénam* (*DIL* "I," 85.9), while the needle itself is called *snaite druinige*. References to embroidery using the related terms *druine, druinech, druinechas* occur in a variety of early sources. Kelly, *Early Irish Farming*, 451, n. 91.

43 Kelly, *Early Irish Farming*, 451.

44 "Ba druiniu cach mnai. Ni faicdis a suili ni nad edais a lama dhi dhruine." Osborn Bergin and R. I. Best, *Tochmarc Étaíne* (Dublin: Royal Irish Academy, 1938), 56–57, §20; Jeffrey Gantz, *Early Irish Myths and Sagas* (London: Penguin Books, 1981), 59.

45 "Air is mo do do thorbu dosli cach ben bes druinech olldaite cid rigna," *CIH*, 2:464.2–3 = *AL* 5:382.3–4; Kelly, *Guide to Early Irish Law*, 78. In these notes, an equals sign indicates the same legal passage as cited both in *CIH* and *AL*.

Luxurious gold embroideries are known from various parts of early medieval Europe.[46] For instance, there are gold-embroidered cuffs on the tunic worn by the lady in grave 49 at Saint-Denis, near Paris (the "Arnegunde" grave), dated to the later sixth or early seventh century.[47] Elaborate embroidery is also found in the late-eighth- to ninth-century Maaseik *casula* (probably "chasuble") of Sts. Harlindis and Relindis (now in Belgium, but possibly embroidered in the south of England)[48] and on the vestments discovered in St. Cuthbert's tomb at Durham.[49] The technique of gold embroidery also seems to have been practised in Ireland, particularly as gold thread, *órsnáithe*, is sometimes specifically mentioned in early texts.[50]

The patterns embroidered on these ancient garments varied. For instance, there are rows of rosettes on the "Arnegunde" tunic from Saint-Denis, while the Maaseik embroideries are richly and densely embellished with interlace and animal ornament, among other patterns. Similar motifs seem to have been embroidered on Irish garments. What appears to be embroidered interlace is depicted at the neck of the Virgin's tunic in folio 7v of the *Book of Kells*, while in "The Cattle Raid of Fróech," which scholars have dated to the eighth century,[51] fifty white tunics are described as being decorated with gold animal interlace (*co túagmílaib óir*),[52] which was probably embroidered (though appliqué is another possibility). This motif is also said to occur on Becfhola's horses' yokes. A relevant recent discovery is the fine quality silk embroidery decorating a linen garment with bird and other patterns from a site with strong Irish connections, Llan-gors crannog, near Brecon in Wales, built at the end of the ninth century, although gold threads were not found there.[53]

---

46 For fuller discussion of the evidence, see Gale R. Owen-Crocker, *Dress in Anglo-Saxon England: Revised and Enlarged Edition* (Woodbridge, UK: Boydell, 2004), 308–16; and Coatsworth, "Stitches in Time," 1–27.

47 Michel Fleury and Albert France-Lanord, *Les Trésors Mérovingiens de la Basilique de Saint-Denis* (Luxemburg: Gérard Klopp, 1998), 163–64, 195–207, fig. II-159.

48 Mildred Budny and Dominic Tweedle, "The Maaseik Embroideries," *Anglo-Saxon England* 13 (1984): 65–96; Helen M. Stevens, "Maaseik Reconstructed: A Practical Investigation and Interpretation of 8th-century Embroidery Techniques," in *Textiles in Northern Archaeology: NESAT III Textile Symposium in York 6–9 May 1987*, ed. Penelope Walton and John Peter Wild (London: Archetype Publications, 1990), 57–60.

49 Elizabeth Plenderleith, "The Stole and Maniples: The Technique," in *The Relics of Saint Cuthbert*, ed. C. F. Battiscombe (Oxford: Oxford University Press, 1956), 375–96.

50 Hillers, "Topos," 29; DIL "S," 296.75.

51 James Carney, *Studies in Irish Literature and History* (Dublin: Dublin Institute for Advanced Studies, 1979), 24; Wolfgang Meid, ed., *Táin Bó Fraích*, Medieval and Modern Irish Series 22 (Dublin: Dublin Institute for Advanced Studies, 1974), xxv.

52 Meid, *Táin Bó Fraích*, 1, §3.20.

53 Hero Granger-Taylor and Frances Pritchard, "A Fine Quality Insular Embroidery from Llan-gors Crannóg, near Brecon," in *Pattern and Purpose in Insular Art: Proceedings of the Fourth International Conference on Insular Art held at the National Museum & Gallery, Cardiff, 3–6 September 1998*, ed. Mark Redknap and others (Oxford: Oxbow Books, 2001), 92–99.

Becfhola's cloak

In the Roman Empire officials likewise wore a tunic with a distinctive heavy cloak (Latin, *paladamentum*) over it, which was fastened by a brooch at the right shoulder. A cloak (Greek, *chlamys*) fastened at the shoulder by a brooch was also part of the costume of important officials in the Byzantine Empire, including the emperor. As figure 1.2 shows, cloaks secured by brooches were also worn over tunics by aristocrats in Rome in the seventh century.[54] Irish aristocratic dress was probably modelled on this type of Mediterranean costume.

Becfhola's cloak or mantle (*brat*) is purple (*corcra*).[55] This is another indication of her royal status. While the Old and Middle Irish tales depict kings, heroes, and Otherworld beings wearing purple cloaks, the Old Irish "Law of the Fosterage Fee" (*Cáin Iarraith*)[56] laid down detailed rules about colours to be worn by the various grades in society.[57] Only the sons of kings were to wear purple (*corcra*), and also, incidentally, blue (*gorm*).[58] Moreover, in some tales a purple cloak, together with its precious brooch, is specifically identified as an emblem of kingship, with the implication that the donning of a purple cloak formed part of royal inauguration ceremonies.[59] An unusually explicit example in the *Book of Leinster*, compiled in the twelfth century from earlier sources, has recently been identified by Breandán Ó Ciobháin.[60] The passage in question concerns a king, Fiacha Fer Mara, conceived incestuously, who as a child was set adrift in the sea in a "boat of one hide." With him were "the marks of a king's son, namely a purple cloak and a golden brooch" (*co slonnud meic ríg .i. bratt corcra co cúaich*[61] *óir*).[62]

Purple was also the colour of power in the Mediterranean, where it was famously extracted at great expense from the shellfish *Murex brandaris* from the Cretan Bronze Age onward. In ancient Rome the emperor wore Tyrian purple, obtained from shellfish

---

54 Francesca Consoli, ed., *Museo Nazionale Romano: Crypta Balbi* (Rome: Electa, per la Soprintendenza Archaeologica di Roma, 2000), 68–69.

55 In early Irish literature, cloaks may be described as being furry, woollen, or silken (*finnach; fo loi; sirecda; srebnaide*), but the most common adjective is *cas*, "woven," usually found in alliterating lists with *corcra* (purple). Hillers, "Topos," 27.

56 This law text deals with the proper treatment of foster-children and the fee payable to their foster-parents. See Kelly, *Guide to Early Irish Law*, appendix 1, no. 19, p. 270; also p. 87.

57 Kelly, *Early Irish Farming*, 263.

58 Sons of lords, in contrast, were to wear clothing which was red (*derg*), grey (*glas*), or brown (*donn*), while sons of commoners were to wear clothing which was dun-coloured (*lachtnae*), yellow (*buide*), black (*dub*), or white (*find*). Kelly, *Early Irish Farming*, 263.

59 Niamh Whitfield, "The 'Tara' Brooch: An Irish Emblem of Status in Its European Context," in *From Ireland Coming: Irish Art from the Early Christian to the Late Gothic Period and Its European Context*, ed. Colum Hourihane (Princeton: Princeton University, 2001), 226; Niamh Whitfield, "More Thoughts on the Wearing of Brooches," in *Irish Art Historical Studies in Honour of Peter Harbison*, ed. Colum Hourihane (Dublin: Princeton University in association with Four Courts Press, 2004), 95–96.

60 Breandán Ó Cíobháin, pers. comm.

61 1 *cúach*, *DIL* "C," 568.56–60.

62 R. I. Best, Osborn Bergin, and M. A. O'Brien, *The Book of Leinster, formerly Lebar na Núachongbála* (Dublin: Dublin Institute for Advanced Studies, 1954), 1:88, §22b.29–30.

of the genera *Murex* and *Purpura*, while in Byzantium the donning of a purple cloak formed part of the inauguration ceremony of the emperor.[63] The adaptation of the same colour symbolism in Ireland is a sign of Classical influence there, and indeed, the Old Irish word for purple dye, *corcur*, is a borrowing from the Latin *purpura*. Philology suggests that it is a very early borrowing, the substitution of "c" for "p" predating the seventh century and possibly being as old as the fifth century.[64]

Murex, of course, was not available in Ireland, but purple dye was extracted locally from dog whelk, *Nucilla lapillus*, formerly *Purpura lapillus*, at a number of places along the west coast, including Inishkea, Co. Mayo,[65] and Dooey, Co. Donegal.[66]

Another possible indigenous source of purple dye was lichen. Recent scientific analysis has revealed traces of a lichen that produces purple dye, perhaps *Ochrolechia tartarea*, on a fragment of imported silk from an early-eleventh-century context at Fishamble Street, Dublin. In this case the silk may have been dyed in its country of origin.[67] Purple can also be made by mixing blue and red, and this approach was widely used in Classical times.[68] Analyses have revealed that some Byzantine silk was dyed purple by mixing indigo (blue) and madder (red), while Islamic dyers used a mixture of indigo and a lichen to obtain a similar purple.[69] Madder (Irish *roid*) was grown in early medieval Ireland exclusively for its dyeing properties, as was woad (Irish *glaisen*).[70] However, it is not known if these substances were used to dye purple textiles in Ireland.

Becfhola's golden brooch

Early Irish sagas suggest that a precious brooch, like the purple cloak it fastened, was part of royal regalia.[71] Brooches are also depicted as prominent insignia of royal status in sculpture, for instance on the eighth- to ninth-century pillar at White Island, Co. Fermanagh, which may represent Christ the King in warrior attire;[72] on the west face of the early-tenth-century Muiredach's cross at Monasterboice, Co. Louth, where

63 Marlia Mundell Mango, "Status and its Symbols," in *The Oxford History of Byzantium*, ed. Cyril Mango (Oxford: Oxford University Press, 2002), 60.

64 Damian McManus, "A Chronology of Latin Loan Words in Early Irish," *Ériu* 34 (1983): 42, 48.

65 Nancy Edwards, *The Archaeology of Early Medieval Ireland* (1990; repr., London: B. T. Batsford, 1996), 82–83.

66 A. Breandán Ó Ríordáin and Étienne Rynne, "A Settlement in the Sandhills at Dooey, Co. Donegal," *Journal of the Royal Society of Antiquaries of Ireland* 91 (1961): 61. I am grateful to Brian Lacey for this information.

67 Elizabeth Wincott Heckett, *Viking Age Headcoverings from Dublin*, Medieval Dublin Excavations 1962–81, ser. B, vol. 6 (Dublin: Royal Irish Academy, 2003), no. DHC 17, 128.

68 George W. Taylor, "Reds and Purples: From the Classical World to Pre-conquest Britain," in Walton and Wild, *NESAT III*, 38.

69 Anna Muthesius, *Studies in Silk in Byzantium* (London: The Pindar Press, 2004), 51.

70 Kelly, *Early Irish Farming*, 264, 267–69.

71 Whitfield, "The 'Tara' Brooch," 225–28; Whitfield, "More Thoughts," 96–97.

72 Helen Hickey, *Images of Stone: Figure Sculpture of the Lough Erne Basin* (Belfast: Blackstaff Press, 1976), 46, fig. 14(d). For another illustration, see Youngs, *Work of Angels*, 89, fig. 2.

Christ is depicted in royal robes;[73] and also on a High Cross at Durrow, Co. Offaly, where the Virgin is identified by a large brooch.[74]

The role of a precious brooch as an emblem of kingship and indication of rank within the regal hierarchy is also reflected in the fragmentary "Law of the Fosterage Fee," where it is stated that gold brooches with crystal or glass "gem-stones" were to be worn by the sons of the king of Ireland and kings of provinces, and silver brooches by the sons of kings of lesser territories.[75] While this passage is not part of the original eighth-century text, but forms part of a commentary, probably added in the eleventh or twelfth century,[76] it probably does reflect earlier sumptuary laws dating to before 1000 (the period when version 1 of "The Wooing of Becfhola" appears to have been composed) for two reasons. First, by the time the commentary was made, the brooch seems to have passed its heyday as the most important piece of jewellery in Irish dress. Second, the use of a precious brooch as a mark of status in Ireland seems to have been longstanding. As is the case with many of the pieces of regalia discussed above, the use of this item as a mark of status seems to derive from the late Roman or early Byzantine world, where brooches of varying degrees of grandeur were also used as insignia of office.[77] The use of the brooch as an emblem of high status in early medieval Ireland is yet another sign of influence from the Mediterranean world.[78]

The abundant finds of brooches from early medieval Ireland range from elaborate examples of gilt silver, decorated with gold filigree and "gems" of various types, to the relatively humble pins of copper-alloy with no inlays. Their diversity is reflected by many words used to denote "brooch" in Old and Middle Irish.[79] One of the commonest is that used to refer to Becfhola's brooch, *delg* (primary meaning, "thorn," a reference to the pin used to secure it).[80] This seems to be a generic term which could be applied to any type of brooch—an ornate gold one like that worn by Becfhola, or a small plain one like that worn by the king, Díarmait, when travelling to Trim, which he offers to Becfhola as her bride-price on the spur of the moment.

The description of Becfhola's brooch is characteristically concise, but it does supply four important pieces of information.

First, as already mentioned, the brooch is of gold (nominative *ór*). This is unlikely to mean that it is made of solid gold. Two such gold dress fasteners are known from ninth-century Ireland, perhaps made of gold imported by the Vikings: a minute one

---

73 Whitfield, "The 'Tara' Brooch," fig. 6; Peter Harbison, *The High Crosses of Ireland: An Iconographical and Photographic Survey* (Bonn: Dr. Rudolf Habelt GMBH, 1992), 1:143–44, 3:fig. 875.

74 Françoise Henry, *Irish Art During the Viking Invasions (800–1020 A.D.)* (London: Methuen, 1967), plate 99.

75 *CIH* 5:1759.165.21–24 = *AL* 2:146–47.

76 Etchingham and Swift, "Terms for Brooch," 46.

77 Dominic Janes, "The Golden Clasp of the Late Roman State," *Early Medieval Europe* 5, no. 2 (1996): 127–53.

78 Whitfield, "The 'Tara Brooch," 225–28.

79 Whitfield, "More Thoughts," 93.

80 *DIL* "D," 19.33.

from Kilfinnane, Co. Clare (more a pin than a brooch),[81] and a more sizable one from Loughan, Co. Derry (weighing 72.2 grams or 2.5 ounces).[82] However, these are exceptions, and the majority of brooches were made of silver or copper-alloy and subsequently gilded.

Second, Becfhola wears her brooch on her breast. This is the typical place for a woman to wear a brooch, according to Old and Middle Irish tales. It was also the correct place for a woman to wear a brooch according to a passage in the law-text "Judgements of Inadvertence" (*Bretha Étgid*),[83] which deals with liability for injuries caused by a brooch (presumably by a projecting pin). A man, in contrast, was to wear his brooch on his shoulder.[84] This distinction is also observed in sculpture from Ireland (fig. 1.3, upper figures) and Scotland, although on men the brooch is sometimes slightly set back to prevent the pin projecting beyond the body.[85] The different ways men and women wore brooches in early medieval Ireland seem ultimately to have originated in the Roman world, as figure 1.2 shows.

Third, the gold on Becfhola's brooch is said to be *láinegair*. This is translated by Máire Bhreathnach as "fully-wrought gold," following one possible meaning listed by the Royal Irish Academy's *Dictionary of the Irish Language*,[86] but a clearer translation is needed.

Láinhecair is a compound adjective, composed of two parts, *lán* and *ecor/ecar*. *Lán* means "full," hence "fully."[87] More open-ended is the second element *ecor/ecar*. The *Dictionary of the Irish Language* suggests on the one hand, "arranging," "disposing," "set in order,"[88] "displayed," "fittingly arranged,"[89] and on the other, "decorated," "inlaid."[90] Bearing in mind the character of the early medieval golden brooches found in Ireland, the following translations may be considered: (1) "Fully decorated," in the sense that it has everything a brooch of the best type should have: good design, gold filigree, elaborate studs, complex chipcarved ornament, subtle underlying geometry, and possibly also ornament on all edges, as in the case of the most splendid brooches that survive, the "Tara" (fig. 1.4) and Hunterston brooches, dated to approximately 700. (2) "Fully decorated" in the narrower sense, that the entire front surface is covered with ornament, as in the case of large brooches of the late seventh to ninth centuries, which do not necessarily contain such de luxe insets, e.g., the Londesborough brooch, which is decorated with gilt chipcarving and studs of

---

81 Raghnall Ó Floinn, "Museum Gets Gold from Christie's," *Archaeology Ireland* 7, no. 25 (Autumn 1993): 10.

82 Michael Ryan, "The Loughan Brooch," in Hourihane, *Irish Art Historical Studies*, 109–25.

83 Kelly, *Guide to Early Irish Law*, appendix 1, no. 33, p. 272.

84 *CIH*, 1:289.25–27 = *AL* 3:290.15.

85 Whitfield, "More Thoughts," fig. 8, shows how the pin projects if the brooch is not worn away from the edge of the shoulder.

86 *DIL* "E," 51.51.

87 *DIL* "L," 46.55.

88 *DIL* "E," 50.62–64.

89 *DIL* "E," 51.3.

90 *DIL* "E," 51.49.

Fig. 1.3: Figures on the Cross of the Scriptures, Clonmacnoise, Co. Offaly. Top: Two warriors, each wearing a tunic and a cloak with a brooch on the right shoulder. Bottom: A cleric in a hooded cloak over a long tunic, and a warrior in a short tunic. Photo: Éditions Zodiaque, by permission.

various types, but has no filigree.[91] Used in this sense the term could, however, hardly be applied to many ninth-century brooches which have large areas of plain metal, such as the Killamery brooch.[92] (3) "Fully inlaid" with gold filigree panels and "gems," again as in the case of the "Tara" and Hunterston brooches (although in this case one might expect the term *intlaisse*[93] to be used).

Finally, the "gems" which decorate Becfhola's brooch are described. This is the second time "gems" are encountered in the saga, and these are very different from

91 Youngs, *Work of Angels*, no. 71.
92 Ibid., no. 80.
93 *Intla(i)sse* is a participle of *ind-slaid*, DIL "I," 290.76–80.

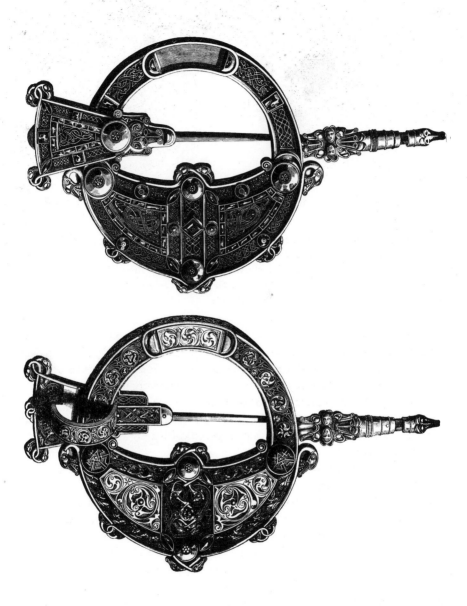

Fig. 1.4: Front (top) and back (bottom) of the "Tara" brooch, omitting the chain, as published in 1852, soon after the discovery of the brooch. Diameter of brooch: 8.6 centimeters (3.4 inches). Engraving: Originally published in *Ornamental Irish Antiquities: Irish Antique Brooches* (Dublin: Waterhouse and Co., 1852), reproduced in the author's article "The Original Appearance of the Tara Brooch," *Journal of the Royal Society of Antiquaries of Ireland* 106 (1976), fig. 4.

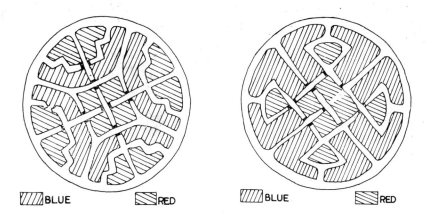

Fig. 1.5: Circular silver grille inlaid into red and blue glass studs in imitation of *cloisonné* enamel, from the Moylough belt-shrine. Each inlay measures 15 millimeters in diameter. Drawing: Michael J. O'Kelly, "The Belt-shrine from Moylough, Sligo," *Journal of the Royal Society of Antiquaries of Ireland* 95 (1965), plates 24 and 25. Copyright © Royal Society of Antiquaries of Ireland, reproduced by permission.

those on Becfhola's sandals, which, it will be recalled, were simply said to be "of precious stones" (*do lic lóghmar*). The brooch, in contrast, is decorated with *mbrechdrad ngem n-illdathach*, in Máire Bhreathnach's translation "shimmering gems of many hues." *Illdathach* indeed conveys the sense that the gems were multi-coloured,[94] but "variegated speckling" is preferable to "shimmering" for *brechdrad*.[95] Barbara Hillers translates the same phrase as "[with] a sprinkling of many-coloured gems,"[96] which more successfully conveys the sense that the gems which decorate the brooch create a variegated, speckled effect.

This is a particularly interesting detail, because it is a very accurate description of the "gems" on a brooch such as the "Tara" brooch (fig. 1.4), which is decorated with a scatter of studs of different colours, many of them multi-coloured. Polychrome glass studs, ornamented with stepped patterns imitating the cell work on Germanic *cloisonné* jewellery, are typical of metalwork of the highest quality from late-seventh-to ninth-century Ireland. Examples occur not only on the back of the "Tara" brooch (fig. 1.4, bottom) but also on the Ardagh chalice. On these objects red and blue glass is juxtaposed, as is gold and blue glass, and gold and amber.[97] Red and blue imitation *cloisonné* studs are also found on the Moylough belt-shrine (fig. 1.5), while polychrome glass studs of even greater variety are found on the magnificent Derrynaflan paten,

94 *DIL* "I," 57.54–55.
95 Nominative, *brechtar*, variegated speckling, *DIL* "B," 170.83.
96 Hillers, "Topos," 34.
97 For excellent colour photographs of the studs, see Michael Ryan, ed., *Treasures of Ireland: Irish Art 3000 B.C.–1500 A.D.* (Dublin: Royal Irish Academy, 1983), front cover and 39 (for the "Tara" brooch), frontispiece and 126–27 (for the Ardagh chalice).

where an even larger palette is employed.[98] Monochrome studs of different colours are also found on an object like the "Tara" brooch (fig. 1.4, top).

The description of the "gems" on Becfhola's golden brooch rings true. It is to be visualized as something similar to the early-eighth-century "Tara" brooch, rather than as a typical late-ninth- or early-tenth-century brooch, which would have been far plainer, and probably made of ungilt silver. It may seem surprising to find a reference to such a brooch in a text which appears to date to the Hiberno-Viking period. However, the presence of a runic inscription of approximately tenth-century date on the back of another magnificent brooch made in c. 700, the Hunterston brooch,[99] demonstrates that such objects remained in circulation for a long period.

Becfhola's neck-rings

Hitherto, we have discussed nothing that cannot be explained in terms of the craft traditions of early medieval Ireland. But when we learn that Becfhola is wearing *munci di ór forlosce ima brágait*, in Máire Bhreathnach's translation, "necklets of refined gold around her neck," we have to look elsewhere. But there is no need to search far afield, because such neck-rings are typical of Viking-age Scandinavia, made of rods of gold, or alternatively silver, twisted or plaited together. A number of such rings, all made of silver, have been found in Ireland (fig. 1.6).[100]

The tenth-century Arab writer, Ibn Fadlan, gave an insight into attitudes toward such neck-rings when he described the appearance of a woman with a party of northern merchants whom he met travelling on the river Volga:

> The women wear neck rings of gold and silver, one for each 10,000 dirhams which her husband is worth.[101]

Becfhola, then, was not alone in wearing more than one neck-ring. Silver rings were more common than gold ones. However, gold neck-rings are also known. The heaviest is from Tissø, Sjaelland, Denmark, which is the largest piece of gold jewellery dating from the Viking Age. It now weighs 1.83 kilograms (about 4 pounds 0.5 ounces), but a small part is missing; it originally weighed about 1.9 kilograms (about 4 pounds 3 ounces).[102] Two smaller examples formed part of the Hoen hoard from Buskerud, Norway, deposited in the 860s.[103] No gold neck-rings have been discovered to date in Ireland. But a number of Viking-age gold finger-rings and arm-rings have been

---

98 Michael Ryan, ed., *The Derrynaflan Hoard: A Preliminary Account* (Dublin: National Museum of Ireland, 1983), 24–25.

99 Youngs, *Work of Angels*, no. 69.

100 Johs. Bøe, *Norse Antiquities in Ireland*, vol. 3 of *Viking Antiquities in Great Britain and Ireland*, ed. Haakon Shetelig (Oslo: H. Aschehoug & Co., 1940), 122–24, figs. 83, 84.

101 H. M. Smyser, "Ibn Fadlan's Account of the Rus with some Commentary and some Allusions to Beowulf," in *Franciplegius: Medieval and Linguistic Studies in Honour of Francis Peabody Magoun, Jr.*, ed. Jess B. Bessinger Jr. and Robert P. Creed (London: George Allen & Unwin, 1965), 96.

102 Else Roesdahl, *The Vikings* (London: Guild Publishing, 1991), 39.

103 Else Roesdahl and David M. Wilson, eds., *From Viking to Crusader: The Scandinavians and Europe 800–1200* (New York: Rizzoli, 1992), no. 26.

Fig. 1.6: Hiberno-Viking silver neck-ring found at Limerick. Diameter: 14.6 centimeters (5.75 inches). Drawing: National Museum of Ireland, by permission.

found there, some of which are quite weighty. The heaviest surviving example is an arm-ring, from Rathedan, Co. Carlow, made of three twined gold rods, which weighs 375 grams (13.2 ounces).[104] Moreover, the ten massive gold arm-rings discovered on Hare Island in Lough Ree on the Shannon in 1802 (sadly melted down soon after they were discovered) constituted the largest gold hoard found in the entire Viking world and together weighed 5 kilograms (about 11

104 Patrick F. Wallace and Raghnall Ó Floinn, *Treasures of the National Museum of Ireland* (Dublin: Gill & Macmillan, 2002), no. 6:18.

pounds).[105] It is probably just an accident of survival that no gold neck-rings have been found in Ireland. Even if they were never worn there, it is unlikely that the *literati* were unaware of the splendid gold neck-rings from other parts of the Viking world.

The gold used to make Becfhola's neck-rings is said to be *forlosce* (a past participle, earlier spelt *forloiscthe*), an adjective also applied to a neck-ring in at least one other saga.[106] Máire Bhreathnach's translation of "refined"[107] is one option which makes sense in this context.

However, an Old Irish gloss to a psalm suggests a subtly different translation. This is *mese l. brathnigthe i. forloiscthe* meaning "examined or judged, i.e. burned (*forloiscthe*)," which is set against *argentum igni examinatum* meaning "silver examined in the fire."[108] On the basis of this gloss the metallurgist Brian Scott has suggested that, with its overriding sense of "burning," *forloiscthe*[109] refers to an ancient method of testing the purity of gold, fire-assaying, whereby gold and silver are tested (and also refined) by being heated in oxidizing conditions in a clay cupel to which lead has been added.[110] Cupellation cannot be used to part silver and gold, and Scott has suggested that, alternatively, *ór forloiscthe* refers to gold de-silvered by cementation, a process whereby salt or sulphur compounds (so-called "vitriols") are added to granulated gold and heated.

In practice, refining, fire-assaying, and de-silvering each produce a similar result, gold of high purity, and the general point about Becfhola's neck-rings seems to be that they are very costly. However, the difficulty of making accurate translations of terms like *ór forlosce* is demonstrated by the fact that both Brian Scott[111] and Breandán Ó Cíobháin[112] have independently suggested that its more usual sense is "gilding."

The golden object on Becfhola's head

The final object worn by Becfhola is the golden *mind* on her head. Máire Bhreathnach translates this as "circlet." *Mind* can simply mean "treasure,"[113] but among its other meanings is "a distinguished badge or emblem of rank, especially one worn on the head, a crown, diadem."[114]

The historian Francis John Byrne has suggested that, in general, the concept of the royal crown was foreign to early medieval Irish kingship.[115] Nevertheless, in the

---

105 James Graham-Campbell, "The Viking-age Silver Hoards of Ireland," in *Proceedings of the Seventh Viking Congress: Dublin, 15–21 August 1973*, ed. Bo Almqvist and David Greene (Dublin: Royal Irish Academy, 1976), 50, plate 3.

106 D. A. Binchy, *Scéla Cano Meic Gartnáin* (Dublin: Dublin Institute for Advanced Studies, 1963), 2, line 34.

107 *DIL* "F," 347.29–30.

108 Whitley Stokes and John Strachan, eds., *Thesaurus Palaeohibernicus: A Collection of Old-Irish Glosses* (1901–3; repr., Dublin: Dublin Institute for Advanced Studies, 1975), 1:71.

109 *Forloiscthe* (*DIL* "F," 347.26) is a participle of *for-loisci*, burns, sets on fire (*DIL* "F," 347.24).

110 Scott, "Goldworking Terms," 248.

111 Ibid., 251.

112 Breandán Ó Cíobháin, pers. comm.

113 Byrne, *Irish Kings*, 22.

114 1 *mind*, DIL "M," 144.5–7.

115 Byrne, *Irish Kings*, 22.

early Irish tale "The Adventures of Nera" (*Ectra Nerai*) a golden head ornament is included among the three insignia of kingship discoveredo by the hero.[116] Moreover, as Byrne also noted, in early texts Irish kings and other notables are sometimes said to wear *minds* as marks of distinction. This practice can hardly have developed in a vacuum, and it was probably ultimately inspired by the wearing of gold fillets or jewelled circlets by dignitaries in other parts of Europe.

A crown or diadem was an important part of the regalia of the early Byzantine emperors and empresses, and this was imitated by some Germanic rulers in areas where the Irish established monasteries. For example, the Langobardic queen Theodolinda had a gem-encrusted gold crown, now at Monza, Italy.[117] Like other queens' crowns of this period, this consists of a circlet, rather than a crown with fleurons such as became fashionable later in the Middle Ages.[118] Anglo-Saxons were also familiar with the crown as a mark of kingship, and crowns and diadems were worn by many of the rulers who issued coins in sixth- to eighth-century Anglo-Saxon England.[119]

Becfhola is not unique in early Irish literature in wearing a golden *mind* on her head. Mallory has noted that such items are also normally described as gold in the Ulster Cycle: There are twenty-seven references to golden *minds*, as opposed to three of silver. In the earliest reference to *minds*, in the Old Irish tale "The Cattle Raid of Fróech," they are said to be of "silver under gilding."[120]

If we are to visualize Becfhola's golden *mind* as a strip of solid metal, then it was probably modelled on the foreign circlets just referred to. But were such metal fillets worn in Ireland before 1000? They may have been, because thin gold bands, often decorated with rows of repoussé pellets, have been found there. The few found in dated contexts have been assigned to the Viking Age or later.[121]

Alternatively, Becfhola's *mind* may be imagined as a woven head-band brocaded with gold thread, as in figure 1.1. This is a possibility, because, as noted above, such bands have been found across Europe from the late Roman period onward. Many were worn as fillets on the head, the majority having a short brocaded central section placed across the forehead. Examples have been discovered in Anglo-Saxon and continental Germanic graves throughout Europe dating from the fifth to eighth centuries. Women's gold head-bands feature in tenth- and eleventh-century Anglo-

---

116 This item is referred to both as a *mionn*, a term related to *mind*, and as a *barr* (*DIL* "B," 37.71). See Kuno Meyer, "The Adventures of Nera," *Revue Celtique* 10 (1889): 218, §8.71; 220, §9.89; 220, §9.91. I am grateful to Elizabeth Seater for this reference.

117 Gian Carlo Menis, *I Longobardi* (Milan: Electa, 1990), no. II.2.

118 Ronald W. Lightbown, *Mediaeval European Jewellery with a Catalogue of the Collection in the Victoria & Albert Museum* (London: Victoria & Albert Museum, 1992), 121–22.

119 Anna Gannon, *The Iconography of Early Anglo-Saxon Coinage Sixth to Eighth Centuries* (Oxford: Oxford University Press, 2003), 42–51.

120 "Co mindaib argdidib fo díor," see Meid, *Táin Bó Fraích*, 2, §3.36; trans. Gantz, *Early Irish Myths and Sagas*, 115.

121 Raghnall Ó Floinn, "A Gold Band Found near Rathkeale, Co. Limerick," *North Munster Antiquarian Journal* 25 (1983): 3–8; Wincott Heckett, *Viking Age Headcoverings*, 7, plate VI; Viginia Glenn, *Romanesque & Gothic: Decorative Metalwork and Ivory Carvings in the Museum of Scotland* (Edinburgh: NMSE Publishing, 2003), 90–91.

Saxon wills.[122] Decorative head-bands seem to have been worn on ceremonial occasions by high-born Frankish ladies in both the Merovingian and Carolingian periods, and are probably what contemporary writers referred to as *vittae*.[123] Tablet-woven head-bands ornamented with gold and silver threads have also been discovered in tenth-century contexts at Birka in Sweden.[124]

Such *vittae* could look very splendid, as Gale Owen-Crocker has explained with reference to early Anglo-Saxon examples:

> the gold ornament consisted of strips of gold foil brocaded into the woven band and then flattened and burnished. The brocading would have resembled solid gold in appearance, and the effect of the gold pattern against the coloured braid, possibly red, would be similar to that of … gold and gilded jewellery inlaid with garnet or coloured glass.[125]

Wool and silk head-bands, "perhaps [the] more informal relations" of golden *vittae*, have been found in Hiberno-Viking contexts in Dublin,[126] while tablet-woven bands using silver and gold threads have also been discovered there, some of which may also have been worn on the head.[127]

A third item which early medieval Irish aristocratic women appear to have worn on their heads was a veil (*caille*).[128] In this they were again following an early medieval Western European fashion,[129] which may have originated in Rome (fig. 1.2, left). In the early Middle Ages, veils were sometimes held in place by metal fillets.[130] It is, therefore, particularly interesting to find that glosses (admittedly dating to the eleventh or twelfth century) to the eighth-century law text "Judgements about Pledge-Interests" suggest an association between the veil and the *mind*, as these two items are listed among the lawful contents of the luxury-bag of a queen or chieftain's wife.[131] So a third possibility is that the *mind*, on occasion, secured a short veil. There is no reference to Becfhola wearing a veil. But it is interesting to note that in the *Book of Kells*, the Virgin on folio 7v seems to wear a barely visible veil held in place by a fillet under a hood.[132] The veil is distinguished by its colour—pinkish purple—from the yellow hood, while the fillet

122 Owen-Crocker, *Dress in Anglo-Saxon England*, 225 n. 99.
123 This information derives from Crowfoot and Hawkes, "Early Anglo-Saxon Gold Braids," 50, 61–64; and Crowfoot, "Early Anglo-Saxon Gold Braids, Addenda," 109–10.
124 Geijer, *Birka III*, 157–75; Geijer, "Textile Finds from Birka," 93–96; I. Hägg, "Einige Bemerkungen über der Birkatracht," in *Textilsymposium Neumünster: Archäeologische Textilfunde*, ed. Lise Bender Jørgensen and Klaus Tidow, NESAT 1 (Neumünster: Textilmuseum Neumünster, 1982), 249–65.
125 Owen-Crocker, *Dress in Anglo-Saxon England*, 96.
126 Wincott Heckett, *Viking Age Headcoverings*, 8.
127 Pritchard, "Silk Braids and Textiles," 151–56; Wincott Heckett, *Viking Age Headcoverings*, 8.
128 *DIL* "C," 28.29–30.
129 E.g. Owen-Crocker, *Dress in Anglo-Saxon England*, 100–2, 157–59, 219–24.
130 Wincott Heckett, *Viking Age Headcoverings*, 7–8, plate V.
131 *CIH* 2:464.14 = *AL* 5:382.18; *CIH* 2:464.17 = *AL* 5:382.21–22; *CIH* 2:465.13–14 = *AL* 5:387.2–3.
132 For good colour reproductions, see Bernard Meehan, *The Book of Kells: An Illustrated Introduction to the Manuscript in Trinity College Dublin* (London: Thames & Hudson, 1994), cover and pl. 7.

on her forehead is represented as a horizontal yellow band ornamented with a row of dots. It is impossible to say if the fillet is made of fabric or gold, but the golden colour suggests the latter, while the row of dots recalls the repoussé pellets on the surviving gold bands, hitherto dated to a slightly later period.

Whatever Becfhola's *mind* was, it was clearly deemed to be an important part of her wardrobe, because there were no fewer than three *minds* among the items Becfhola claimed she had to retrieve when setting off to rendezvous with the king's foster-son, whom she was trying to seduce.

Becfhola's wardrobe

The quantity of garments Becfhola told her husband that she had left behind on her travels is the final indication of her wealth and status. The number of tunics and brooches she wished to retrieve (seven in version 1, eight in version 2)[133] together with the three *minds* noted above, may be an example of what Kenneth Jackson called "the tendency to exaggeration which is inherent in [early Irish] literature as a whole."[134] Nevertheless, there is evidence from the early Irish laws for the possession of extensive wardrobes by those of high status. The tract on status, *Críth Gablach*, named the number of clothes the well-off farmer (*bóaire*) and his wife were allowed to own: four garments each.[135] There is, unfortunately, no mention of the clothing of other classes of society in this text in its surviving form, but the clear implication is that those of higher rank could own more, and presumably better quality, clothes. The "Law of the Fosterage Fee" also indicates that a person of high rank should have many fine, new clothes, while one of lowly rank should have a few old clothes.[136] Again, the passage in question comes from a commentary probably added in the eleventh or twelfth century,[137] but it may reflect earlier customs.

DESCRIPTION OF FLANN

Following is the description of Flann, together with Máire Bhreathnach's translation:

Co n-accae in [n]-óclach imon teinid oc urgnam na muici; inar sirecdai ime co nglanchorthair 7 co circlaib óir 7 arcait; cennbarr di ór 7 argut 7 glaine ima chenn; mocoil 7 fithisi óir im cach ndúal dia fult co braine a dá imdai; dá uball óir for dégabal a mongi; mét ferdornn ceachtar n-aí; a chlaideb órduirnn ara chris 7 dá shleg coicrindi i ttarrlethor a scéith co cobruid fhindruine fair; brat ildathach leis; a dí láim lána di

133 M. Bhreathnach, "*Tochmarc Becfhola*," 82, 85, §5.
134 Kenneth Hurlstone Jackson, *A Celtic Miscellany: Translations from the Celtic Literatures* (Harmondsworth: Penguin Books Ltd., 1971), 28.
135 D. A. Binchy, ed., *Críth Gablach* (Dublin: Dublin Institute for Advanced Studies, 1979), 8, §15.198–99; Eoin MacNeill, "Ancient Irish Law: The Law of Status or Franchise," *Proceedings of the Royal Irish Academy* 36C (1923): 291, §90.IV.312.
136 *CIH* 5:1759.165.25–36 = *AL* 2:149.
137 Colmán Etchingham, pers. comm.

fhailgib óir 7 arcait co a dí uillinn.[138]

[She saw a warrior cooking a pig by the fire. He was clad in a silken tunic with a bright border, embroidered with circular designs of gold and silver. A helmet of gold, silver and crystal was on his head, clusters and loops of gold around every lock of his hair, which hung down to his shoulder-blades. Two gold balls were at the parting of his braids, each one of them the size of a man's fist. His golden-hilted sword on his belt. His two five-barbed spears lay on his shield of belly-leather which was embossed in *findruine*. A cloak of many hues beside him. His two arms were laden to the elbows with gold and silver bracelets.][139]

As one who is about to fight his relatives for his patrimony, Flann is presented as a warrior, but, like Becfhola, he is dressed to impress (fig. 1.1, right).

Flann's tunic

Flann's tunic is identified as an *inar*, which was probably shorter than the *léine*, and more convenient for Flann as a warrior about to do battle. But the precise nature of the *inar* is unclear. The *Dictionary of the Irish Language* is noncommittal, defining the *inar* as

> evidently, sometimes at least, a short tunic ... worn sometimes next to the skin ... sometimes worn with, and apparently over, a *léine*.[140]

In the written sources the *inar* is associated with both men and women. The garment appears to predate the Viking era, because it is mentioned in as early a text as "The Cattle Raid of Fróech," which, as noted above, is dated to the eighth century.[141] Knee-length tunics are sometimes depicted on High Crosses, e.g., by the warrior facing the cleric on the Cross of the Scriptures at Clonmacnoise, Co. Offaly (fig. 1.3, lower right). Perhaps this is how one should imagine the *inar*.

Two interesting pieces of information are given about Flann's *inar*. First, it is silken (*sirecdai*). This is not necessarily wholly unrealistic. In Byzantium, while production of silks of different weaves was an imperial monopoly and the most elaborate silks were not for export to the barbarians of Northern Europe, plainer silks were traded there.[142]

Reference has already been made to the silk threads used to embroider textiles discovered in ninth-century context with Irish connections at Llan-gors crannog in Wales, and also to silken woven bands discovered during excavations at Dublin, but other silk items have also been discovered in Ireland. In all, over a hundred fragments of silk were found from among household debris in Dublin, exhibiting a wide variety

---

138 M. Bhreathnach, "*Tochmarc Becfhola*," 73, §6.
139 Ibid., 78, §6.
140 *DIL* "I," 201.70, 79, 83.
141 Meid, *Táin Bó Fraích*, 9, §20.235; Gantz, *Early Irish Myths and Sagas*, 121.
142 Wincott Heckett, *Viking Age Headcoverings*, 106.

of construction techniques including the use of different types of looms. Silk occurred there both as unworked thread and as fragments of finished goods. Some woven silk cloths were folded and stitched to make caps; other pieces of woven silk were worn as scarves or ribbons. There were also silk tabbies and some patterned silks.[143] Fragments of silk were also discovered during excavations in Waterford, another town founded by the Vikings.[144]

Evidence for the presence of silk in Hiberno-Viking towns is building up. There are several references in the annals and sagas to various types of imported cloth, including silk.[145] As Elizabeth Wincott Heckett has commented:

> Perhaps one has been too ready to discount as hyperbole the description in the Sack of Limerick in 967 AD: "They followed them also into the fort and slaughtered them on the streets and in the houses … their blooming silk-clad young women" Perhaps conspicuous consumption was a feature of [Hiberno-Viking towns]?[146]

Silk found in Ireland could, in theory, have originated in several places, including Baghdad, Spain, Egypt, or China. Some may have been brought into Ireland by the Vikings. Silks from the East were also traded through Rome, and Irish pilgrims to Rome may have brought silks back to Ireland, or may alternatively have acquired them in the textile trading town of Pavia in northern Italy, near the Irish monastery at Bobbio.[147]

Indeed, silk may have been imported into Ireland even before the Hiberno-Viking period. Silk of high quality was famously transparent. In the Roman period this shocked Seneca the Elder, who warned of the consequences of going out "naked hardly less obviously than if you had taken off your clothes."[148] In the eighth- to ninth-century *Book of Kells*, illuminated in a Columban monastery probably in Kells or Iona, the Virgin appears to be wearing a silken garment, because her legs and breasts are plainly visible under her thin dress. The limbs of the two flanking figures in the so-called "Arrest of Christ" on folio 114r in the same manuscript[149] are also visible, suggesting that they too wore silk.

These images, of course, may have been copied from exemplars, and so do not provide absolute proof that silk was imported into Ireland in the eighth or early ninth century. However, the spread of Christianity led to an influx of cloth into

143 This passage derives from Pritchard, "Silk Braids and Textiles," 149–61, and Wincott Heckett, *Viking Age Headcoverings*, 91–98, 105–6.

144 Wincott Heckett, "Textiles, Cordage, Basketry," 749–51.

145 Wallace, "Economy and Commerce," 220.

146 Wincott Heckett, "Textiles, Cordage, Basketry," 751. The quotation derives from James Henthorn Todd, *Cogadh Gaedhel re Gallaibh: The Wars of the Gaedhil with the Gaill, or the Invasions of Ireland by the Danes and Other Norsemen* (London: Longmans, Green, Reader, and Dyer, 1867), 78–79.

147 Wincott Heckett, *Viking Age Headcoverings*, 106–8; Wincott Hecket; "Textiles, Cordage, Basketry," 749–53.

148 Frances Wood, *The Silk Road: Two Thousand Years in the Heart of Asia* (London: British Library, 2004), 30.

149 Meehan, *The Book of Kells*, fig. 54.

England from the seventh century onward, including silk,[150] and the same thing probably happened in contemporary Ireland. In any event, silk clearly was worn in the Hiberno-Viking period, when "The Wooing of Becfhola" seems to have been composed. Flann's silken tunic, then, may have had some basis in reality, although whether garments were made entirely of silk or merely silk-trimmed is unclear. There is no archaeological evidence from Ireland or Britain for silk robes (except vestments) before their appearance in the tomb of Edward the Confessor (d. 1066).[151] On the other hand, in the late-sixth- to early-seventh-century so-called Grave of Queen Arnegunde at Saint-Denis, near Paris, a knee-length silk dress and an ankle-length silk tunic were found.[152]

The second thing we are told about this garment is that it had a "bright border, embroidered with circles of gold and silver" (*co nglanchorthair 7 co circlaib óir 7 arcait*). It has already been mentioned that animal interlace is said to decorate Becfhola's chariot yokes. The circle (nominative singular *circul*)[153] is the second decorative motif referred to in the tale.

There has to be some doubt as to precisely how the circles were embroidered. But it is likely that the text should be interpreted literally and that the embroidery consisted of a simple row of circles, since this motif appears on the hems of the tunics worn by figures on some late-ninth- to early-tenth-century Irish High Crosses, e.g., both the cleric and warriors on the Cross of the Scriptures at Clonmacnoise, Co. Offaly (fig. 1.3, bottom), and on both figures in the "Flight into Egypt" at Durrow.[154] Moreover, rows of large circles are also illustrated on the hems of garments in Carolingian manuscripts such as the Stuttgart Psalter,[155] while similar borders, though with smaller circles, appear in Ottonian art.[156] Continental influence on Irish clothing is not as unlikely as it might seem. The Irish Annals recorded the deaths of Charlemagne in 813 and of Louis the Pious in 840,[157] while Peter Harbison has long argued for a strong Carolingian contribution to Irish sculpture.[158]

In view of the above, a more remote possibility is that this is an allusion to one of the other principal motifs of early medieval Irish art, circular ornament in the so-called Ultimate La Tène style. This archaic motif, based on subtle geometric patterns

---

150 Elisabeth Crowfoot, Frances Pritchard, and Kay Staniland, *Textiles and Clothing c. 1150–c. 1450* (London: HMSO, 1992), 82–86.

151 Gale Owen-Crocker, pers. comm.

152 Fleury and France-Lanord, *Les Trésors Mérovingiens*, fig. Il–130–3.

153 *DIL* "C," 200.41–43.

154 Henry, *Irish Art During the Viking Invasions*, plate 99.

155 Max Martin, "Kleider Machen Leute," in *Die Alamannen* (Baden-Württemberg: Theiss, 1978), fig. 386.

156 Henry Mayr-Harting, *Ottonian Book Illumination: An Art-historical Study* (London: Harvey Miller, 1991), vol. 1: plates xx, xxv; vol. 2: figs. 56, 60. I am grateful to Gale Owen-Crocker for this information.

157 William M. Hennessy, *Chronicum Scotorum: A Chronicle of Irish Affairs from the Earliest Times to A.D. 1135* (London: Longman, Green, Reader, and Dyer, 1866), 128–29, 142–43. I am grateful to Peter Harbison for calling my attention to this.

158 E.g. Peter Harbison, "The Carolingian Contribution to Irish Sculpture," in *Ireland and Insular Art A.D. 500–1200*, ed. Michael Ryan (Dublin: Royal Irish Academy, 1987), 105–10.

of circles and spirals, originated in the Celtic Iron Age[159] and continued to be developed at least up to the early tenth century, when it appears on High Crosses such as Muiredach's cross at Monasterboice. Circular patterns in the Ultimate La Tène style also abound on early medieval manuscripts and metalwork from Ireland, and it would be surprising if it were not also one of the principal patterns used in contemporary embroidery.

Flann's cloak

Flann is busy cooking when spotted by Becfhola, and has taken off his cloak (*brat*), which is mentioned only toward the end of the passage, when we are told it is lying beside him (though he is shown wearing it in figure 1.1). It seems, however, that his cloak is to hand around the clock, and at night is used as a blanket. We know this because when Becfhola tries, unsuccessfully, to seduce Flann, we are told "she slipped in beneath his cloak, between him and the wall."[160] There is linguistic evidence that the cloak was also used as a blanket in Anglo-Saxon England,[161] while this custom persisted in some communities until relatively modern times.[162]

The importance of the cloak in everyday life is further illustrated by an incident at the end of the tale when clerics appear before the king, Díarmait, bearing treasure from the bodies of the warriors killed in Flann's battle for the island. This breaks church rules about Sunday travel:

> "What then," cried Díarmait, "the clergy travelling on a Sunday!" He drew his cloak about his head so that he might not see them at all.[163]

In contrast to Becfhola, who wears a purple cloak, Flann's cloak is said to be *ildathach*, "of many colours," a term applied earlier to the "gems" on Becfhola's brooch. As Barbara Hillers has noted, cloaks are often said to be a single colour, ranging in order of frequency from purple (*corcra*), to green (*úaine, úainide*), red (*derg*), blue (*gorm*), black-grey (*dub-glas*), brown (*donn*), grey (*liath*), and dun (*odarda*). However, words like multi-coloured (*ildathach*), differently (?contrastingly) coloured (*saindathach*), and speckled/variegated (*brecc*) are also used to describe cloaks.[164] These words perhaps suggest woollen textiles made of multi-coloured yarn, or alternatively plaids.

On Muiredach's cross at Monasterboice the soldiers on either side of Christ have striped trousers.[165] Elaborate woollen plaids have been discovered in later

---

159 For a definition of this style, see Peter Harbison, *The Golden Age of Irish Art: The Medieval Achievement 600–1200* (London: Thames and Hudson, 1999), 13–14.
160 "Dos-léic-si foa brat-som, etarru 7 fraigh." M. Bhreathnach, "Tochmarc Becfhola," 74 and 78, §8.
161 Owen-Crocker, *Dress in Anglo-Saxon England*, 109.
162 Elizabeth Wincott Heckett, pers. comm.
163 M. Bhreathnach, "Tochmarc Becfhola," 76 and 80 §12.
164 Hillers, "Topos," 26–27.
165 FitzGerald, "Insular Dress," 258, fig. 22.

Roman Iron Age contexts in Northern Europe,[166] while stripe and check patterns have been identified on a few textiles from Anglo-Saxon contexts.[167] Although pieces of woollen textiles are sometimes found in excavations in Ireland, as far as I am aware there is no clear evidence as yet of multi-coloured fabrics, but early medieval Irish art generally is very sophisticated, and there is no reason to suppose that woven textiles did not sometimes display colour combinations.

Flann's headdress

Although Flann has taken off his cloak when seen by Becfhola, he has not removed a richly decorated *cennbarr* from his head. Máire Bhreathnach translates this as "helmet." While she may be correct, the usual term for "helmet" is *cathbarr*,[168] while the usual meaning assigned to *cennbarr* is "headdress," "cap," or "fillet."[169] This seems to be another item which denotes high status.

Some *cennbarrs* were clearly envisaged as being made of textile, because in "The Cattle Raid of Fróech," bright green headdresses (plural dative, *cenbarraib úanidib*)[170] are said to be worn by 150 Otherworld women. Flann's headdress, on the other hand, is described as being *di ór 7 argut 7 glaine*, "of gold, silver, and crystal (or perhaps glass)."

Should we follow Máire Bhreathnach and visualize a splendid Viking-age metal helmet (as shown on the ground in figure 1.1), or alternatively, something like the Anglian helmet from Coppergate in York,[171] with the difference that it was decorated with gemstones, as well as precious metals? Or are we to suppose instead that the *cennbarr* consisted of a textile band with gold and silver thread, to which one or more gemstones were attached (as worn by Flann in figure 1.1)?

It is impossible to say on present evidence. While no helmets have been discovered to date from early medieval Ireland, they were clearly known there, as Viking-style helmets are depicted on soldiers guarding the body of Christ on the Cross of the Scriptures at Clonmacnoise.[172] On the other hand, admittedly later Scandinavian sagas suggest that it was perfectly acceptable for Viking warriors to wear head-bands. In *Njal's Saga*, King Harold Gormsson presents Gunnar with "a head-band studded with gold,"[173] and when Skarp-Hedin visits the Althing,

---

166 Evert Kramer and others, eds., *Kings of the North Sea AD 250–850* (Newcastle upon Tyne: Tyne & Wear Museums, 2000), 108–9.

167 Owen-Crocker, *Dress in Anglo-Saxon England*, 304–5.

168 *DIL* "C," 90.65.

169 *Cennbarr* (*cenn* + *barr*), *DIL* "C," 130.62. The first element, *cenn*, refers to the head (*DIL* "C," 120.15); the second element, *barr*, may mean a tiara, diadem, or helmet (*DIL* "B," 37.71).

170 Meid, *Táin Bó Fraích*, 9, §20.235–36; Gantz, *Early Irish Myths and Sagas*, 121.

171 Dominic Tweddle, *The Anglian Helmet from 16–22 Coppergate*, The Archaeology of York: The Small Finds 17/8 (London: Council for British Archaeology for the York Archaeological Trust, 1992).

172 FitzGerald, "Insular Dress," 258, fig. 23.

173 Magnus Magnusson and Hermann Pálsson, *Njal's Saga* (Harmondsworth: Penguin Books, 1960), 91.

His hair was combed well back and held in place by a silk head-band. He looked every inch a warrior.[174]

Furthermore, woven headdresses with attached gemstones were worn in medieval Europe from at least the sixth century, when one was placed in the "Princess" grave in Cologne Cathedral.[175] This type of headdress continued to be worn as an ornament and mark of rank throughout the Middle Ages,[176] and may also have existed in Ireland in the early medieval period, although no examples have hitherto been recognised in the archaeological record.

The final point about Flann's *cennbarr* is that it is adorned with the third type of "gem" to be referred to in this tale, *glaine*, which the *Dictionary of the Irish Language* translates as "crystal" or "glass."[177] Máire Bhreathnach favours the former meaning. Polished quartz crystals do indeed occur on Irish metalwork of the highest quality dating to the eighth or ninth century: on the underside of the Ardagh chalice[178] and on the tip of the handle of the Derrynaflan strainer.[179] If the term is to be translated as "crystal," this raises Flann's *cennbarr* to the level of the very best surviving artefacts from the period.

The alternative translation, "glass," does not, however, suggest that the *cennbarr* is inferior. As already explained, true gemstones are rare in early medieval Irish metalwork, and many of the finest objects are decorated with polychrome or, less commonly, monochrome glass studs. Given that one meaning of *glaine* is "clearness,"[180] it could be that here the term is used to denote a clear glass stud, which, like that on an eighth- to ninth-century Crieff mount from Scotland, looks very like rock-crystal.[181] However, the term may simply refer to a translucent glass stud of any colour. Each of these three types of studs occurs on early medieval Irish metalwork, so this third reference to a "gem" in the tale is again consistent with the archaeological record.

Flann's hair ornaments

Flann's appearance is also greatly enhanced by his long hair and his golden hair ornaments. The first objects decorating Flann's locks (or curls)[182] are the *mocoil* (Máire Bhreathnach's "clusters"), nominative singular *mocol*. The *Dictionary of the Irish Language* suggests that "the allusion may be to spherical ornaments attached to plaits of hair,"[183]

---

174 Ibid., 248.

175 Crowfoot and Hawkes, "Early Anglo-Saxon Gold Braids," 79.

176 Lightbown, *Mediaeval European Jewellery*, 112, 133.

177 1 *glaine*, DIL "G," 90.24.

178 Ryan, *Treasures of Ireland*, no. 51a.

179 Ryan, *The Derrynaflan Hoard*, 33, plate 75.

180 1 *glaine*, DIL "G," 90.5.

181 R. Michael Spearman, "The Mounts from Crieff, Perthshire, and Their Wider Context," in *The Age of Migrating Ideas: Early Medieval Art in Northern Britain*, ed. R. Michael Spearman and John Higgitt (Edinburgh: National Museums of Scotland & Alan Sutton Publishing, 1993), 138.

182 2 *dúal*, DIL "D," 420.39.

183 DIL "M," 154.79–80.

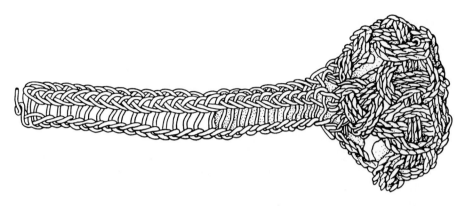

Fig. 1.7: Gold, bun-shaped woven-wire ball attached to a gold chain from Carlisle Cathedral. Length: approximately 3.3 centimeters (1.3 inches). Drawing: Carlisle Archaeological Unit, by permission.

proposing, among other meanings "a mesh, network, web,"[184] "a globe, sphere or rounded mass,"[185] or "bunches and weavings of gold."[186]

This is highly suggestive of a type of woven wire ball found in Ireland, the Isle of Man, Britain, and Iceland in contexts dating to the late ninth to late tenth centuries, the period when "The Wooing of Becfhola" seems to have been composed. These small, bun-shaped balls are generally of silver, but in Dublin copper-alloy wire was used, while gold wire was employed in an example found at Carlisle (fig. 1.7). Woven wire balls of this type were put to various uses. A silver example acted as a stop on the chain of a (now lost) kite-brooch from Clonmacnoise in the Irish Midlands.[187] They form terminals on the thongs of the metal scourge from the late-ninth-century hoard from Trewhiddle, Cornwall.[188] They were also used as decorative edgings for garments discovered in graves in the Isle of Man.[189] The woven wire cone-shaped objects recently discovered as part of a hoard from Dunmore Cave, Co. Kilkenny, probably also decorated clothing.[190] Such woven balls, then, were put to a number of uses. Could they also have acted as hair ornaments? If worn in this way they may have trapped individual hairs, but some discomfort may have been

184 *DIL* "M," 154.67.
185 *DIL* "M," 154.77.
186 *DIL* "M," 154.79.
187 Niamh Whitfield, "The Waterford Kite-brooch and its Place in Irish Metalwork," in Hurley, Scully, and McCutcheon, *Late Viking Age and Medieval Waterford*, 501, plate 40f.
188 David M. Wilson, *Catalogue of Antiquities of the Later Saxon Period* (London: British Museum Publications, 1964), no. 91.
189 James Graham-Campbell, "Tenth-century Graves: The Viking-age Artefacts and their Significance," in *Excavations on St. Patrick's Isle, Peel, Isle of Man, 1982–88: Prehistoric, Viking, Medieval and Later*, ed. David Freke (Liverpool: Liverpool University Press, 2002), 88–89, 96. The most up-to-date discussion of bun-shaped, woven wire balls from the Isle of Man, Britain, and Ireland is to be found here.
190 Wallace and Ó Floinn, *Treasures*, no. 6:1.

considered a price worth paying for wearing gold in one's hair.

The second ornaments in Flann's tresses are the *fithisi* (Máire Bhreathnach's "loops"), nominative singular *fithis*, which, according to the *Dictionary of the Irish Language*, means "following a circular course,"[191] or alternatively "a loop or ring (of metal or other material)."[192] In this case it is unlikely that actual coiled wire, such as that which survives attached to one of the Dunmore cones,[193] would have been placed in hair, because it would have snagged and tangled. More practicable would have been gold-thread cordings, ribbons, or other narrow wares which might be tied and knotted.[194] Such fragile items have not hitherto been recognized in the archaeological record, but the English twelfth-century *Psalter of Henry of Blois* shows Mary Magdalene with her hair in two long sections wrapped and bound with what appears to be a spiral of ribbon, with tassels at the ends.[195]

Finally, there are golden balls (*uball*)[196] at the parting in Flann's hair (speculatively illustrated in figure 1.1). It is not clear if these are constructed in the same way as the *mocoil*, but we are told that they are enormous. The extant bun-shaped, woven balls are generally small, typically 1.7–2.4 centimeters (0.67–0.94 inches) wide, like the eighteen examples found in one of the graves in the Isle of Man. However, the cone-shaped woven wire objects from Dunmore Cave come in three sizes, ranging from the very small to larger ones which measure 4.1 centimeters (1.6 inches) across. This is hardly the "size of a man's fist," the dimensions attributed to the two golden *uball*, but perhaps one should allow for some hyperbole in descriptions of a handsome warrior like Flann.

Small hair ornaments of this type are not depicted in art. However, the plaited beards of some high-status figures on Irish High Crosses (fig. 1.3, upper left) suggest that men were interested in elaborate coiffures.

Flann's arm-rings

Finally, Flann has one type of ornament which is undoubtedly in the Hiberno-Viking, rather than native Irish, tradition: His two arms (*láim*) were laden to the elbows (*uillinn*) with gold and silver bracelets (*fhailgib*).

It may seem rather impractical for a warrior to load himself down with such heavy items before going into battle, as Flann plans to do at this point in the story. However, such jewellery was undoubtedly worn on occasion, because the existence of Hiberno-Viking gold arm-rings of various types is very well established in Ireland. The earlier discussion of Becfhola's neck-rings already made reference to the Rathedan arm-ring and to the ten massive gold arm-rings discovered on Hare Island. Other

---

191 *DIL* "F," 156.64–65.
192 *DIL* "F," 157.16.
193 Wallace and Ó Floinn, *Treasures*, no. 6:1.
194 Robin Netherton, pers. comm.
195 London, British Library, MS Cotton Nero C iv, 24r; one reproduction appears in Janet Backhouse, *The Illuminated Manuscript* (Oxford: Phaidon, 1979), plate 17.
196 "Any globular object, a ball," *DIL* "U," 46.81.

Fig. 1.8: Hiberno-Viking silver arm-ring, broad-band type, from Cushalogurt, Co. Mayo. Diameter: 7 centimeters (2.75 inches). Drawing: National Museum of Ireland, by permission.

examples have been discovered at Edenvale Caves, Co. Clare, and Dublin.[197]

Flann's silver arm-rings are also entirely plausible, because silver arm-rings were by far the commonest products of the Hiberno-Viking tradition (fig. 1.8). Over one hundred are known from silver hoards in Ireland, where they were sometimes cut into fragments which could be later melted down and recycled. Several different types have been identified, the most important in terms of sheer numbers being the broad-band type. Like the neck-rings, they seem to have been manufactured for the storage and circulation of silver, and their target weight of 26.15 grams (0.92 ounces) is very close to the most important weight unit of the lead scale-weights from tenth-century Dublin. Their purity was obviously a matter of concern, because they sometimes display small nicks and pecks, a characteristic Scandinavian method of testing for plated forgeries.[198]

Gold and silver arm-bands, like neck-rings of precious metal, were worn in the Viking Age as a way of displaying wealth. Moreover, since most payments were made in silver according to weight, this was a practical way of carrying riches. If a smaller sum were needed, then the jewellery could simply be cut up, which probably explains

197 Wallace and Ó Floinn, *Treasures*, nos. 6:18 and 6:8.
198 I am grateful to John Sheehan for this information. This passage derives from his "Early Viking Age Silver Hoards from Ireland and their Scandinavian Elements," in *Ireland and Scandinavia in the Early Viking Age*, ed. Howard B. Clarke, Máire Ní Mhaonaigh, and Raghnall Ó Floinn (Dublin: Four Courts Press, 1998), 178–79.

the large number of fragmentary arm-rings in Irish silver hoards of the late ninth to tenth centuries.

A very large number of individual arm-rings may be found together in a single hoard, for instance, ten in the Hare Island hoard, as already mentioned. This does not in itself prove that an individual could own many arm-rings, but Flann's possession of such a large number suggests that this may have been the case.

Another interesting aspect of "The Wooing of Becfhola" is that while Flann wears arm-rings, Becfhola does not. But there is no way of telling if this was the general rule, because Irish arm-rings are found in hoards and not graves, so there is no archaeological evidence to associate them with either sex. Evidence from other parts of the Viking world is also inconclusive.

Finally, the word *lám* can mean "hand" as well as "arm,"[199] while the term *fail* can mean finger-ring as well as arm-ring.[200] So it could be that Flann wears finger-rings as well as arm-rings. In the Hiberno-Viking period these were like miniature versions of some of the most common type of arm-ring, and could be made of (relatively) broad bands[201] or twisted or plaited rods.[202]

Additional information about male attire

While Flann is the only male to warrant a full description in the saga, there is additional information about men's finery in the final episode of "The Wooing of Becfhola," referred to above, in which a group of clerics presents Díarmait with metal found on the bodies of Flann's dead brothers and of the warriors they defeated. Máire Bhreathnach translates the passage as follows:

> However, they left behind as much gold and silver as two of us could carry, of all that was beneath their cloaks (*fo mbrotaib*) and about their necks (*ima mbráigdib*) and on their shields (*ima scíathaib*) and on their spears (*imma ngóae*) and about their swords (*imma claidbiu*) and on their arms (*ima láma*) and on their tunics (*ima n-innara*).[203]

Evidently, the dead warriors, like Flann, each wore an *inar* (rather than a *léine*, the type of tunic Becfhola wears) and a cloak. An item of precious metal was associated with their cloaks. This was probably a brooch to keep the cloak in place (as in figure 1.1), an inference made more likely if the preposition *fo* is translated as "through"[204] or "on,"[205] rather than "under."[206] Flann presumably also had a brooch, but as he was not wearing his cloak, it is not mentioned. The dead warriors have, in addition,

---

199 *DIL* "L," 35.54, 36.26.
200 1 *fail*, *DIL* "F," 20.82. The adjective may means "having bracelets or rings"; see 1 *failgech DIL* "F," 22.37.
201 E.g., one from the Shanmullagh hoard, Co. Armagh; see Cormac Bourke, *Patrick: The Archaeology of a Saint* (Belfast: HMSO, 1993), 25 (top).
202 E.g. Wallace and Ó Floinn, *Treasures*, nos. 6:8 and 6:18.
203 M. Bhreathnach, "Tochmarc Becfhola," 76 and 80, §12.
204 *DIL* "F," 169.4.
205 *DIL* "F," 169.78.
206 *DIL* "F," 167.66.

precious metal on their tunics, perhaps embroidery of gold or silver. They also have weaponry embellished with gold and silver, like Flann, swords, spears, and shields. Again like Flann, they wear arm-rings and perhaps also finger-rings. Intriguingly, they have, in addition, gold and/or silver "about their necks." Are we to understand that the other warriors, in contrast, do have such valuable (and heavy) items around their necks, and if so, does this suggest that in Ireland, neck-rings were worn by both men and women? Archaeology, unfortunately, cannot answer this question, because neck-rings (like arm-bands) have not been found in graves. In any case, these dead warriors, like Flann, seem to have been dressed as ceremonial icons, rather than as men with practical clothing for battle.

CONCLUSION

The version of "The Wooing of Becfhola" under discussion is composed in early Middle Irish, a form of the language which predates the year 1000. However, the manuscripts in which the text survives are much later. This may lead to doubts about the authenticity of descriptions in the text of dress and accessories and to the suspicion that they have been tampered with by later redactors.

Like J. P. Mallory's earlier survey of objects described in the Ulster Cycle of Tales, this review suggests that the material culture described is of approximately the same date as the language of the text in which it has been recorded.

It is not possible to be certain that every object described was worn by the Irish elite in the centuries immediately before 1000. For instance, there are now few traces in the Irish archeological record of the fragile gold brocaded head-bands worn in other parts of Europe, a headdress which may be the *mind* worn by Becfhola. However, this may simply be due to the lack of grave goods in Irish burials. Other objects described, such as *findruine* shoes, may be fanciful. But it is possible that shoes decorated with metal strap-ends or metalwork mounts were worn by the elite in Ireland, as they were elsewhere in parts of Europe. Alternatively, the narrators may just have been inspired by their knowledge of the clothing of foreign dignitaries.

Nevertheless, a remarkably large number of objects referred to in "The Wooing of Becfhola" can be matched in the surviving archaeological record from early medieval Ireland. Some items, such as Becfhola's neck-rings and Flann's arm-rings, seem to date to the later ninth or tenth centuries, when this version of the text appears to have been composed. Other objects, such as Becfhola's brooch, seem to represent objects manufactured in the late seventh and eighth centuries, i.e., roughly the period in which the action takes place. Here the narrator may have been referring to heirlooms worn by his contemporaries, or alternatively may have been making use of a formulaic description inherited from earlier storytellers. In either case the descriptions of the items in "The Wooing of Becfhola" are drawn from a repertory of objects familiar to the narrator of this and other tales of approximately the same date as the best examples of their type.

The Embroidered Word:
Text in the Bayeux Tapestry

Gale R. Owen-Crocker

The Bayeux Tapestry, at 68.38 metres long (224 feet 4 inches), is the largest surviving medieval textile. This embroidered narrative frieze,[1] almost certainly designed in Canterbury, England,[2] and generally believed to have been made there,[3] was probably

A shorter version of this article, "The Scene and the Unseen: Text in the Bayeux Tapestry," was presented as a paper in May 2005 at the International Congress on Medieval Studies at Kalamazoo, Michigan. I am grateful for advice given on that occasion by members of the audience, particularly George Brown, Elizabeth Coatsworth, and Jacqueline Stodnick, and also for guidance on manuscript punctuation by my colleague Alexander Rumble.

1 The object is technically an embroidery, not a tapestry, but the name "Bayeux Tapestry" is firmly established; therefore I retain it. The history and technicalities of the terminology are discussed in Nicole de Reyniès, "Bayeux Tapestry, or Bayeux Embroidery? Questions of Terminology," in *The Bayeux Tapestry: Embroidering the Facts of History*, ed. Pierre Bouet, Brian Levy, and François Neveux (Caen: Presses universitaires de Caen, 2004), 69–76.

2 The Bayeux artist borrows images from manuscripts known to have been in Canterbury in the eleventh century. This relationship with the Canterbury scriptoria, demonstrated by Francis Wormald, "Style and Design," in *The Bayeux Tapestry: A Comprehensive Survey*, ed. Frank Stenton (1957; rev. ed., London: Phaidon, 1965), 25–36, has been further developed by C. R. Dodwell and Peter Clemoes, *The Old English Illustrated Hexateuch*, Early English Manuscripts in Facsimile 18 (Copenhagen: Rosenkilde and Bagger, 1974), 72–73; David J. Bernstein, *The Mystery of the Bayeux Tapestry* (London: Weidenfeld and Nicolson, 1986), 39–46; C. Hart, "The Canterbury Contribution to the Bayeux Tapestry," in *Art and Symbolism in Medieval Europe: Papers of the 'Medieval Europe Brugge 1997' Conference* 5, ed. Guy de Boe and Frans Verhaeghe (Zellik, Belgium: Instituut voor het Archeologisch Patrimonium, 1997), 7–15; and Hart, "The *Cicero-Aratea* and the Bayeux Tapestry," in *King Harold II and the Bayeux Tapestry*, ed. Gale R. Owen-Crocker (Woodbridge, UK: Boydell, 2005), 161–78. Their findings and some of my own are discussed in Gale R. Owen-Crocker, "Reading the Bayeux Tapestry through Canterbury Eyes," in *Anglo-Saxons: Studies Presented to Cyril Roy Hart*, ed. Simon Keynes and Alfred P. Smyth (Dublin: Four Courts, 2005), 243–65.

3 This is the majority view. There are claimants for a continental origin, including, most recently, Wolfgang Grape, *The Bayeux Tapestry: Monument to a Norman Triumph*, trans. David Britt (Munich: Prestel, 1994), and George Beech, *Was the Bayeux Tapestry Made in France? The Case for Saint-Florent of Saumur* (New York: Palgrave Macmillan, 2005). Arguments about provenance have been largely based on artistic style; Beech offers documentary evidence for an eleventh-century textile workshop at the Loire monastery and personal contacts between its Breton abbot and Duke William. Presumably technical analysis of the linen and wool more sophisticated than that undertaken in 1982–83 could offer scientific evidence of the place of origin.

commissioned for Odo, bishop of Bayeux, the half-brother of Duke William of Normandy,[4] between 1066 and the 1080s.[5] Its pictorial record of events leading up to the Norman Conquest of England is accompanied by an explanatory inscription,[6] mostly taking the form of *tituli* (surtexts along the top of the main register), comprising 2,226 characters and symbols, the longest known text of its kind.[7] The inscription is transcribed and translated in table 2.1, with an approximation of the spacing and punctuation; uncial letters are there represented with a mixture of lower case and Greek letters. Punctuation and uncials are not represented in quotations in the body of this article for typographical reasons.

THE TEXT: LETTERING, SPELLING, LANGUAGE

The majority of the inscription's letters are square capitals, with a scattering of uncial forms. There appears to be no consistency in the use of the uncials: though the frieze is made out of nine pieces of linen,[8] some of which were evidently worked in separate locations, the distribution of the lettering does not give any clear indication that

4 This is the general opinion; Andrew Bridgeford, in *1066: The Hidden History of the Bayeux Tapestry* (London: Fourth Estate, 2004), argues that Eustace of Boulogne was the patron, and Beech advocates King William.

5 Odo of Bayeux features in both text and graphics. The Tapestry has been in Bayeux, France, since at least the fifteenth century. The significant dates relate to the Battle of Hastings, which features in the Tapestry (1066), Odo's first imprisonment (1082), and his final banishment from England (1088).

6 Commentators on the inscription in the facsimile editions have been content with a brief description, transcription, and translation. Francis Wormald, "The Inscriptions with a Translation," in Stenton, *The Bayeux Tapestry*, 177–80, is effectively dismissive of interest in anything but the content of the text: "All [letters and abbreviations] can ... be found in inscriptions or display script in MSS. Neither the forms of the letters nor the abbreviations throw any light on the origin of the work" (177). Both Wormald and David M. Wilson, *The Bayeux Tapestry* (London: Thames and Hudson, 1985), 172–73, helpfully expand the Latin abbreviations. The language is analysed by René Lepelley, "A Contribution to the Study of the Inscriptions in the Bayeux Tapestry: *Bagias* and *Wilgelm*," in *The Study of the Bayeux Tapestry*, ed. Richard Gameson (Woodbridge, UK: Boydell, 1997), 39–45 (first published in 1964 as "Contribution à l'étude des inscriptions de la Tapisserie de Bayeux," *Annales de Normandie* 14: 313–21), and as part of a wide-ranging discussion by Ian Short, "The Language of the Bayeux Tapestry Inscription," *Anglo-Norman Studies* 23 (2001): 267–80. Syntax is analysed briefly in Peter Clemoes, "Language in Context: *Her* in the 890 Anglo-Saxon Chronicle," *Leeds Studies in English* 16 (1985): 27–36, at 31 and 33–34 n. 9; and Rouben C. Cholakian, *The Bayeux Tapestry and the Ethos of War* (Delmar, NY: Caravan Books, 1998), 33–45.

7 Medieval textile inscriptions in northwest Europe, both embroidered and woven, are enumerated in Elizabeth Coatsworth, "Text and Textile," in *Text, Image, Interpretation: Studies in Anglo-Saxon Literature and Iconography within Their Insular Context in Honour of Éamonn Ó Carragáin*, ed. Alastair Minnis and Jane Roberts (Turnhout, Belgium: Brepols, forthcoming).

8 Isabelle Bédat and Béatrice Girault-Kurtzeman, "The Technical Study of the Bayeux Tapestry," in Bouet, Levy, and Neveux, *The Bayeux Tapestry*, 83–109, at 84–86. The Tapestry was previously thought to consist of eight panels.

different scribes wrote the separate sections.[9] Neither is there any pattern in the variant spellings of recurrent names—Edward, William, and Wido (Guy of Pontieu).

The language of the text is Latin. Other near-contemporary textile inscriptions are also Latin,[10] but this choice of language for the Bayeux Tapestry is interesting since the work is not biblical and does not have overtly religious subject matter, though it includes two churches, two priests, and a bishop, and, arguably, a moral message. Its materials are linen and wool, not the silk and spun gold of ecclesiastical vestments and other luxury textiles with inscriptions. If the composer were Anglo-Saxon, since that culture had a well-established tradition of vernacular prose composition, he might have used the Old English language to convey secular subject matter, as was the case in the *Anglo-Saxon Chronicle*. The choice of Latin is more consistent with Norman patronage—a Norman lord would not have wanted an English text—and this, together with strong indications of Norman French influence on the Latin,[11] suggests that the essential content was dictated by a Norman (by or on behalf of the patron). However, the characteristically English stylistic detail of using the adverb *Hic* plus a verb,[12] together with the forms of certain names, some spellings, and Old English letters,[13] also the error of transcription at Scene 22 which transformed Latin *hic* ("here") into Old English *hie* ("they") implies that the person who wrote it down was English.

DIFFERENT HANDS: SCRIBES AND EMBROIDERERS

Palaeographers studying manuscripts are usually able to distinguish different hands. In contrast, Bayeux Tapestry scholars have not, so far, suggested that there were different scribes at work. There are, in fact, subtle differences between similar letters. For example, at Scene 17 the *e* letters, both Roman and uncial, in the top line of the *titulus* have elegant serifs with tiny points; those in the lower two lines have straight

9 Preferences relate to areas larger than individual sections: "In panels I–IV ... uncial-type forms are significantly predominant, whereas in panels V–VIII [IX] they are never in the majority." Short, "Bayeux Tapestry Inscription," 270.

10 Coatsworth, "Text and Textile," passim.

11 Short, "Bayeux Tapestry Inscription," identifies the influence of French pronunciation on the spellings *Wilgelmvm, Wilgelm, Willem, Edward,* and *Edwardvm* (271). Certain Latin words and phrases probably derived from medieval French: *arena, benedicere, caballi, cadere, caro, confortare, exire de navibvs, fodere, iste/isti, ministrare, ministri, navigare, navigivm, nvntiare, palativm, parabolare, porrigere, sacramentvm facere, se preparare, simul, tener, trahere, un* (273). Short also suggests French influence in the absence of inflexions on names (272) and mixture of tenses (273).

12 Clemoes, "Language in Context," 27, 29. First manifested as *Her* in the *Anglo-Saxon Chronicle* and found in the English translations of Latin captions to illustrations in copies of Prudentius's *Psychomachia* (Cambridge, Corpus Christi College, MS 23 and London, British Library, MS Cotton Cleopatra C viii), this construction does not appear in continental annals or in the Latin originals of the *Psychomachia* captions.

13 Lepelley, "Study of the Inscriptions," notes as Anglo-Saxon the forms *Bagias* and *Wilgelm* (cf. note 11); the spellings *ceastra, Eadwardus,* and *Willelm*; the letter "eth" (Ð); and the Tironian nota (7) for "and." *At* instead of *ad*, and the letter "ash" (Æ) are also Old English.

Table 2.1: The Bayeux Tapestry inscription: Translation, parts of speech, and symbols

Sc	Inscription	Translation	Noun or Pronoun	Prep	Adj	Verb	Adv or Conjun	Symbol
1	EDVVARD REX:	King Edward	Edward Rex					••
2	VBI:hAROLÐ DVX: ANGLOVM: ETSVMILITES: EQVI TANT: ADBOS hAm:	Where Harold duke of the English and his soldiers ride to Bosham.	Harold dux Anglorum milites Bosham	ad		equitant	ubi	•• •• •• ••• ••
3	ECCLESIA:	church	ecclesia					••
4	HIC hAROLD:··MARE· NAVIGAVI T:·	Here Harold navigated the sea	Harold mare			navigavit	hic	•• •• •
5	ETVE LIS:VENTO:PLENIS VE= =NIT:INTE RR A: VVIÐONIS COMITIS	and, with the wind full in his sails, came to the land of Count Guy.	velis vento terra Widonis Comitis	in		venit	et	•• = = •• ••
6	HAR OLD:𝜏 hIC:.APPREhENDIT:VVIDO: HAROLDV:	Harold / Here Guy arrests Harold	Harold Haroldu[m]			apprehendit	hic	•• •• ••• 𝜏
7	ETD VX IT:EV M ADBEL REM:	and led him to Beaurain	eum Belrem	ad		duxit	et	••
8	ETI BI EVM:TEN VIT:	and held him there.	eum			tenuit	et ibi	••

#	Inscription	Translation						
9	VBI:hARO LD:7VVIDO:PA RABO LANT:	Where Harold and Guy talk.	Harold Wido			parabolant	ubi	:: 7 ::
10	VBI:NVNTII:VVILLƐLMI: DVCIS:VENERVNT:ADVVIDO Nē TVROLD	Where the messengers of Duke William came to Guy. Turold	nuntii Willelmi Ducis Widone[m] Turold	ad		venerunt	ubi	:: :: ::
11	NVN TII:VVILLELMI	William's messengers	nuntii Willelmi					::
12	†HIC VENIT:NVNTIVS:ADWIL GELMVM DV CEM	Here a messenger came to Duke William.	nuntius Wilgelum Ducem	ad		venit	hic	† ::
13	HIC:WIDO:AD DVXIT hAR OLDVm ADVVILGELM VM: NORMANNO RV M: DVCƐM	Here Guy led Harold to William Duke of the Normans.	Wido Haroldum Wilgelmum Normannorum Ducem			adduxit	hic	:: :: ::
14	HIC:DVX:-VVILGELM : CVMhAROLDO:VENIT:ADPA LATIV SVV̄	Here Duke William came with Harold to his palace.	Dux Wilgelm Haroldo palatiu[m]	ad	suu[m]	venit	hic	:: -:: ::
15	VBI:VNVS:CLƐRICVS:ƐT:- ƐLFGY VA	Where a cleric and Ælfgyva ….	clericus Ælfgyva		unus		ubi et	:: :-

Sc	Inscription	Translation	Noun or Pronoun	Prep	Adj	Verb	Adv or Conjun	Symbol
16	hIC·VVILLEM:DVX: ET·EXERCITVS: EIVS :VE NERVNT:ADMONTE MICHAELIS	Here Duke William and his army came to Mont-Saint-Michel	Willem Dux exercitus Monte[m] Michaelis	ad	eius	venerunt	hic et	: : : : :
17	ET hIC:TRANSIERVNT:FLVMEN: COSNONIS: hIC:hAROLD:DVX:TRAhEBAT: EOS:- DEARENA	and here they crossed the River Couesnon. Here Duke Harold pulled them from the sand	flumen Cosnonis Harold Dux eos arena	de		transierunt trahebat	et hic hic	: : : : :
18	ET·VENERVNT AD DOL: ET:CONAN:- FVGA VER TIT:- RED NES	and they came to Dol and Conan took flight. Rennes	Dol Conan fuga Rednes	ad		venerunt vertit	et et	: : :- :-
19	hICMILITES VVILELMI:DVCIS:PVG NANT:CONTRA DINA NTES:-	Here Duke William's soldiers fight against the inhabitants of Dinan	milites Wilelmi Ducis Dinantes	contra		pugnant	hic	: :-
20	ET:CVNAN:CLAVES:POR REXIT:-	and Conan surrendered the keys.	Cunan claves			porrexit	et	: :-

No.	Inscription	Translation						Braille
21	hIC:WILLɛLM: DɛDIT: HA ROL DO: ARMA	Here William gave arms to Harold.	Willelm Haroldo arma			dedit	hic	[braille]
22	hIɛVVILLEL M VɛNIT:BAGIAS	[Here] William came to Bayeux	Willelm Bagias			venit	hie [*sic*]	[braille]
23	VBI hAROLD:SACRAMɛNTVM: FECIT:- VVILLɛLMO DVCI:-	where Harold made an oath to Duke William.	Harold sacramentum Willelmo Duci			fecit	ubi	[braille]
24	hIChAROL D:DVX:- RɛVERSUS: ɛST ADANGLICAM:TERRAM:-	Here Duke Harold returned to England	Harold Dux terram	ad	Anglicam	reversus est	hic	[braille]
25	ET VENIT:AD:ɛDVVARDV:- RɛGɛ M:-	and came to King Edward.	Edwardu[m] Regem	ad		venit	et	[braille]
26	hIC PORTA TVR:CORPVS:EADWARDI: REGIS:AD:ɛCCLɛSIAM:SCI PETRI AP[ĩ]	Here the body of King Edward is carried to the church of St. Peter the Apostle.	corpus Eadwardi Regis ecclesiam S[an]c[t]i Petri Ap[osto]li	ad		portatur	hic	[braille]
27	hIC ɛADVVARDVS:REX INLECTO : ALLOQVIT:FIDE LES:-	Here King Edward in bed speaks to the faithful	Eadwardus Rex lecto fideles	in		alloquit[ur]	hic	[braille]

Sc	Inscription	Translation	Noun or Pronoun	Prep	Adj	Verb	Adv or Conjun	Symbol
28	EThI C: DEFVNC TVS ɛST	and here he is dead.			defunctus	est	et hic	∵
29	hIC DEDERVNT:hAROLDO: CORO NÃ: REGIS	Here they have given the king's crown to Harold.	Haroldo corona[m] regis			dederunt	hic	⋮⋮
30	hICRɛ SIDET:hAROLD RɛX:AN GLORVM: STIGANT ARChI EP̄S	Here sits Harold, king of the English. Archbishop Stigand	Harold Rex Anglorum Stigant Archiep[iscopu]s			residet	hic	⋮⋮
31		None						
32	ISTIMIRANT STELLÃ	These [people] wonder at the star.	isti stella[m]			mirant		
33	hAROLD	Harold	Harold					
34	hIC:NAVIS:ANGLI CA:VENIT.INTɛR RAM WILLɛLMI:DV CIS	Here an English ship came to the land of Duke William.	navis terram Willelmi Ducis	in	Anglica	venit	hic	⋮⋮⋮
35	HIC:WILLɛLM DVX:IVSSIT NAVɛS ⋮ EDI FICARE:	Here Duke William commanded ships to be built.	Willelm Dux naves			iussit edificare	hic	⋮⋮
36	hIC TRAhVNT:NAVES:ADMA RE:-	Here ships are dragged to the sea.	naves mare	ad		trahunt[ur]	hic	⋮⋮·-

No.	Inscription	Translation						
37	ISTI PORTANT:ARMAS:ADNAVES: εThIC TRAhVNT CARRV·M CVMVINO:ETARM IS:-	These [people] carry arms to the ships and here drag a cart with wine and arms.	isti armas naves carrum vino armis	ad cum		portent trahunt	et hic et	: : • : : · -
38	†hIC:VVILL ELM: DVX INMAGN O:NAVIGIO: MAR ε TRAN SIVit ETVENIT ADPεVEN SÆ:-	Here Duke William crossed the sea in a big ship and came to Pevensey.	Willelm Dux navigio mare Pevensæ	in	magno	transivit venit	hic et	† : : : : · :·
39	hIC εXεVNT:CABALLı DεNAVIBVS:-	Here horses get out of the ships	caballi navibus	de		exeunt	hic	: : · -
40	εThIC:MI LITES: FESTINA VERV NT:hεSTINGA: VTCIBVM.RAPERεNTVR :	and here soldiers hastened to Hastings to plunder food.	milites Hestinga cibum			festinaverunt raperentur	et hic ut	: : • : : · :·
41	HIC:EST:VVAD AR D:	Here is Wadard.	Wadard			est	hic	: : · :·
42	hIC:COQVI TVR:CARO ET hIC: MINISTRAVεRVN MINISTRI	Here meat is cooked and here they waited on. Waiters	caro ministri			coquitur ministraverunt	hic et hic	: : · :·
43	hICFECERVNT:PRANDIVM: ET·hIC:EPISCOPVS:CIBV:ET: POTV̄: BE NE DIC IT.	Here they made a meal and here the bishop blesses the food and drink.	prandium episcopus cibu[m] potu[m]			fecerunt benedicit	hic et hic et	: : • : : · : :

Sc	Inscription	Translation	Noun or Pronoun	Prep	Adj	Verb	Adv or Conjun	Symbol
44	ODO:EPS: ROTBERT:- WIL LELM:	Bishop Odo, Robert, William	Odo ep[iscopu]s Rotbert Willelm					∴ :-∴
45	ISTƐ: IV SSIT:VTFO DERƐTVR:CASTELLVM: AT:HESTENGA CEASTRA	This [man] has commanded that a castle should be thrown up at Hastings. Castle	iste castellum Hestenga ceastra	at		iussit foderetur		. ∴ ∴
46	HIC:NVN TIATVMES T: WILLELM DEhARO LD:	Here [information] is reported to William about Harold.	Willelmo Harold	de		nuntiatum est	hic	∴
47	hIC DOMVS:IN CEN DITVR:	Here a house is set on fire.	domus			incenditur	hic	∴
48	hIC:MILI TE S: EXIƐRVNT:DƐhESTƐNGA: ET:VENE R VNT ADPRƐLIVM:CON TRA:hAROL DVM·REGE ⫶	Here soldiers left Hastings and came to the fight against King Harold.	milites Hestenga prelium Haroldum Rege	de ad contra		exierunt venerunt	hic est	∴ ∴ ∴ ∴ ⫶
49	HIC:V VILLƐLM:DVX INTERROGAT:VITAL.: SIVI DISSƐT EXƐR CI TV̄ HAROLDI	Here Duke William questions Vital if he has seen Harold's army.	Willelm Dux Vital exercitu[m] Haroldi			interrogat vidisset	hic si	∴ ∴

#	Latin (inscription)	English	Words		Verbs		Marks
50	ISTE NVNTIAT:HA RO LDVM REGẼ DEEXER CITV VVILELMI DVCIS	This [man] reports to King Harold about Duke William's army.	iste Haroldum rege[m] exercitu[m] Wilelmi Ducis	de	nuntiat		:.
51	HIC WILLELM:DVX ALLOQVI TVR:SV IS:MILITI BVS:VT· PRℰPARA RENTSE: VI RILI TER ETSAPIENTE R: ADPRℰ LIVM: CONRA:AN GLORVM EXER CI TA	Here Duke William exhorts his soldiers that they should prepare themselves manfully and wisely for the fight against the English army.	Willelm Dux se prelium Anglorum exercitu[m]	ad contra	alloquitur prepararent	hic ut viriliter sapienter	:: :: ·:· :: ·:·
52	hIC CECI DℰRVN T LℰVVINE ℰT:GYRD:FRATRE S:hARO L DI REGIS:	Here Leofwine and Gyrth, brothers of King Harold, were killed.	Lewine Gyrð fratres Haroldi Regis		ceciderunt	hic et	:: ::
53	hIC CℰCI DERVN SIMVL:ANGLI ℰT FRA NCI:INPRℰLIO:-	Here English and French were killed at the same time in the fight.	Angli Franci prelio	in	ceciderunt	hic simul et	:: :-
54	hIC·ODO EPS:BACVLV̄. TℰNℰNS: CONFOR:- TAT PVE ROS	Here Bishop Odo, holding his staff, 'encourages' the boys.	Odo Ep[iscopu]s baculu[m] pueros		tenens confortat	hic	· ·· ·:-

Sc	Inscription	Translation	Noun or Pronoun	Prep	Adj	Verb	Adv or Conjun	Symbol
55	hICEST:- DVX VVILEŁ E CIVS	Here is Duke William [?] Eustace	Dux Wile[m] E…cius			est	hic	·:·
56	hIC:FRAN CI PVGNAN ETCƐCI DƐ RVNT QVIƐRANT:CVM hAROLDO:-	Here the French fight and have killed those who were with Harold.	Franci qui Haroldo	cum		pugnant ceciderunt erant	hic et	∴ ∴
57	hIC hARO L D:-REX:- INTERFƐC TVS:EST	Here King Harold has been killed	Harold Rex			interfectus est	hic	·:· ·:· ·:
58	ETFVGA:VE RTERVN ANGLI	and the English have turned to flight.	fuga Angli			verterunt	et	··

ET hIC: TRANSIERVNT : FLVMEN: COSNONIS: ETVENERVNT
hIC: hAROLD:DVX: TRAhEBAT:EOS : ⁓

DEARENA

Fig. 2.1: The Bayeux Tapestry, Scene 17: "… and here they crossed the River Couesnon. Here Duke Harold pulled them from the sand." At the right edge is a portion of Scene 18, with caption beginning "And they came …" Illustrations by Gale R. Owen-Crocker, after David M. Wilson, *The Bayeux Tapestry* (London: Thames and Hudson, 1985).

bars (fig. 2.1). This might invite us to consider whether the two lower lines, in part smaller, and rather wobbly in arrangement, were an addition to fill the empty space in the graphics, and written by a different person. The absence of any remains of the original cartoon, replaced by embroidery which itself may have been executed by different hands, necessarily complicates the issue of distinguishing scribes, at this point and throughout the Tapestry.

Nevertheless, occasional clues suggest that parts of the inscription were laid out by different people. For example, the *tituli* at Scenes 12 and 38 each open with a cross.[14] It was quite normal practice for Anglo-Saxon inscriptions to *begin* with a cross,[15] but crosses part way through an inscription are not usual. The cross and Scene 38 immediately follow the third seam (Wilson, plate 39); the insertion of a cross suggests that someone began his task at this point and that the workshop producing the fourth section was different from that working on the third. It may be significant that the inscription to Scene 37, which concludes the third piece of linen, is neatly but tightly spaced into three tiers which finish in line with the last figure in the graphics, just before the end of the piece of linen. The inscription concludes with the two-dots-and-a-dash punctuation mark which is sometimes used elsewhere in the Tapestry to indicate that there is more to come (see fig. 2.2). The inscription following the cross is more spread out.

14 The scenes are numbered in an early modern hand on the linen backcloth of the Tapestry and may be found in the folding reproductions published by the Ville de Bayeux titled *La Tapisserie de Bayeux*, which present the Tapestry as a continuous frieze. Plate numbers cited in this article are from the colour facsimile, Wilson, *The Bayeux Tapestry*.
15 There is no cross at the opening of the Tapestry. However, the beginning is heavily restored and some details may have been lost.

Fig. 2.2: The Bayeux Tapestry, Scene 44 and the beginning of Scene 45: "Bishop Odo, Robert, William. This man …" The two-dots-and-a-dash sign indicates that the caption to Scene 44 is continued on the line below and distinguishes it from the start of the caption of the next scene.

Scene 12 (Wilson, plate 12) is more complicated: The cross opens the penultimate section of the inscription on the first piece of linen, preceding the first seam by some distance. It seems that a different writer took over the inscription at this point and saw himself as beginning here; or that the same scribe began a new stint of work here. The upper border has dipped at this point and the birds and beasts depicted in it are large. The inscription is accordingly forced into smaller letters and is very intermittent, being fitted in round a tree, a sword, hands, spears, and birds' heads. It seems likely that the first workshop completed the main register and the upper border, leaving the inscription (and possibly the lower border) incomplete.[16] The inscription may have been filled in by the scribe of the second workshop, which was responsible for the second section of linen and for joining it to the first; but without seeing the back of the Tapestry, one cannot ascertain if the inscription at this point was stitched independently of the main register, which would support my point.[17]

16 Gale R. Owen-Crocker, "The Bayeux 'Tapestry': Invisible Seams and Visible Boundaries," *Anglo-Saxon England* 31 (2002): 257–73, at 262–63.

17 The back of the Tapestry is covered by a lining, and the whole object is enclosed in a climate-controlled display case at all times. The back was photographed in 1982–83, but only a few of the photographs have been published. Bédat and Girault-Kurtzeman ("Technical Study," 97) assert "the entire embroidered strip (upper and lower borders, inscriptions and central scenes) was embroidered at the same time," but on the evidence of published images I remain unconvinced about the borders and open-minded about the consistency of method throughout the Tapestry.

There is a major change in the embroidery at Scene 43 (Wilson, plate 48), soon after the fourth seam, when the lettering starts to be written in alternate red and black, an innovation which suggests a new workshop. Scene 43, though it does not advance the narrative, is important structurally, as I have demonstrated elsewhere.[18] Its inscription, *ET HIC EPISCOPVS CIBV[M] ET POTV[M] BENEDICIT*, "and here the bishop blesses the food and drink," is very upright and large. This contrasts with the smaller, sloping letters of *HIC FECERVNT PRANDIVM*, "Here they made a meal," which precedes it. The difference indicates the adjacent *tituli* were the work of different hands.[19] I have suggested elsewhere[20] that the scenes of pillage and food preparation were not original to the Tapestry design but were inserted to make the feast appear at a specific, measured point. This part of the inscription, then, may also have been an afterthought.

The contrasting colours continue, sometimes in blocks of alternating letters, sometimes with a word or two in each colour. At Scene 52 (Wilson, plate 63), the first new *titulus* after the sixth seam,[21] the colours change to black and yellow with intermittent red letters. They continue, mostly in letters of alternating colour, until Scene 57, Harold's death (Wilson, plate 71). At this point green is introduced to the inscription and there are some words in black, some in the lighter greenish shade, to the present limit of the Tapestry. (The end is missing.) The change of colour at Scene 57 may, again, relate to a different production team: The episode of Harold's death also contains a seam, the eighth, although it is invisible from the front of the Tapestry.[22]

LETTERING, LAYOUT, AND PUNCTUATION: CONTRASTS, PARALLELS, AND INDIVIDUALITY

The demonstrable relationship between the Tapestry's images and illuminated manuscripts naturally invites comparison between the Tapestry inscription and manuscript writing. However, the inscription omits some features found in manuscript text. The Tapestry does not use *litterae notabiliores* (larger or decorated letters)[23] to

18 Gale R. Owen-Crocker, "Telling a Tale: Narrative Techniques in the Bayeux Tapestry and the Old English Epic *Beowulf*," in *Medieval Art: Recent Perspectives: A Memorial Tribute to C. R. Dodwell*, ed. Owen-Crocker and Timothy Graham (Manchester: Manchester University Press, 1998), 40–59, at 52–54; Owen-Crocker, "Brothers, Rivals and the Geometry of the Bayeux Tapestry," in Owen-Crocker, *King Harold II*, 109–123, at 115–16.

19 An alternative possibility is that the inscription of *Hic fecervnt prandivm* was set out using a template (perhaps leather) which had got pulled out of shape.

20 Owen-Crocker, "Brothers, Rivals," 120.

21 *Exercitv[m]*, the last word of the preceding *titulus*, is embroidered in black, after the seam.

22 The eighth seam is said to be 2.43 metres (8 feet) from the end; Bédat and Girault-Kurtzeman, "Technical Study," 86, diagram 1. This is based on an overall measurement of 68.38 metres (224 feet 4 inches). However, other published measurements and the measurements of the facsimiles from which scholars are obliged to work vary considerably, according to the tension of the Tapestry in different situations, and the exact position of this seam is not clear to me.

23 M. B. Parkes, *Pause and Effect: An Introduction to the History of Punctuation in the West* (Aldershot: Scolar, 1992), 305.

mark the opening of the inscription or any of its parts,[24] and although the text is expressed in short statements, the layout does not reflect that structure as it would in a liturgical text,[25] since the long narrow shape of the frieze demands that in all but a few cases the text be written in a continuous line.

Rather, the Tapestry writing resembles inscriptions on stone sculptures. There is a particularly close parallel in the text on an eleventh-century grave-cover found at St. Augustine's Abbey, Canterbury, where the Tapestry itself was probably designed.[26] The incised letters on the grave-cover, predominantly Roman capitals "made up of slender, even strokes which terminate in small serifs,"[27] would have appeared very similar to those of the Tapestry especially if the writing was picked out in colour, a possibility strongly suggested from the evidence of paint remaining on more than a third of Anglo-Saxon sculptures in southeast England.[28] Like the Tapestry, the St. Augustine's carving includes uncial lettering.[29]

The Tapestry uses some marks of punctuation which are found in manuscripts, especially the *punctus* (a single point), the double *punctus* (colon), and variants of the two-dots-and-a-dash (:-) or two-dots-and-a-tilde (:~) combination. The latter sometimes functions as a symbol of continuation, especially where the text follows on beneath, which is unusual in the Tapestry as a whole (see fig. 2.2, also Scene 15; Wilson, plate 17), and sometimes where there is continuous action over several graphic images, as at Scenes 24–25 (Wilson, plates 26–28). In other places, such as at the end of Scene 25 (Wilson, plate 29), the symbol seems to be used simply as an alternative to the double *punctus*, discussed below. In general, the symbols are not used syntactically as in literary or liturgical manuscripts. Instead the text is laid out in continuous script[30] with a double *punctus* often used to mark word division. In this respect the Tapestry

24 Clemoes, "Language in Context," 35 n. 28, notes that in the successive instances of *Her* in the Parker Chronicle, "each initial H was made prominent by size, shape, and spacing," whereas there is no such treatment of the successive *Hic* in the Tapestry.

25 Liturgical text is arranged *per cola et commata*, a format by which "at the beginning of each breath group a new line was started, new lines not corresponding to such a beginning being indented." Peter Clemoes, *Liturgical Influence on Punctuation in Late Old English and Early Middle English Manuscripts*, Old English Newsletter *Subsidia* 4 (1952; reprinted and corrected, Binghamton, NY: CEMERS SUNY-Binghamton, 1980), 10.

26 St. Augustine's 2; Dominic Tweddle, Martin Biddle, and Birthe Kjølbye-Biddle, *Corpus of Anglo-Saxon Stone Sculpture*, vol. 4, *South-East England* (Oxford: Oxford University Press, 1995), 128–31, ills. 24–28.

27 John Higgitt, "The Inscriptions in Latin Lettering," in Tweddle, Biddle, and Kjølbye-Biddle, *Corpus*, 108–113, at 113.

28 Ibid.

29 The e of the last word, *fecit*, is uncial; Tweddle, Biddle, and Kjølbye-Biddle, *Corpus*, ill. 28. Mixed lettering appears to be typical of sculpture at this period in southeast England: an eleventh-century carving in Old English from London (All Hallows 1) includes a half-uncial letter and the runic "wynn" among its Roman capitals; and a Latin inscription on an Anglo-Norman grave-cover from Stratfield Mortimer, Berkshire, uses Old English "ash" and "wynn" (219, 336).

30 This *scriptio continua*, in which words were divided by points known as "interpuncts," had been used in older Latin manuscripts but is not characteristic of early medieval manuscript writing. Parkes, *Pause and Effect*, 10.

again used a technique found in contemporary sculptured inscriptions, rather than contemporary manuscript writing.[31]

The Tapestry scribe, or the embroiderers, did however use certain individual symbols in a way which, I suggest, reflects the emphasis the makers placed on persons and events. Three times the early appearance of Harold, the future English king, is marked by a symbol consisting of three dots in a triangular shape (Scenes 4 and 6; Wilson, plates 4, 6). A triple *punctus* (three dots arranged vertically), which is not in the usual scribal repertoire, marks the journey of Harold three times at Scene 2 (Wilson, plate 2) and occurs at other points, with slight variations, marking out William, the death of King Edward, the order to build ships, the capture of food supplies, and the opening of William's *viriliter et sapienter* speech (Scenes 14, 27, 35, 40, 51; Wilson, plates 15–16, 30, 34, 45, 58). Most are significant occasions: William and Harold, the major protagonists of the narrative, are here depicted riding in some splendour, while the deathbed of King Edward, the decision to invade England, and the invasion's culmination in the Battle of Hastings were major events in recent history. Only the capture of food supplies is mundane; but if we recall that the Norman pillage was at the expense of the English, the matter was not unimportant to them, and the triple mark may have given it an ironic emphasis.

The embroiderers also evidently expressed themselves by utilising a greater variety of embroidery stitches than has been hitherto appreciated. Until very recently, it was assumed that embroidery in chain stitch and split stitch was not original to the Tapestry, and that any work in these stitches should be identified as repair and reconstruction. A technical study of the Tapestry published in 2004 provides evidence to the contrary.[32] The study includes an analysis of the stitching employed on the inscription *HIC DEDERVNT HAROLDO CORONA[M] REGIS*, "Here they have given Harold the king's crown" (Scene 29, fig. 2.3). While most of the Tapestry's inscription is worked in a single row of stem stitch, this statement that Harold was given the crown shows some special effect in almost every letter, variously double stem stitch, chain stitch, double chain stitch, and split stitch. Only the g and s of *REGIS* are simple stem stitch.[33] Furthermore, uniquely in the Tapestry, this *titulus* uses a "suspension" to indicate abbreviation over the A of *CORONA*. Elsewhere the Tapestry uses a straight horizontal bar to indicate the nasal inflexion (M), but this sign, which resembles a little crown, may be a deliberate witticism or emphasis. Not only was Harold's reception of the crown the climax of the career of the last English king, it was an important issue politically that Harold did not seize the crown but was offered it by the councillors of the land.

Immediately after Harold's coronation, the threatening appearance of Halley's comet in the upper border is explained by *ISTE MIRANT STELLA[M]*, also placed in

---

31 The continuous script divided by colons is found, for example, on the St. Augustine's grave-cover (see note 26) and also on a roughly contemporary runic inscription on a grave-marker from St. Paul's Cathedral, London. Tweddle, Biddle, and Kjølbye-Biddle, *Corpus*, 226, ill. 350.

32 Bédat and Girault-Kurtzeman, "Technical Study," 93.

33 Bédat and Girault-Kurtzeman, "Technical Study," 96, diagram 4.

Fig. 2.3: The Bayeux Tapestry, Scene 29: "Here they have given Harold the king's crown."

the border. Here the lettering, which has been monochrome black up to this point, becomes two-tone, yellow and a dark colour (possibly green), with only the two Ls of *STELLA[M]* monochrome; however, the Ls are not black, but yellow, like the tail of the adjacent comet. The two-tone effect is continued in the first three letters of *HAROLD*, the name above the heads of the distressed king and the man who speaks to him urgently, no doubt interpreting the celestial occurrence in pessimistic terms.

It seems that the embroiderers appreciated the importance of these scenes and enhanced them with their own sign language. This differed from the way manuscript scribes typically enhanced their writing (with attention to initial letters or special decoration appended to the letters), and included a wider range of "special effects" than was available to the sculptor in stone. It is now clear that experiment and creativity played a larger part in the embroidery work than was previously believed. Examination of facsimiles shows that, as with Scene 29, some letters elsewhere in the inscription are clearly not in single stem stitch (for example, in fig. 2.1, the thick letters of *COSNONIS* and the diagonal of the first N in *VENERVNT*); these effects may or may not reflect thematic significance. There is clearly research to be done on this matter, but until the photographs of the back of the Tapestry are made available, observations can only be tentative.

FUNCTION AND POSITION OF THE TEXT

Much of the text consists of sentences characterised by the use of words localising the narrative in time or place: *hic* ("here") and *ubi* ("where").[34] Alternatively the inscription is used for labelling, mostly giving names. In the usual *titulus* position there is *EDVVARD REX* at the start and an isolated *HAROLD* as the Englishman stands in his ship, and again as the comet threatens his reign. What may be the torn remains of the name *Eustacius* (*E CIVS*) is in the upper border of Scene 55 (Wilson, plate 68).[35]

William's messengers are labelled, *NVNTII VVILLELMI*, at Scene 11. The three seated figures of William and his brothers are named, *ODO EP[ISCOPU]S ROTBERT WILLELM*, at Scene 44 (fig. 2.2). The roof of the building allows little space here, and the scribe is forced to write William's name beneath it, on either side of his head. We *read* the scene left to right: Odo, William, and Robert; but the scribe obviously *laid out* the inscription in the sequence Odo, Robert, William, since he placed the two-dots-and-a-dash symbol after the name of Robert as a mark of continuation to show that there was more to come of this inscription below, distinguishing it from the *titulus* of the next scene, which is uncomfortably close.

Other names are inserted into the main register alongside figures. The naming of Stigand, archbishop of Canterbury, at Harold's coronation (Scene 30; Wilson, plate 31) may be deliberate anti-English propaganda. Stigand's appointment was uncanonical and he was excommunicate. Norman writers claim that Stigand crowned Harold, and hence that the coronation was invalid; but English sources suggest that Harold was well aware of Stigand's position, asserting that the archbishop of York officiated at the coronation, as he had done for other consecrations during Harold's reign.[36] The name *TVROLD*, a man who was probably a vassal of Odo and later one of his tenants in Kent,[37] is also inserted into the main register (Scene 10; Wilson, plate 11), as is the place-name *REDNES*, "Rennes" (Scene 18; Wilson, plates 21–22). *ECCLESIA*, "church," is rather unnecessarily written above the church at Bosham (Scene 3; Wilson, plate 3), and *MINISTRI*, "waiters," next to the servants delivering the Hastings feast (Scene 42; Wilson, plate 47). The latter inscription is tautologous and somewhat clumsy since the text above reads *ET HIC MINISTRAVERVNT*, "and

---

34 *Ubi* is used in the first and second sections of linen only. Its last appearance is at Scene 23, Harold's oath, as recognised in Short, "Bayeux Tapestry Inscription," 271.

35 This interpretation is particularly advocated in Bridgeford, *1066*, especially 191–93.

36 Barbara English, "The Coronation of Harold in the Bayeux Tapestry," in Bouet, Levy, and Neveux, *The Bayeux Tapestry*, 347–81, at 377–78.

37 Charles Prentout, "An Attempt to Identify Some Unknown Characters in the Bayeux Tapestry," in Gameson, *Study*, 21–30 (first published in 1935 as "Essai d'identification des personnages inconnus de la Tapisserie de Bayeux," *Revue Historique* 176:14–23).

here they waited on." *MINISTRI* was perhaps an addition to fill space. Like the inscription following it, *HIC FECERVNT PRANDIVM*, "Here they made a meal," *MINISTRI* is in smaller letters with a pronounced slope and so may have been inscribed by a different hand. It was probably embroidered later too: It is in red, a colour which only begins to feature in the *tituli* (on alternate letters) above the feast itself.[38]

VOCABULARY, SYNTAX, RHETORIC

Despite its length, the inscription is remarkable for the poverty of its vocabulary and syntax. As is apparent from table 2.1, the majority of the words are proper nouns and titles. Adjectives are confined to the necessary "English" (twice), "dead," some possessives meaning "his," the numeral *unus*, perhaps reflecting the Old English *an* or Old French *un*, both of which can mean "a certain" as well as "one"—this is at Scene 15 where a cleric and Ælfgiva stand to vex posterity[39]—and the sole gratuitous example, *magno*, recording that William crossed the Channel in a big ship. In contrast the verbs are varied and precise, unlike the allusive, flowery style of contemporary literature: They include *equitant*, "they rode"; *incenditur*, "they set fire to"; and *festinaverunt*, "they hastened."

Only two sections of the inscription have any rhetorical character. The first (fig. 2.4) comes as Harold crosses the sea: *ET VELIS VENTO PLENIS VENIT IN TERRA VVIDONIS COMITIS*, "and with the wind full in his sails came to the land of Count Guy."[40] Not surprisingly, wind and sail are often found associated together in literature, both in Old English[41] and in Latin, where the words have a pleasing alliteration (*ventus* and *velum*, respectively), which was exploited particularly in poetry[42] but also in prose.[43] In isolation the graphics of this scene would seem to

---

38 A photograph of the back of the embroidery at this point demonstrates that the stitching of *MINISTRI* is not connected to anything else in the scene. Bédat and Girault-Kurtzeman, "Technical Study," 97, plate 20.

39 For an up-to-date resumé of theories as to the identity of Ælfgiva, see Catherine E. Karkov, "Gendering the Battle? Male and Female in the Bayeux Tapestry," in Owen-Crocker, *King Harold II*, 139–47, at 142 n. 13.

40 Uniquely in the Tapestry, the writer inserts a double hyphen, twice (*VE= =NIT*), to ensure that the necessary splitting of *venit* over two lines does not interfere with the continuity of his rhetorical burst.

41 *Beowulf*, lines 1905–8. F. Klaeber, ed., *Beowulf and the Fight at Finnesburg*, 3rd ed. (Boston: D. C. Heath, 1950), 71.

42 It can be found in Horace, Lucan, Lucretius, Ovid, and Vergil. The closest parallel to the Bayeux Tapestry text is Ovid, *Metamorphoses*: "Et quoniam magno feror aequore plenaque ventis / vela dedit: nihil est toto, quod perstet, in orbe" (And since I am embarked on the boundless sea and have spread my full sails to the winds, there is nothing in all the world that keeps its form). Ovid, *Metamorphoses*, with an English translation by Frank Justus Miller, 3rd ed., vol. 2, Loeb Classical Library, Ovid in Six Volumes 4 (Cambridge, MA: Harvard University Press: 1984), 366–67.

43 An example is by the Anglo-Saxon scholar Bede: "uentorum furores uela non sustinent" (the sails could not resist the fury of the winds). Bertram Colgrave and R. A. B. Mynors, eds., *Bede's Ecclesiastical History of the English People* (Oxford: Oxford University Press, 1969), 54–55 (I.17).

Fig. 2.4: The Bayeux Tapestry, Scene 5: "… and, with the wind full in his sails, came to the land of Count Guy."

suggest the English sailors were in full control, handling the anchor and posting a lookout as if they knew where they were going. The appearance of a hostile Guy of Pontieu is a complete surprise. Nothing supports William of Malmesbury's explanation that this was a fishing trip that went wrong.[44] Only the caption with its reference to the wind opens the possibility that the English were blown off course.[45]

The second rhetorical *titulus* comes at Scene 51 (Wilson, plates 57–61). It paraphrases William's rallying speech immediately before the battle: *HIC WILLELM DVX ALLOQVITVR SVIS MILITIBVS VT PREPARARENT SE VIRILITER ET SAPIENTER AD PRELIVM CONTRA ANGLORVM EXERCITV[M]*, "Here Duke William exhorts his soldiers that they should prepare themselves manfully and wisely for the fight against the English army." This is the longest "statement" in the Tapestry and the only one to use the conjunction *ut* and a subordinate clause. Other captions are made continuous by the use of *et* ("and"), but they link parallel main clauses and bridge separate graphic scenes. Although the graphic situation is improbable—William

44 William of Malmesbury, *Gesta Regum Anglorum: The History of the English Kings*, ed. and trans. R. A. B. Mynors, Rodney M. Thomson, and Michael Winterbottom, vol. 2, Oxford Medieval Texts (Oxford: Clarendon, 1999), 416–17 (228, 3–4).

45 I have considered the possibility that a reference to wind in the sails could alone imply a sudden storm, since *velis* and *ventus* are often used together in this context (see the Bede quotation above, also, for example, Ovid, *Metamorphoses*, 154–55); but I concluded that it could not, since the formula is frequently used descriptively, and metaphorically, as in the Ovid quotation at note 42. Lucretius even uses similes of wind in the sails to explain the human body, and magnetism! See Lucretius, *De Rerum Natura*, with an English translation by W. H. D. Rouse, Loeb Classical Library (Cambridge, MA: Harvard University Press, 1992), 436–37 (Book 4, lines 896–97) and 568–69 (Book 6, lines 1031–33). It was evidently a literary commonplace. In *Beowulf* references to wind in relation to a voyage always mark favourable conditions.

addressing his army, from the rear, on a moving horse—the text is entirely appropriate in both sentiment and style. The ideal that a hero should possess both wisdom and physical courage is a literary *topos* which can be found from classical (Greek and Latin) literature to Old English and Old French, notably in *Beowulf* and the *Chanson de Roland*.[46] The dual virtues are prominent also in the Bible and were especially popularised by Isidore of Seville. The grammatical construction in the Tapestry, which expresses the *topos* by means of adverbs (rather than nouns or adjectives), appears to be unusual. However, the rhetorical use of *sapienter* in conjunction with a matching adverb is a stylistic device used by the orator Cicero.[47] The adverbial *viriliter* is rare, but is characteristic of exhortations in the Vulgate Bible of St. Jerome,[48] an association which adds a moral dimension to the familiar concept of "fortitude," and a biblical tone to the Duke's speech.

TEXT AND GRAPHICS

It is clear that the Tapestry images were laid out first and the inscription fitted round them: Words were split, and the scribe or scribes were economical of space where necessary, making some letters smaller than others (see table 2.1, Scenes 38, 44, 48); eliding N and T (Scenes 42, 43, 51, 53, 56, 58) and also N and E (Scene 52); fitting an O inside an M (Scene 46); and making frequent use of abbreviations, usually indicated by a bar above the word, sometimes by a bar across a letter and by other signs each used only once (Scene 29) or twice (Scenes 27, 36).

The graphics are organized into scenes divided by trees and buildings. Generally these observe the unities of time and place: Alternate scenes show people travelling to a place and people actually at that place. The inscriptions occasionally override this. For example, Scene 4, Harold's embarkation, captioned *HIC HAROLD MARE NAVIGAVIT* shows men leaving a building at Bosham, loading a small boat, pushing it from the shore, and then rowing it out (Wilson, plates 4–5). Scene 5 shows the men in a larger ship, with a figurehead and sail. The inscription, though, makes no distinction between this "scene" and the previous one, continuing with *et*: *ET VELIS VENTO PLENIS VENIT IN TERRA VVIDONIS COMITIS* (fig. 2.4).

46 R. E. Kaske, "*Sapientia et fortitudo* as the Controlling Theme of Beowulf," in *An Anthology of Beowulf Criticism*, ed. Lewis E. Nicholson (Notre Dame, IN: University of Notre Dame Press, 1963), 269–310 (first published in 1958 in *Studies in Philology*, 55:423–57).

47 I note that translators avoid the adverbial construction. Closest to the Bayeux Tapestry text is "et sapienter et fortiter" (with wisdom and courage), in Cicero, *Letters to his Friends*, with an English translation by W. Glynn Williams, vol. 1, Loeb Classical Library (Cambridge, MA: Harvard University Press, 1952), 30–31 (Book 1.7.5), but the construction is characteristic of this author; see also, for example, "humaniter et sapienter et amabiliter in me" (humanity, wisdom, and a regard for myself), Cicero, *Letters to Atticus*, with an English translation by D. R. Shackleton Bailey, Loeb Classical Library (Cambridge, MA: Harvard University Press, 1999), 174–75 (Book 14.13a).

48 For example, St. Paul to the Corinthians: "Vigilate, state in fide, viriliter agite, et confortamini" (Watch, stand in the faith, do manfully, and be strengthened), I Corinthians 16:13. *The Vulgate New Testament with the Douay Version of 1582* (London: Samuel Bagstone and Sons, 1872).

The opening of military action, and hence of the Brittany campaign proper, is attached by both inscription and graphics to the preceding episode of the river crossing and the quicksand rescue. The *titulus* for Scene 17 (Wilson, plates 19–20), placed immediately below the upper border, *ET HIC TRANSIERVNT FLUMEN COSNONIS*, "and here they crossed the river Couesnon," continues without a gap into that for Scene 18, the siege of Dol (Wilson, plates 20–21), *ET VENERVNT AD DOL ET CONAN FVGA VERTIT*, "and they came to Dol and Conan took flight"; while the description of Harold's heroism at the quicksand comes like a digression beneath it, occupying not only the space underneath *–SIERVNT FLUMEN COSNONIS* of Scene 17 but also the area below the *ETVE–* of Scene 18 (fig. 2.1).[49] Unusually, there is no tree or building to mark the transition. There is a gap between Harold's shield at the extremity of Scene 17 and the horse's tail which begins Scene 18, although the tail projects back under the preceding scene's inscription, below the S of *COSNONIS* and the *T: EOS* concluding *TRAHEBAT EOS*. A few stitch holes in the blank linen indicate that there may once have been some embroidery there, but they do not form any recognisable shape.

Some scenes are not mentioned in the inscription. The *artist* creates a pair of Last Suppers: The first occurs before Harold's voyage to France and, like Christ's Passover meal, takes place in an upper room (Scene 3; Wilson, plates 3–4); the second, on the eve of the Battle of Hastings (Scene 44; Wilson, plate 48), is based on a Last Supper illustration in the St. Augustine Gospels, Cambridge, Corpus Christi College MS 286. The graphic designer makes a major parallel and contrast between the two suppers; but the *lack of caption* for the first feast suggests it was not part of the original plan, the oral commission. Similarly, the inscription records William ordering ships, the loading of them, and their launch, but makes no mention of their construction. The graphics show Odo advising his brother, which is not implicit in the inscription, and a long sequence of tree felling, plank planing, and boat building without any explanatory words (Scene 35; Wilson, plates 34–36).

Conversely, the inscription may hint at more than the graphics. At Scene 6, Harold has arrived in Brittany, and at Scene 7, he is arrested by Guy of Pontieu (Wilson, plates 6–8). Awkwardly placed over the latter scene is the caption relating to the next: *ET DVXIT EVM AD BELREM*, "and led him to Beaurain." The inscription continues (Wilson, plate 8) over the bunched English and French riders following Harold: *ET IBI EVM TENUIT*, "and held him there [or 'then']." In isolation the statement that Harold was "held" might imply that he was imprisoned by Guy, a situation only loosely suggested by the group of English and French crowded round him (at the end of Scene 8; Wilson, plate 9). However, it is claimed by the Norman historian William of Poitiers that the men of Pontieu habitually ambushed, imprisoned, and tortured wealthy travellers.[50] Possibly the person who dictated the Tapestry caption intended to convey a cruel captivity of this kind. If Harold had been

---

49 See my comments on the script, above, beginning on page 37.
50 R. H. C. Davis and Marjorie Chibnall, eds., *The "Gesta Gvillelmi" of William of Poitiers* (Oxford: Clarendon, 1998), 68–69 (i.41).

shown victimised by Guy, William's rescue of him would have reflected well on the Duke (a pro-Norman interpretation of events); as it is, Harold, though suffering the humiliation of removing his sword, is shown (Scene 9; Wilson, plate 9) in parley with his captor more like an aristocratic hostage than a degraded prisoner (in keeping with an English estimate of his worth). However, the interesting suggestion has been made to me that the captions might have been inserted the wrong way round: that "and led him to Beaurain" was intended to caption the horseback journey, while "and then held him" belongs with the previous scene and the words "Here Guy arrests Harold."[51] The caption has been fitted round spears and heads, and the M of *DUXIT EVM* has a shortened upright to accommodate an angled spear, but it is worth noting that the spacing of the letters in the words is exactly the same at the start of both clauses: *ETD*[spear]*VX*[spear] and *ETI*[spear]*BI*[spear], respectively, and that the space for the initial I of *IBI* is rather wide and could have accommodated a D. There is no certainty that the person responsible for transferring the cartoon of the inscription to the linen would have been able to read Latin, or even that he or she was literate (though the generally high standard leads me to think that the person understood the text).

THE CREATIVE PROCESS

The Bayeux Tapestry's words reflect various stages in the creative process: communicating the original conception orally; writing down the text; creating stencils or templates of the letters (or selecting them from an existing stock); working out the position of the text in relation to the graphics; transferring the text to the cloth; embroidering it; and finally reading it to expound the narrative. The constant use of *hic* ("here") and *ubi* ("where") clearly aided the ultimate interpretive process,[52] but it is possible that it also reflects the conceptual level: that the sequence of events to be depicted was determined at the earliest stage of the design. I would suggest that the patron or his creative agent specified certain episodes and places that were to be included, and these were laid out by the designer in a meaningful relationship, not, at this stage, with geometric precision, but in such a way as to establish basic parallels and contrasts—Harold's sea journey to France and its counterpart, the Normans' invasion voyage to England; the Brittany campaign and the Battle of Hastings—and that this was achieved through dictation by a Norman speaking Latin to an Englishman who wrote it down. Perhaps at the earliest stage the conception was indicated by gesturing about a room. The detailed graphic design was to expand the work into many subtleties; some of these were later accommodated into the inscription, and some were not.

---

51 I am grateful to my son Peter Crocker for this suggestion.

52 See Clemoes, "Language in Context," 31: "Applied to successive year numbers or pictures [the written Her/Hic formula] had a 'voice' like that of a guide on a conducted tour"; also Richard Brilliant, "The Bayeux Tapestry: A Stripped Narrative for Their Eyes and Ears," in Gameson, *Study*, 111–37, especially 137 and 112, fig. 1 (first published in 1991 in *Word and Image* 7:93–125).

The text raises various questions about the making of the Tapestry. To what extent did the graphic design anticipate inscriptions? In the case of Harold's feast at Bosham there is no space for text, which may mean the scene was not part of the original plan, as suggested above, or may simply mean that no space was left for it. Were some of the inscriptions composed *ad hoc*, such as the caption to the Ælfgiva scene,[53] where the scribe either did not understand the significance of the image, or conversely knew it so well that a mere allusion was thought sufficient?

The design of the Tapestry seems to have brought together experts from different fields, some of whom had detailed knowledge of Canterbury manuscripts, though different individuals seemingly exploited different codices in their borrowings for the Tapestry graphics.[54] The inscription evidently utilised the expertise of craftsmen accustomed to writing inscriptions for sculptures, though the person(s) who laid out the inscription on the cloth may also have been familiar with the punctuation of manuscripts. Did the "sculptor" work on the textile, or did he merely supply templates of letters to expert tracers? Did the experts work together as a team, or in sequence? Did the full development of the inscription immediately follow the initial dictation by the Norman patron or his agent, or did its final manifestation succeed creation of the graphics?

Did the first workshop complete all its work, including the embroidery, before the second workshop's section was even laid out? If, as the latest published research asserts, the whole width of the Tapestry (borders, main register, and inscription) was embroidered simultaneously, I cannot think of any other way in which the second workshop could have completed the bottom border and the inscription on the first piece of linen, as they almost certainly did. This would negate the usual assumption that several *ateliers* were working simultaneously to complete the enormous project, and supports my suspicion that the first section of linen was individual, perhaps a prototype, which was completed before the others and only subsequently linked to the second section.[55]

---

53 "Where a cleric and Ælfgiva ..."

54 The main register particularly corresponds to pictures in the Old English illustrated Hexateuch, London, British Library, MS Cotton Claudius B iv. The bottom border exploits other Canterbury manuscripts, some of which are also copied on an ivory book cover. See Owen-Crocker, "Reading the Bayeux Tapestry," passim, and Hart, "The *Cicero-Aratea*," 176–78.

55 This suggestion is made on the basis of the very different treatment of the bottom border in the first section (with genre scenes and fables in long sequences); the way in which a scene end and the first seam coincide and the disjunction in the upper border at the join; and my deduction, based on the overall design of the Tapestry, that the object was designed as a square, and the first section made to fit a specific wall (see Owen-Crocker, "Brothers, Rivals," 116–18 and fig. 8; also Chris Henige, "Putting the Bayeux Tapestry in its Place," in Owen-Crocker, *King Harold II*, 126–37, especially 128). Short, in "Bayeux Tapestry Inscription," also concluded the first section was individual and completed first.

"De Fil d'Or et de Soie": Making Textiles in Twelfth-Century French Romance

Monica L. Wright

Cloth and clothing held a privileged place in the romances of twelfth-century France. The writers from this period, which marked the birth of romance as a literary genre, used textiles in a great many ways and for a great many narrative purposes, providing lengthy descriptions of characters' clothing, depicting scenes of dressing and undressing, and even including scenes in which characters make cloth. Yet cloth and clothing do not appear to be simply ornaments in these literary works. Cloth and clothing were so important for these writers, and the writers were able to use them so inventively, precisely because textile had a special relationship both with the society of the day and with the new literary conventions that emerged with the rise of romance.[1] Moreover, an examination of some textual instances that depict the production of textiles—or, in some cases, the refusal to produce them—shows how changing social norms about the gender roles in textile production created ambivalence in both society and literature.

The making of clothing and fabric was of tremendous importance for medieval society: It helped form and solidify complex social bonds, both within families,

A version of this paper was presented in May 2004 at the International Congress on Medieval Studies at Kalamazoo, Michigan.

1 As Eugène Vinaver noted in *Form and Meaning in Medieval Romance* (Cambridge: Modern Humanities Association, 1966), romance's narrative form is comparable to that of a tapestry, with a complex intricate structure that would unravel if there were "a single cut across it, made at any point" (10). Moreover, the technique of romance composition closely resembled weaving: Pre-existing material was refashioned through amplification and embellishment to render it pleasing to a new audience. Although such refashioning occurred in other genres, romance composition was distinct in its heavy reliance upon clothing signifiers. The writers' use of clothing included far more than the articulation of class, gender, profession, or state of being: They used clothing to structure their works, to open and close narrative threads, and to inscribe dynamism into their portraits of characters. For a discussion of Chrétien's use of clothing in his romances, see my article "Their Clothing Becomes Them: The Narrative Function of Clothing in Chrétien de Troyes," *Arthurian Literature* 20 (2003): 31–42. Chrétien's use, while often more ingenious than that of his contemporaries, exemplified the innovative role clothing played in romance generally.

especially from generation to generation, and among different families.[2] Gifts of cloth and clothing, among other valuables, created these social ties, while the manufacture of cloth was often a shared experience. It is indeed no surprise that today we still refer metaphorically to the "fabric of society." The industries providing the raw materials for cloth production included a great variety of different vocations, starting with farming, raising livestock, and manufacturing dyestuffs. Merchants and traders transported goods to where they were needed. Production required the work of spinners, weavers, dyers, finishers, and other skilled and unskilled laborers. The people involved in these commercial relationships were diverse, from different backgrounds and social classes and both sexes. In a very real sense, therefore, cloth bound society together.

Traditionally, spinning, weaving, cutting, and sewing fell into the domain of women's work.[3] Yet, by the mid-twelfth century, a slow, complex shift had begun to occur. As cloth production was steadily becoming an industry of professionals and thus increasingly organized, and as the technology that supported such production was advancing and becoming more complicated, men began to take over certain formerly female-dominated occupations within the manufacturing process.[4] This

2 Cloth manufacture itself has traditionally been reserved for "spinners, weavers, dyers, and finishers [who] harness the imagined blessings of ancestors and divinities to inspire or animate the product, and draw analogies between weaving or dyeing and the life cycle of birth, maturation, death, and decay. The ritual and discourse that surround its manufacture establish cloth as a convincing analog for the regenerative and degenerative processes of life, and as a great connector, binding humans not only to each other but to the ancestors of their past and the progeny who constitute their future." The importance of clothing for such societies cannot be overstated. Annette B. Weiner and Jane Schneider, eds., *Cloth and Human Experience* (Washington: Smithsonian Institution Press, 1989), 3.

3 Andrée Lehmann has pointed out that, despite widespread changes in the gendering of certain cloth-producing activities, women continued to be the only practitioners of certain trades such as silk spinning and weaving, hemp and flax dressing, and the production of silk items and garments. See Lehmann, *Le Rôle de la femme dans l'histoire de la France au moyen âge* (Paris: Berger-Levrault, 1952), 436. Moreover, attitudes about female involvement in these activities tended to be based primarily on whether the work was commercial, in which case men were favored, or whether it was private, for household uses, in which case women were favored, as Ruth Mazo Karras noted in her essay "'This Skill in a Woman is By No Means to Be Despised': Weaving and the Gender Division of Labor in the Middle Ages," in *Medieval Fabrications: Dress, Textiles, Cloth Work, and Other Cultural Imaginings*, ed. E. Jane Burns (New York: Palgrave Macmillan, 2004), 89–104. Karras attests that the "connection of textile work with female virtue was not strong enough that it excluded men from commercial weaving, because virtuous textile production for women was noncommercial" (103).

4 During the course of the Middle Ages, men began to join with women in such enterprises as commercial embroidery, spinning, and weaving, although women continued to exert a strong presence in these fields. Other trades, however, began to be more and more taken over by men who were organized into guilds, such as furriers, tailors, tapestry makers, and dyers (Lehmann, *Rôle de la femme*, 436–37). Guild membership tended to be reserved for males, even though some women participated in guilds; as Maryanne Kowaleski and Judith M. Bennett have explained, "most skilled 'women's work' never came under guild structure and supervision." Moreover, the guilds to which women tended to belong centered on the textile trades, and, within those guilds, women most often remained second-rank guild members, that is, on a par with boys, old men, and disabled men; see "Crafts, Guilds, and Women in the Middle Ages:

shift in the gender assignments of tasks appears to have first taken root, very predictably, in the larger production centers, such as in the large northern cities of Paris, Ghent, and Bruges, and to have started as early as the eleventh century, when the horizontal treadle loom began to replace the vertical loom in commercial production.[5] It is important to specify, however, that changes of this nature occur over time, and it was certainly the case that at the same time that men were taking over certain occupations in cloth manufacture, women continued to have a significant presence in them for quite a while.[6] In fact, this shift took several centuries to complete. Moreover, despite this phenomenon occurring in the urban cloth centers, spinning, cutting, and sewing, as well as private cloth production, continued to be primarily female tasks until well after the twelfth century. It is therefore not surprising that we should see gender ambivalence about these tasks manifest in the romances of the period.

The writers of twelfth-century romance in France respond to this type of gender ambivalence concerning cloth production by playing with convention. They do so to create new literary conventions that better reflect societal changes occurring around them. Because there was room for both female and male participants in the tasks and trades, a certain degree of flexibility rather than rigidity with regard to the gender assignment of clothmaking might be anticipated. Indeed, two textual examples give evidence of just such an attitude.

First, in the Occitan romance *Jaufré*,[7] the protagonist encounters a knight who gives him the choice of fighting him in battle or passing unharmed if he agrees to

Fifty Years after Marian K. Dale," in *Sisters and Workers in the Middle Ages*, ed. Judith M. Bennett et al. (Chicago: University of Chicago Press, 1989), 12, 14–15. David Herlihy sees evidence that by the late eleventh century the kinds of fabric produced had begun to fall along gender lines as well, with men taking over wool production in certain geographic areas while women continued to produce linen in those same areas; see *Opera Muliebria: Women and Work in Medieval Europe* (Philadelphia: Temple University Press, 1990), 92. What is clear is that the changes to gender assignment of cloth production in the Middle Ages, from an almost entirely female realm in the Carolingian period to a male-dominated commercial model by the advent of the early modern period, followed an irregular, chaotic pattern of development, in which the gendering of cloth production varied greatly according to geographic location, type of activity involved, and type of fabric produced.

5 The advantages of the horizontal treadle loom are multiple. Worked by two people, it allows for greater fabric widths and lengths and therefore more efficient production, as well as making certain weaving techniques possible. Elisabeth Crowfoot, Frances Pritchard, and Kay Staniland, *Textiles and Clothing c. 1150–c. 1450* (London: HMSO, 1992), 22–23.

6 Martha C. Howell has noted the discrepancy from city to city in late medieval northern European cities regarding women's involvement in market production, including the production of textiles. She found evidence that over the course of the high medieval and late medieval periods, women had progressively less access to what she terms "high labor status," meaning those professional activities that conferred both social status and higher pay, and that most often women participating in high-status work were consigned to marginal positions, secure in only a few conditions, by the late Middle Ages. "Women, the Family Economy, and the Structure of Market Production in Cities of Northern Europe during the Late Middle Ages," in *Women and Work in Preindustrial Europe*, ed. Barbara A. Hanawalt (Bloomington: Indiana University Press, 1986), 201.

7 Clovis Brunel, ed., *Jaufré: Roman arthurien du XIIIe siècle en vers provençaux* (Paris: Société des Anciens Textes Français, 1943).

certain conditions, one being that he never again wear clothes that he has not made himself: "ni vestiment / Non portes si el nol teisia" (vss. 1448–49). Although the list of conditions contains items that do not involve Jaufré's making his own clothes, such as never again riding a horse or cutting his hair or nails, the making of clothing is the one he seizes on as most absurd. He asks: "E si no sai far vestimens?" [And if I do not know how to make clothes?] (vs. 1455), to which the White Knight responds that he will have him taught: "Eu t'o farai mot ricamens … enseinar, / Teiser e cozir e talar" [I will have you most expertly taught to weave and sew and cut] (vss. 1456–58).[8] Jaufré insists that he would have too much difficulty learning (vss. 1461–62), but the White Knight believes it would take a strong man like Jaufré only seven years to learn (vss. 1463–64). In the end, Jaufré prefers to fight the knight, thereby reasserting his knighthood instead of giving in to the knight's strange conditions. Interestingly, Jaufré does not seem to fear any kind of social demotion from knightly status involved in taking on work that was traditionally associated with women, but rather worries about his ability to learn this type of work. It appears that Jaufré is rather accepting of, or at the very least not outraged by, the gender ambivalence that the knight is proposing, even though he fights him to avoid his proposition. It is seemingly not the reversal of gender roles that so bothers Jaufré about the knight's proposition, but his own perceived lack of competence and the prospect of wasting precious time.

An important counterexample to Jaufré's acceptance of gender ambivalence occurs in *Enéas*[9] with the character of Camille, the queen of Vulcane and a female knight. Camille does not accept gender ambivalence; she simultaneously defies and insists upon it.[10] The text makes clear that Camille is no typical woman of her day, preferring war to traditional women's work:

> el fu toz tens norrie an guerre
> et molt ama chevalerie
> et maintint la tote sa vie.
> Onc d'ovre a feme ne ot cure,
> ne de filer ne de costure.
> (vss. 3968–72)

[She was all the time trained in war and loved knighthood well and practiced it all her life. Never did she care for women's work: spinning and sewing.]

Her nonconformist attitude, in addition to her great skill as a warrior, occasionally attracts criticism from male knights. One such scene occurs when Tarcon, a Trojan knight, taunts her during a battle, saying that she should lay aside her arms because war is not women's work:

> "Laissiez ester desmesurance,
> metez jus l'escu et la lance

8 All translations are my own.
9 J. J. Salverda de Grave, ed., *Enéas: Roman du XIIe siècle* (Paris: Champion, 1925).
10 Camille's very name is imbued with the gender ambivalence that her character embodies: Her name is both a masculine and a feminine name in French.

et le hauberc, qui trop vos blece,
et ne mostrez vostre proëce.
Ce ne est pas vostre mestier,
mes filer, coldre et taillier;
en bele chanbre soz cortine
fet bon esbatre o tel meschine."
(vss. 7081–88)

["Calm this excessiveness, put down the shield and the lance and the hauberk that hurts you too much, and do not show your prowess. This is not your profession, but spinning, sewing, and cutting are; a young woman makes a better battle in a nice bedchamber behind the bedcurtain."]

Tarcon is making three assertions in his taunt. First, he states that war is not women's work; secondly, he informs her of what is—spinning, sewing, and cutting; finally, he suggests that if Camille does want to make war, she, as a woman, should be doing it between the sheets. He is thus in turn telling her that she is unfit to be a knight, that her work is inappropriate to her sex, and that she needs to be put in her place. Moreover, in all three of his assertions, he makes references to attire or cloth that are emblematic of the relative social positions he is proposing. The hauberk represents the knightly class from which women are normally excluded. The making of cloth and clothing symbolizes the women who master a craft and have the possibility of becoming economically autonomous; these women sometimes even escape masculine control. Finally, the bedcurtain evokes the traditional role of women as wives and producers of children, a type of production that very rarely assures female autonomy. Tarcon's suggestions, then, progressively demote Camille, removing her autonomy and her equal status with men and reducing her to a sex object.

Camille, however, refuses Tarcon's "advice," preferring instead to kill him. She wins the battle and fights it on her own terms, as a knight in armor, reasserting her status and prowess as knight. She moreover refuses any essentialist reading of her womanhood, stating that what Tarcon suggests comes naturally to women, at least in her own case, does not. She is a knight, like it or not. Whereas Jaufré's refusal to engage in the making of clothing is not a real rejection of women's work, since he worries simply about his own incompetence, Camille's refusal takes on a different tenor, as she brandishes her incompetence in female endeavors as another weapon. Both of these cases show the burgeoning social ambivalence with regard to gender roles in the making of cloth.

Just as these characters helped to question and redefine gender roles in a changing society, the emergence of romance was redefining and expanding literary conventions. The writers' portrayal of women in distress who make textiles was instrumental to this process.

In depicting the making of cloth in their romances, writers were also providing a deft metaphor for the very process in which they themselves were engaging. The weavers of romance depicted weavers of tapestry and makers of fine cloth, all of whom push the meaning of their labor to its very fullest in order to create new

65

meanings. In a sense, the writers depicted themselves and their projects in the acts of these characters. The process of making cloth and clothing was indeed the most natural place for writers to demonstrate their own process of creating meaning through manipulation of the existing vestimentary code by which social meanings were attached to attire.[11]

Because skill in producing textiles created the potential for material gains in this society, clothing and cloth manufacture theoretically provided some women with a degree of economic autonomy from men. Twelfth-century society had reservations about the existence of powerful women and often resisted acceptance of them, just as Tarcon fears Camille's power and rejection of traditionally conceived womanhood. An example of an abused woman who gains and exerts power through the production of textiles in order to overcome her misfortune is Chrétien de Troyes' protagonist in his Ovidian rewriting *Philomena*.[12] Philomena's textile skills, evoked three times in the short narrative poem, is also her saving grace. Her expertise is unmistakable:

> Avuec c'iert si bone ovriere
> D'ovrer une porpre vermoille
> Qu'an tot le mont n'ot sa paroille.
> Un diaspre ou un baudequin
> Nes la mesniee Hellequin
> Seüst ele an un drap portreire.
> > (vss. 188–93)

[Also, she was so skilled at working red *poupre* that the world contained no equal. She knew how to depict in cloth—in *diaspre* or in *baudequin*—even the followers of Harlequin.]

Although she has many other skills, this is the one that will save her life. Philomena's sister Procné marries Tereus, who soon takes an illicit liking to his new sister-in-law. Once Tereus has raped Philomena, he cuts out her tongue to prevent her from telling what has happened to her.[13] Then he hides her away, entrusting her

---

11 Romance of the twelfth century relied upon the use of old tropes in new settings, old characters in new stories, and old plots in new forms. A parallel to this process is the fact that romance writers used simultaneously the vestimentary code—that is, "standard" meanings of clothing, for example if a man is dressed like a wealthy man then he is a wealthy man— alongside more innovative ones, such as the use of clothing to convey meanings other than gender, class, or profession, creating new meanings for old forms.

12 Chrétien de Troyes, *Philomena: Conte raconté d'après Ovide*, ed. C. de Boer (Paris: Librairie Paul Geuthner, 1909).

13 E. Jane Burns has analyzed *Philomena* in terms of female responses to rape, positing that the two sisters react to Tereus' rape of Philomena in such a way that rejects the "narrative plots of virginal beauty that progress seamlessly from attraction, love, and passion to seduction, abduction, violation" and effectively changes "the path of myth, calling into question cultural stereotypes of the beautiful maiden and nurturing mother." "Raping Men: What's Motherhood Got to Do With It?" in *Representing Rape in Medieval and Early Modern Literature*, ed. Elizabeth Robertson and Christine M. Rose (New York: Palgrave, 2001), 129.

to a peasant woman who supports herself through spinning and weaving. The text describes her as "une vilainne / Qui vivoit de sa propre painne, / Car filer et tistre savoit" [a commoner who lived on her own (made her own living) for she knew how to spin and weave] (vss. 869–71). This self-sufficient woman unknowingly provides Philomena with the means to escape, reunite with her sister, and regain her own status. Philomena has full access to the woman's spinning and weaving tools and supplies, and one day, she decides to make a tapestry communicating her plight to her sister (vss. 1083–99). The old woman, who is unaware of Philomena's motivations, procures for her whatever she needs for her task:

> La vieille ne li contredist,
> Mes mout volantiers li eida
> Et trestot quanqu'ele cuida
> Qui a tel uevre covenist
> Porchasier et querre li fist.
> Trestot li quist son aparoil,
> Tant que fil inde et fil vermoil
> Et jaune et vert a plante ot,
> Mes el ne conut ne ne sot
> Rien de quanque cele tissoit;
> Mes l'uevre li abelissoit.
> (vss. 1108–18)

[The old woman did not impede her but helped her very willingly, and she quickly sought out and found all that she thought necessary for such a task. Soon she (Philomena) asked for the loom and placed threads of indigo, red, yellow, and green on it, but she (the old woman) knew nothing about what she was weaving; but she embellished the work.]

Meanwhile, Tereus has led Procné to believe that Philomena has died. In response to this news, Procné has mourning clothes brought to her (vs. 1005). Her action reflects the peasant woman's bringing materials to Philomena, inasmuch as both actions involve specialized cloth imbued with precise meaning brought out on Philomena's account. Procné's grief is furthermore so great that she swears never to remove her mourning clothes (vss. 1007–8). Later, however, when the peasant woman offers her the tapestry, her grief ends because she learns her sister is alive, although the story she reads from it enrages her. In effect, she trades one cloth for another, one state of being for another: Her powerlessness before the death of her sister transforms, through the message of the tapestry, into a position of power. She is now able to save her sister and to exact revenge upon her husband for the suffering he has inflicted upon them both.[14] Therefore, in this short narrative poem, three women are

---

14 Burns has fully analyzed Procné's murderous dinner and its importance for rewriting the narrative of rape and thus reconfiguring the power relationships within the text. Procné's violent meal, in which she kills her own son, cooks his flesh, and serves him to his father for dinner, reads as a destructive counterpoint to Philomena's constructive act of weaving, but both acts are part and parcel of the same revenge plot. Ibid., 143ff.

empowered through the making of cloth.[15]

This striking example of female empowerment through the manipulation of cloth is interesting especially in light of the importance of gifts to establishing social bonds in medieval society. Twelfth-century French aristocratic society was organized by the gift economy, meaning that gifts formed the basis for complex social ties; the gift economy stood in contrast to the emerging profit, or mercantile, economy by which exchanges of goods were conducted for profit rather than for the formation of social bonds.[16] Philomena's act, when considered in this way, takes on even more significance. She manipulates cloth and meaning in the same way that writers manipulated vestimentary conventions, using cloth and its place in the medieval gift economy. Her gift certainly creates the opportunity for her bonds with her sister to be renewed, but it is more than a simple reaffirmation of this relationship. She uses the cloth actually to transmit a crucial message to her sister, which must be seen as the most extensive and interesting manipulation possible of cloth.

In other words, in the same way that twelfth-century writers sometimes used clothing at face value, Philomena uses the gift to impart her desire to re-establish bonds with her sister. Yet just as the writers used clothing signifiers to force the old conventions to take on new, contextually based meanings, Philomena uses her cloth gift to create and convey meaning by working a message directly into it. Moreover, her handiwork creates a meaning that is readable without reliance upon the vestimentary code: Its manufacture represents a truly innovative use of textile to convey meaning. The significance of tapestry weaving in this poem is multiple and wide-ranging—it exacts revenge, rights wrongs, and restores Philomena to her former

15 Burns likens this female complicity to a tacit rejection of a male-dominated body of knowledge that objectifies women: "This collaborative women's work substantially redefines the intersection of knowledge and sight that constructs the medieval portrait of female beauty under a desiring male gaze." The sisters subvert conventional conceptions of both women's crafts and motherhood and thereby redefine gender roles and the expectations associated with them. Ibid., 141.

16 Lester K. Little, in *Religious Poverty and the Profit Economy in Medieval Europe* (Ithaca: Cornell University Press, 1978), defines the gift economy in the following way: "In a gift economy, goods and services are exchanged without having specific, calculated values assigned to them. Prestige, power, honor, and wealth are all expressed in the spontaneous giving of gifts; and more than just expressed: these attributes are attained and maintained through largess" (4). Through homage, feudal society was based on a system of reciprocal relations between persons of different social classes; one of the most important means for solidifying these ties was gifts, and in particular, gifts of clothing, armor, or cloth. Patrick Geary speaks specifically of the importance of the gift in the context of social relations in Europe during the Middle Ages: "Between equals or near-equals, cordial relationships were created and affirmed by the exchange of gifts. Between individuals or groups of differing status, the disparity of the exchanges both articulated and defined the direction and degree of subordination." In this system, a vassal swore homage to a lord who gave his protection in return, and often a gift from the vassal to the lord accompanied this exchange. "The goal of gift-giving was not the acquisition of commodities but the establishments of bonds between giver and receiver, bonds that had to be reaffirmed at some point by a countergift." "Sacred Commodities: the Circulation of Medieval Relics," in *The Social Life of Things: Commodities in Cultural Perspective*, ed. Arjun Appadurai (Cambridge: Cambridge University Press, 1986), 173.

place with her sister—but it also has the additional role of providing a metaphor for the new process of signification in which the romance writers were engaging.[17]

Chrétien's *Chevalier au lion*, or *Yvain*, offers another example of the innovations in the process of signification.[18] While in *Philomena* women gain power through the making of cloth, the *tisseuses* episode in *Yvain* provides a counterexample to this phenomenon. Yvain discovers a large group of enslaved young noblewomen who toil endlessly making cloth and clothes. There are three hundred of these *tisseuses*, whose condition is deplorable; yet they produce clothing of great value. Coming upon them, Yvain

> vit puceles jusqu'a trois cenz
> qui diverses oevres feisoient:
> de fil d'or et de soie ovroient
> chascune au mialz qu'ele savoit;
> mes tel povreté i avoit
> que deslïees et desceintes
> en i ot de povreté meintes;
> et as memeles et as cotes
> estoient lor cotes derotes
> et les chemises as dos sales
>
> (vss. 5188–97)

[saw as many as three hundred maidens who were engaged in diverse tasks: they worked with golden thread and silk, each to the best of her ability; but they were of such poverty that many of them were bare-headed and ungirdled due to their poverty; and at their breasts and sides their garments were torn and the chemises on their backs were dirty.]

The contrast between the quality of the materials they produce and the way they themselves are dressed is striking. When Yvain shows concern over their treatment, one of the *tisseuses* explains their situation in some detail:

> "toz jorz dras de soie tistrons,
> ne ja n'en serons mialz vestues;
> toz jorz serons povres et nues,
> et toz jorz fain et soif avrons.
> ja tant chevir ne nos savrons
> que mialz en aiens a mangier.
> Del pain avons a grant dongier
> au main petit, et au soir mains,
> que ja de l'uevre de noz mains
> n'avra chascune por son vivre

---

17 The similarities between cloth production and literary composition are stressed by Jean Renart in his early-thirteenth-century romance *Le Roman de la Rose*, when he likens textual embellishment to the process of dyeing fabric with kermes to increase its worth, as well as to the process of embroidery. *Le Roman de la Rose, ou de Guillaume de Dole*, ed. Félix Lecoy (Paris: Champion, 1962), vss. 8–11, 14.

18 Chrétien de Troyes, *Chevalier au lion (Yvain)*, ed. Mario Roques (Paris: Champion, 1960).

que quatre deniers de la livre;
et de ce ne poons nos pas
assez avoir viande et dras
car qui gaaigne la semainne
vint solz n'est mie fors de painne."

(vss. 5292–5306)

["We will always weave silk cloth, never will this make us better dressed; we will always be poor and naked, and always will we be hungry and thirsty. We will never be able to earn enough to afford better food. We have so little bread: little in the morning, less at night, for never through our handiwork will any of us have more to live on than four deniers for the pound; and with that, we cannot have enough food or clothing, for anyone who earns twenty sous in a week is not spared misery."]

Clearly, these women have been denied the economic fruits of their labor.[19] Whereas spinning, weaving, and sewing normally would provide at least some economic stability and self-sufficiency for women, these *tisseuses* live a life of abject poverty while the males for whom they work reap the benefits.

Mes bien sachiez vos a estros
que il n'i a celi de nos
qui ne gaaint cinc solz ou plus.
De ce seroit riches uns dus!
Et nos somes ci an poverte,
s'est riches de nostre desserte
cil por cui nos nos traveillons."

(vss. 5307–13)

["But, know this well, there is not one of us who does not do the work to earn five sous or more. With this sum, even a duke would be rich! And we are in poverty, he is rich through our product, the one for whom we work."]

Not only are these noblewomen forced to engage in manual labor, but they are also subjugated to male greed. This image of noble femininity is doubly unseemly: The *tisseuses'* nobility is undermined by involvement in the ignoble profit economy, and they are economically raped through their captors' masculine exploitation.

The situation of these poor ladies is a notable irony in the romance, for their work provides to others what they themselves are denied. Their vocation should, but does not, grant them some hope for an improved economic situation; they have a valued skill. But, rather than elevate them in this way, their work simply accentuates

---

19 According to Herlihy, the sweatshop depicted here by Chrétien has its roots in the early medieval tradition of the *gynaeceum* as a living and work space in which indentured women produced cloth, weaving and dyeing it. This kind of women's workshop was already in decline by the time Chrétien was writing in the second half of the twelfth century, giving way to the rapid development of the commercial production of cloth and of the cloth trade. Herlihy thus interprets the combination of servile and salaried labor described in this scene—Chrétien's *tisseuses* are slaves, yet paid in pittance wages—as a mixing of old and new economic orders (*Opera Muliebria*, 75–102).

their lack. The tattered state of their clothing, moreover, borders on nudity, and this near-nudity represents their powerlessness, vulnerability, and lack of social status. Yvain is, in fact, in the process of atoning for his own devaluing of a woman—his failure to keep his promise to Laudine—and he is sensitive to the plight of these women perhaps because of his prior mistake through which he himself had fallen into nudity.[20] The interest that he takes in these women and his ultimate liberation of them help Yvain along his redemptive path. He understands that despite their truly valuable work, they themselves remain unjustly devalued and economically disadvantaged. Thus, in this episode, Chrétien distorted the earning potential of making cloth, transforming it instead into a cruel irony.

Moreover, Chrétien depicted noblewomen engaged in mercantile activity within the profit economy. This image would have been shocking for the noble audience of romance, since the nobility of the twelfth century considered such engagements to be ignoble. All of the characters vilify the forced mercantile activity of these ladies even more than they do their captivity, and the narrator himself acknowledges the injustice. Fortunately for the young ladies, the situation is rectified by the hero. Ultimately, what originates as a subversion not only of vestimentary conventions (the ladies are dressed in rags) but also of the notion of nobility (they are engaged in manual labor for profit) becomes reinscribed into the clothing signifying system, giving it an enhanced degree of expressivity and narrative purpose. Their act of making luxury clothing while imprisoned and dressed in rags has meaning if for no other reason than that it gives Yvain the opportunity to liberate them, but it has, like Philomena's act, the additional meaning of providing a model of the manipulations of conventions that became inscribed into the signifying system by the writers of romance. Chrétien demonstrated his skill at weaving narrative even as he presented a shocking, unconventional image to his audience and in the same way that he challenged and changed literary conventions with the creation of romance.

In each of the examples examined, characters in distress attain resolution to their immediate situation through making, or refusing to make, textiles. The distress of these characters reflects the discomfort of a society undergoing reorganization, including the reassignment of textile production from its traditional place in the home and hands of women to the masculine and mercantile domain. Women's work was becoming men's professions, while the societal function of textile was shifting from the gift economy to the profit economy. In these romances, though, women have remarkable and important textile transactions, and their acts rearticulate and

---

20 Not long after Yvain's marriage to Laudine, he takes his leave of her to venture out into the world with Gauvain to pursue *aventures*. His new bride consents to his leaving only upon his acceptance of the condition that he return in one year. When he later misses that deadline, his lady sends her handmaiden to reclaim the ring she had given him as a love token, thereby withdrawing her love. Yvain is reduced to madness and nudity upon this news. Once he recovers from this diminished state, he must spend the rest of the romance atoning for his offence by never again failing to keep his word, regardless of the circumstances. It is in this process that Yvain gains back his lady's love, and the *tisseuses* episode figures prominently on his redemptive path.

reaffirm the values of tradition and the gift economy, all the while offering expanded possibilities for new conventions to emerge to account for new realities. Thus, romance both challenged and reaffirmed traditional values and conventional forms. Just as textile was at the heart of romance, so romance came to occupy a central place in the changing fabric of society.

Biffes, Tiretaines, and Aumonières: The Role of Paris in the International Textile Markets of the Thirteenth and Fourteenth Centuries

Sharon Farmer

Historians of Western medieval textiles tend to emphasize two major centers of production in the thirteenth and fourteenth centuries: the Low Countries and Northern Italy. From the twelfth century until the first quarter of the fourteenth, the towns of Flanders, Artois, Brabant, and Champagne dominated international markets in the production of luxury and middle-level wool cloth.[1] By the twelfth century, luxury silks from the Northern Italian town of Lucca were being sold at the Champagne fairs of Northern France. By the early fourteenth century, Lucchese silks dominated the northern aristocratic market for silks, and Lucca had been joined by three other Italian silk-weaving towns—Venice, Genoa, and Bologna. By the thirteenth century, Italian woolens and cottons were also being sold internationally.[2]

While historians have acknowledged that Paris—the largest city in Western Europe—also had a cloth industry and that it played a major role in the emergence of the tapestry-weaving industry at the beginning of the fourteenth century, the full extent and the unusual range of Parisian textile production has generally been ignored. By the second half of the thirteenth century, Paris was at the top of the field in the production and export of middle-level woolens called *biffes*; it had a very significant linen industry with an international market; and it had a small but significant silk

A version of this paper was presented in May 2004 at the International Congress on Medieval Studies at Kalamazoo, Michigan.

1 For a good discussion of the output and markets of these towns, as well as those of Normandy, Paris, and the Parisian suburb of Saint-Denis, see Patrick Chorley, "The Cloth Exports of Flanders and Northern France During the Thirteenth Century: A Luxury Trade?" *Economic History Review*, new series 40 (1987): 349–79.

2 On Northern Italian silk-making towns, see Florence Elder De Roover, "Lucchese Silks," *Ciba Review* 80 (June 1950): 2902–30; Luca Molà, *The Silk Industry of Renaissance Venice* (Baltimore: Johns Hopkins University Press, 2000); Luca Molà, Reinhold C. Mueller, and Claudio Zanier, eds., *La seta in Italia dal Medioevo al Seicento* (Venice: Marsilio, 2000). On cotton, see Maureen F. Mazzaoui, *The Italian Cotton Industry in the Later Middle Ages, 1100–1600* (Cambridge: Cambridge University Press, 1981). On wool, see Hidetoshi Hoshino, *L'arte della lana in Firenze nel basso Medioevo: Il commercio della lana e il mercato dei panni fiorentini nei secoli XIII-XV* (Florence: Leo S. Olschki, 1980).

industry, which, by the early fourteenth century, was selling cloth to the royal courts of England and France. Along with Arras, Paris dominated the tapestry industry in the first half of the fourteenth century, and it was also well known for its small luxury textile items, such as silk almspurses and silk belts.

The purpose of this article is to bring together the evidence for the market of Parisian textiles in order to demonstrate just how significant Paris was as a textile center during the second half of the thirteenth and the first four decades of the fourteenth centuries. I focus on this period because the sources are too scant before the middle of the thirteenth century, and most of the Parisian textile industries suffered a radical decline with the onset of the Hundred Years' War, which began in 1337. Sources for this discussion include a broad array of published materials as well as an examination of the unpublished royal wardrobe accounts of England and the household accounts of the count and countess of Artois, which cover the period 1302 to 1329.

WOOLENS

In terms of their market, Parisian woolens have received perhaps more attention than any of the other Parisian textiles. In an important doctoral thesis, Roger Gourmelon argued convincingly from street name evidence and residential patterns in the Parisian tax assessments of the late thirteenth century that the Parisian wool industry predated the mid-twelfth century.[3] Building on this evidence, Jean-François Belhoste has suggested that the Parisian wool industry must have originated in the eleventh century, when the introduction of the horizontal loom stimulated the rise of all of the great northern European centers of textile production.[4]

By the mid-thirteenth century, Paris was known for its *biffes*, which were mid-level woolens. Indeed, Parisian *biffes* were the earliest to be specified in Genoese contracts, in 1239, and they were the most frequently mentioned *biffes* in those contracts.[5] Parisian *biffes*, along with those of its suburb Saint-Denis and of the Champagne town of Provins, dominated the international market for this type of cloth in the second half of the thirteenth century.[6] We find Parisian *biffes* in thirteenth-century records from Aragon, Castile, Portugal, Genoa, Venice, Florence, Siena, Marseilles, and Provins, and in early-fourteenth-century records from Grasse. These fabrics were bought by large aristocratic households for servants' clothing, and by more modest knights and demoiselles for their own use.[7]

---

3 Roger Gourmelon, "L'industrie et le commerce des draps à Paris du XIIIe au XVIe siècle" (doctoral thesis, Ecole des Chartes, 1950; available at Paris: Archives Nationales, 76 Mi 10), 34–36.

4 Jean-François Belhoste, "Paris, Grand centre drapier au moyen âge," in *Fédération des Sociétés historiques et archéologiques de Paris et de l'Ile-de-France: Mémoires* 51 (2000): 42–44.

5 Chorley, "Cloth Exports," 365.

6 Ibid., 366. Provins, it should be noted, produced luxury cloth, *biffes*, and a variety of other cloths (359).

7 Ibid., 351, 352, 355–58.

The Parisian tax assessment from 1300 lists 360 wool weavers. Through a comparison of names in the 1299 and 1300 tax lists, Gourmelon estimated that there were about 400 master wool weavers in Paris.[8] Parisian *biffes* were 38 Champagne ells (or 47 Flemish ells) in length.[9] According to John Munro, the average late medieval Flemish weaver produced 840 Flemish ells (equivalent to about 679 Champagne ells or 640 yards) each year.[10] Assuming that the production rate of Parisian weavers was about the same, its 400 weaving workshops produced around 7,150 pieces of cloth each year. This was slightly less than one-fifth the total output of ells in Provins, which at its height in the 1270s is believed to have produced about 50,000 pieces annually, each of which was 28 Champagne ells in length; and it was slightly more than one-fourth the output of ells in Chalons, which produced about 36,000 pieces that were 30 Champagne ells in length.[11] At its height, Provins must have had nearly 2,100 weaving workshops, and Chalons must have had around 1,600.

With 400 master weavers, each of whom needed a worker to work beside him at the broadloom, and all of the other workers needed to turn raw wool into finished cloth (the most important being fullers and dyers), Paris' wool industry would have employed at least 1,700 people, in Gourmelon's estimation.[12] The number of Parisian wool workers would have been even larger if all of the wool had been combed and spun in Paris, but apparently a substantial amount of wool arrived in Paris already spun.[13]

TIRETAINE

Most historians of cloth production in the thirteenth and early fourteenth centuries have ignored the wool products of an important suburb of Paris, Saint-Marcel, which was situated outside the southeastern walls of the *rive gauche*, along the stream known as the Bièvre, which facilitated dyeing and fulling.[14] It is difficult to determine just how large this industry was.

The most important textile product of Saint-Marcel was called *tiretaine*. Most textile historians have assumed that *tiretaine* was a low-priced, low-status, lightweight cloth made with a warp of linen and a weft of wool.[15] Evidence from royal and aristocratic account books suggests, however, that we need to rethink the value, the

---

8 Gourmelon, "L'industrie," 37–39.

9 Chorley, "Cloth Exports," 355.

10 John Munro, "Textile Technology," in *The Dictionary of the Middle Ages*, ed. Joseph R. Strayer (New York: Scribner, 1988), 11:704.

11 Chorley, "Cloth Exports," 355, 366.

12 Belhoste, "Paris, Grand centre drapier," 36–37.

13 Gourmelon, "L'industrie," 56.

14 Belhoste ("Paris, Grand centre drapier," 47) mentions that it was a center of cloth dyeing in the early fourteenth century.

15 Félix Bourquelot, *Études sur les foires de Champagne, sur la nature, l'étendue et les règles du commerce qui s'y faisait aux XIIe, XIIIe, et XIVe siècles*, Mémoires présentés par divers savants à l'Academie des Inscriptions et Belles-lettres de l'Institut Impérial de France, ser. 2, vol. 5, pts. 1–2 (1865; repr., Le Portulan: Le Manoir de Saint-Pierre-de-Salerne, 1970), 1:239; Hoshino,

status, and, in some instances, the fiber of *tiretaine*. An ordinance of the *tiretainiers* of Saint-Marcel, probably dating from the late thirteenth century, indicates that *tiretaine* was indeed frequently made with linen and wool.[16] Moreover, evidence from household accounts indicates that this was indeed a lightweight cloth, suitable for use as summer clothing, and almost always lined with some sort of silk; I have found only one example of an outfit made of *tiretaine* and lined with fur.[17] In 1304 and 1315, Countess Mahaut of Artois wore *tiretaine* on Pentecost, the day that she presented her livery of summer clothing to her retainers.[18] Mahaut, and her father before her, made most of their purchases of *tiretaine* during the summer months.[19] It seems, however, that *tiretaine* was not always made with linen and wool. On one occasion, Mahaut of Artois's account book mentions a purchase of twenty-six ounces of *tiretaine sur soie*, suggesting that in this one instance either the fabric was made entirely of silk or it had a warp of silk rather than linen.[20] Silk cloth was almost always sold by the ounce rather than by length.

Evidence in a number of sources suggests that there was a broad range of prices for *tiretaines*. Mahaut of Artois paid between four and twenty-four sous per ell for *tiretaines* of differing qualities. Both the lowest-priced and the highest-priced *tiretaines* in her accounts were from Florence.[21] Sources also indicate that *tiretaine* was sometimes dyed with kermes, the extremely expensive dye that was used to dye the most luxurious of all medieval woolens, scarlet. In 1268, buyers for the English king who were shopping in Paris bought two *tiretaines* dyed with kermes;[22] in 1328, the inventory of

L'arte della lana, 83, 126–27. C. Leber repeated the dominant definition, but admitted that some fabrics identified by this name must have been of luxury quality. Leber, comp., *Collection des meilleurs dissertations, notices et traités particuliers relatifs à l'histoire de France* (Paris: G.-A. Dentu, 1838), 19:79.

16 Geneviève Souchal, "Études sur la tapisserie Parisienne: Règlements et technique des tapissiers sarrasinois, hautelissiers et nostrez (vers 1260–vers 1350)," *Bibliothèque de l'École des Chartes* 123 (1965): 91–92.

17 Silk linings: Archives Départementales de Pas-de-Calais, ser. A (henceforth, Pas-de-Calais A), 199, 96v (household account of Countess of Artois, 1304); 270, 19r (household account of Countess of Artois, 1310); 334, 24r (household account of Countess of Artois, 1315, transcribed by Véronique Gérard and others, untitled thesis on the Court of Mahaut of Artois, Mémoire de maîtrise, Université de Nanterre, 1971, vol. 2, available for consultation in the Salle Diplomatique, Institut de recherche et histoire des textes, Paris); "Compte du bailliage d'Artois" (1304–5), in *Documents et extraits divers concernant l'histoire de l'art dans la Flandre, l'Artois et le Hainaut avant le xve siècle*, ed. C. Dehaisnes (Lille: Impr. L. Danel, 1886), 161; "Inventaire et vente après décès des biens de la reine Clémence de Hongrie, veuve de Louis le Hutin, 1328," in *Nouveau recueil de comptes de l'Argenterie des rois de France*, ed. L. Douët-D'Arcq (Paris: Librairie Renouard, 1874), 70–71 (four "robes" of *tiretaine* of Saint-Marcel, lined with taffetas, cendal, and tartar). Fur lining: "[Testament de] Blanche, fille du roi de Sicile et femme de Robert, fils ainé du comte de Flandres," in Dehaisnes, *Documents*, 63.

18 Pas-de-Calais A 199, 94v; A 334, 24r.

19 Pas-de-Calais A 162, 43r; A 199, 96v; A 270, 16v; A 334, 28v (transcribed by Gérard et al., vol. 2); A 374, 28v, 29r (transcribed by Gérard et al., 3:154, 155).

20 Pas-de-Calais A 270, 19r.

21 Pas-de-Calais A 199, 96v (24 sous/ell, 1304); A 270, 16v (4 sous/ell, 1310).

22 Samuel Lysons, "Copy of a Roll of Purchases Made for the Tournament of Windsor Park, in the sixth Year of Edward the First," *Archaeologia* 17 (1814): 309.

goods belonging to Clemence of Hungary, the deceased widow of the French King Louis X, included an outfit of black *tiretaine* of Saint-Marcel, which was also dyed with kermes.[23]

The higher-priced *tiretaines* were almost always worn by royalty or by the highest members of the aristocracy, rather than by servants or retainers, who always wore cloth of lesser quality than that worn by their employers. In 1269, Blanche, the daughter of the King of Sicily and wife of the eldest son of the Count of Flanders, bequeathed to a woman named Vivien *ma reube de tiretaine* ("my outfit of *tiretaine*"), which was lined with miniver (*menu vair*), one of the most prized furs in the Middle Ages.[24] On Pentecost in 1304, Mahaut of Artois wore an outfit of *tiretaine* for which the fabric alone cost £28.[25] Mahaut wore *tiretaine* again in 1306 and 1315, and in 1326 she wore *tiretaine* of Saint-Marcel.[26] In 1306 and 1315 she also purchased *tiretaine* for her son Robert—in the latter case, it was *tiretaine* of Saint-Marcel, which he and his companions wore to the feast of the king's coronation.[27] In 1328, when the French Queen Clemence of Hungary died, four of her thirty-five garments were made of *tiretaine* of Saint-Marcel. They were all dyed in different colors.[28] Sometime between 1335 and 1342, the French king's wardrober bought a coat lined with *tiretaine* for the king.[29] It seems, then, that some *tiretaines* were considered luxury cloth.

The Parisian tax assessments indicate that there were at least two weavers of *tiretaine* working in the suburb of Saint-Marcel by 1292.[30] Nevertheless, in the sources I have examined, *tiretaine* that was produced in Saint-Marcel is not mentioned before 1315. Up until then, the most frequently mentioned place of origin for high-quality *tiretaine* was Florence. Florentine *tiretaine* is mentioned in the 1294 accounts of the countess of Flanders, in the 1302 inventory of goods of Raoul of Nesle, the Constable of France, and in the 1304 and 1310 accounts of Mahaut of Artois.[31] I have found no mention of Florentine *tiretaines* in Northern French households after 1314. However, we learn from the account books of Mahaut of Artois that several Florentine drapers who had settled in Saint-Marcel were now producing and marketing *tiretaines*. Twice in 1315 and twice in 1326, Mahaut bought *tiretaine* of Saint-Marcel from "Berthmien Cresseten" or "Berthelot Castanis" (apparently the same person); and two times in

23 "Inventaire et vente après décès," 70.

24 "[Testament de] Blanche," 63.

25 Pas-de-Calais A 199, 94v.

26 Pas-de-Calais A 222, 26r; A 334, 24r (transcribed by Gérard et al., vol. 2); A 458, 24r.

27 Pas-de-Calais A 222, 26r; A 334, 28v (transcribed by Gérard et al., vol. 2).

28 "Inventaire et vente après décès," 70–71.

29 Leber, *Collection des meilleurs dissertations*, 19:79.

30 Hercule Géraud, ed., *Paris sous Philippe-le-Bel d'après des documents originaux et notamment d'après un manuscrit contenant "Le Rôle de la Taille" imposée sur les habitants de Paris en 1292*, reproduced with a new introduction and index by Caroline Bourlet and Lucie Fossier (Tubingen: Max Niemeyer, 1991), 176.

31 "Recettes et depenses faites par Jacques le receveur pour l'hotel de madame la comtesse de Flandre," in Dehaisnes, *Documents*, 85; "Inventaire des biens de feu Raoul de Nesle, connètable de France," in Dehaisnes, *Documents,* 137; Pas-de-Calais A 199, 96v; A 270, 16v.

1319 she bought *tiretaine* of Saint-Marcel from "Jacques Faves" (or Feves).[32] In 1317 she had paid this same Jacques Faves £216 to dye eleven white *camelins* and one *drap fin* of Brussels with kermes.[33] Berthmien Cresseten and Jacques Faves were two of four Florentines—the brothers "Jaquinus Quercitanus" and "Berthelinus Quercitanus" (Latin for Berthmien Cresseten), "Jacobus Fava" (Latin for Jacques Faves) and "Colinus Usimbardus"—who had settled in Saint-Marcel sometime before 1317, when the French king granted them the rights and privileges of French townsmen (*burgenses nostros et regni nostri Francie facimus*).[34] Berthmien was already residing there in 1292.[35]

It thus seems clear that the high-quality *tiretaines* that came to be associated with the Parisian suburb of Saint-Marcel had their origins in the earlier *tiretaines* of Florence, and that sometime around 1314 the *tiretaines* of Saint-Marcel began to supplant Florentine *tiretaines* in Northern aristocratic courts. It is also clear that the Italian draper/dyers of Saint-Marcel were using kermes as well as other dyes. We can thus infer that they were at the top of the economic hierarchy in their profession. The one Parisian dyer who had the right to use kermes in 1313 was one of the two most wealthy dyers in the tax assessment of that year.[36]

Textile production in Saint-Marcel may have suffered in the second half of the fourteenth century, due to the ravages of the Hundred Years' War. When it was reestablished, in the mid-fifteenth century, the patterns resembled those of the early fourteenth century: The men who founded the new industry were Italian draper/dyers—the well-known Gobelins and Canayes. Once again, moreover, they used kermes.[37]

LINENS

At the end of the thirteenth century, the linen industry of Paris was apparently smaller than the wool industry in terms of numbers of weavers, but it already played a major role in supplying the most important royal and aristocratic households of northern Europe, and its size may have grown toward the end of the fourth decade of the fourteenth century, as the wool and silk industries began to decline. The tax assessments of the years 1296–1300 reveal an average of twenty-four linen weavers per year, half of whom were women.[38]

32 Pas-de-Calais A 334, 28v (transcribed by Gérard et al., vol. 2); A 374, 28v, 29r (transcribed by Gérard et al., 3:154, 155); A 458, 24r, 30v.

33 Jules-Marie Richard, *Une petite-nièce de Saint Louis: Mahaut, comtesse d'Artois et de Bourgogne (1302–1329)* (Paris: H. Champion, 1887), 396. *Drap fin* is "fine cloth." *Camelin* was a type of wool cloth, of varying quality; see Bourquelot, *Études*, 262–66.

34 Jules Marie Édouard Viard, ed., *Documents Parisiens du règne de Philippe VI de Valois (1328–1350)* (Paris: H. Champion, 1899), 1:104–5.

35 Géraud, *Paris sous Philippe-le-Bel*, 176.

36 Belhoste, "Paris, Grand centre drapier," 36.

37 Ibid., 47.

38 Janice Archer, "Working Women in Thirteenth-Century Paris" (Ph.D. diss., University of Arizona, 1995), 252. I am including *tisserand de linge*, *tisserand de toile*, and *telier* in this total.

Parisian linens—especially bed linens, altar cloths, and veils, but also linen cloth used in various items of clothing—were highly prized by the English royal court throughout the fourteenth century and by the Papal court during its entire stay in Avignon (1307–1417), most especially during the years 1317–32 and 1342–60.[39] The Countess of Artois also made most of her linen purchases in Paris, and a good proportion of those purchases were probably Parisian linens.[40]

A single purchase record for the English royal court for the year 1301–2 shows the king's household purchasing 832 ells of Parisian *mappa* (napery—i.e., table linens and altar cloths).[41] A purchase record from 1303–4 reveals the same household purchasing 878 ells of Parisian *mappa* as well as 22 *tuallii* (toweling, altar cloths, or head coverings) from Paris.[42] By the 1320s and 1330s, when we can get a global picture of the English kings' annual purchases from the Great Wardrobe accounts, the English royal household was purchasing annually well over 1,000 ells of Parisian *mappa*, several hundred to over 1,000 ells of Parisian *tela* (linen cloth), and several hundred ells of long and short Parisian *manuterga* (fine linen towels).[43]

Quantities purchased as well as price hierarchies in the English royal accounts indicate that at the beginning of the century, Paris was a major supplier of *mappa*, but that the royal household was willing to pay more for *mappa* from Dinant, and occasionally for English linen. In 1301–2 and 1303–4, the English king's buyers paid between 6.6d. and 10d. per ell for Parisian *mappa*, between 5d. and 14d. for *mappa* from Dinant, and, on one occasion, 13d. for some unspecified English *mappa*.[44]

By the 1320s and 1330s, however, Paris had clearly established itself with the English royal household as the most prized producer of both *mappa* and *manuterga*, with slightly less expensive products from Rouen filling out the demand.[45] In 1323–24, the English royal household paid 10d. for each ell of Parisian *mappa* and between 7d. and 8d. for that from Rouen.[46] In 1331–32, the same household paid between 12d. and 14d. for each ell of Parisian *mappa*, and 10d. for that from Rouen.[47]

39 Anne Sutton, "Some Aspects of the Linen Trade c. 1130s to 1500, and the Part Played by the Mercers of London," *Textile History* 30 (1999): 157, 165, 166; Robert Delort, "Note sur les achats de draps et d'étoffes effectués par la chambre apostolique des papes d'Avignon (1316–1417)," *École française de Rome, Mélanges d'archeologie et d'histoire* 74 (1962): 232.

40 I have examined most of the surviving Artois household accounts from 1300–1328: Pas-de-Calais A 162, A 178, A 199, A 222, A 261, A 263, A 270, A 280, A 293, A 298, A 448, A 458, A 470, A 474. For the following accounts, I examined the transcriptions of Gérard et al.: A 316, A 329, A 334, A 351, A 361, A 368, A 374, A 378, A 386, A 396, A 403.

41 London, National Archives, E 101/359/18.

42 London, National Archives, E 101/366/4.

43 In 1333, for instance, the Great Wardrobe account records purchases of 1,509 ells of *mappa* of Paris, 930 ells of long *manuterga* of Paris, 169 pieces of short *manuterga* of Paris, 135 ells of *mappa* of Rouen, 1,080 ells of *tela* from Reims, 1,399¾ ells of *tela* from Paris, and 1,513 ells of English *tela*. London, National Archives, E 361/9, rot. 13.

44 London, National Archives, E 101/359/18; E 101/366/4.

45 See note 43.

46 London, National Archives, E 101/379/12.

47 London, National Archives, E 101/386/5.

In the area of linen cloth (*tela*), Reims was at the top of the status hierarchy in terms of price, with Parisian linen coming in second, and English linens coming in third (see table 4.1). Quantities of linen cloth from Reims, Paris, and England were often about equal in the Great Wardrobe Accounts. In 1333–34, for instance, the Great Wardrobe account records purchases of 1,080 ells of *tela* from Reims, 1,399¾ ells of *tela* from Paris, and 1,513 ells of English *tela*.[48]

TAPESTRIES AND FURNISHINGS

Historians of medieval tapestries agree that, along with Arras, Paris played a major role in the emergence of commercial tapestry weaving in Western Europe in the late thirteenth and early fourteenth centuries.[49] However, they do not agree in their interpretations of the evidence concerning the evolution of tapestry-weaving techniques in that early period. By the fifteenth century—the period for which most of the physical evidence survives—two techniques had emerged: that using the *haute lisse*, or vertical loom, and that using the *basse lisse*, or horizontal loom. The most prized tapestries were those made on a *haute lisse* loom. With both loom types, tapestry weavers worked with several shuttles, each carrying a wool yarn of a different color, and they passed each shuttle only as far as its color was needed, rather than sending a single shuttle from selvage to selvage, as is the case with conventional weaving. The warp yarn provided the strength of the material, but it was not visible once the tapestry was completed.[50]

Guild statutes from Paris from the 1260s highlight two distinct techniques for producing *tapis*, but the distinctions between the two do not seem to correspond to the distinctions between the later *basse lisse* and *haute lisse* techniques for tapestries. One of the thirteenth-century guilds consisted of *tapissiers de tapiz sarrasinois* ("makers of Saracen *tapis*"); a second consisted of *tapissier(s) de tapis nostrez* ("makers of our *tapis*," meaning, apparently, native French *tapis*).[51] The word *tapis* was used to describe any textile that was employed for furnishings, wall hangings, or upholstery; thus it is

---

48 London, National Archives, E 361/9, rot. 13.

49 J. Lestocquoy, *Deux siècles de l'histoire de la tapisserie (1300–1500), Paris, Arras, Lille, Tournai, Bruxelles* (Arras: Commission départementale des monuments historiques du Pas-de-Calais, 1978), 12–17; Adolfo Salvatore Cavallo, *Medieval Tapestries in the Metropolitan Museum of Art* (New York: Metropolitan Museum of Art, 1993), 63–65. Cavallo argues that Bruges, Brussels, Ghent, Lille, Louvain, Valenciennes, and London were also centers of tapestry-making in the fourteenth century, but for the period before the outbreak of the Hundred Years' War in 1337 he cites evidence for only Ghent and Brussels, and that evidence does not give any indication of the extent of the tapestry industry in those two towns. Tapestry-makers were also active in Germany in the twelfth and thirteenth centuries, but they were not working within an organized commercial industry (73–74).

50 Anna G. Bennett, "Tapestry, Art of," in *Dictionary of the Middle Ages*, 11:593–94.

51 René de Lespinasse and François Bonnardot, eds., *Les métiers et corporations de la ville de Paris, XIIIe siècle* (Paris: Imprimerie nationale, 1879), 102, 106 (*titres* 51 and 52). On the meaning of *nostrez*, see Souchal, "Études sur la tapisserie," 38–39.

Table 4.1: Pennies/ell for *tela* (linen cloth) purchased by the English royal household, 1323–35

Place of origin	1323–24	1325–26	1329–30	1331–32	1334–35
Reims	9–10	7½–15	12–16	12–18	24–30
Paris	4–5	6–10	5½–12	8–12	8–12
England	3½	3 ½		4–7	4–5
Straill' (locale uncertain)	4				
Leg' (probably Liège)		7½–8			

Sources: London, National Archives, E 101/379/12; E 101/381/9: E 101/384/6; E 101/386/5; E 101/387/13.

not clear that either of these guilds made tapestries. Geneviève Souchal has argued that the term *tapiz sarrasinois* referred to a technique known as knotted pile (used both then and now in Oriental carpets),[52] and that the term *tapis nostrez* referred to furnishing fabrics that were woven in the conventional way, with a single shuttle that passed from one selvage to the other.[53] However, other textile historians maintain that the evidence is too scanty for us to recover the precise meanings of these two terms.[54] The fact that one of the Parisian techniques was identified with the Muslims finds a parallel in Germany, where tapestries were known as "heathen's work" (*Heidnischwerk*).[55] The earliest surviving woven tapestries from Germany date from the eleventh century; the earliest knotted-pile tapestry, from the mid-twelfth century.[56]

A set of revisions to the statutes of the makers of *tapiz sarrasinois*, which dates from around 1290, indicates that by then a new group of tapestry makers had arisen or arrived in Paris, perhaps from Arras. An accord between the two groups, drawn up in 1303, reveals that the new tapestry makers were using the *haute lisse* technique.[57] This is the earliest piece of written evidence from anywhere in Europe for the emergence of the *haute lisse* technique. A purchase order from the household of Mahaut of Artois, dated 1313, is our earliest mention of a *haute lisse* tapestry.[58] It indicates that by then *haute lisse* tapestries were being made not only in Paris, but also in Arras.

As historians have already noted, the household account books and administrative records of Mahaut of Artois indicate that in the first three decades of the fourteenth century, tapestries and furnishing fabrics were sold, and probably produced, in both Paris and Arras. Only in the case of a few of Mahaut's purchases in Arras, however,

---

52 Rosamond Mack, *Bazaar to Piazza: Islamic Trade and Italian Art, 1300–1600* (Berkeley: University of California Press, 2002), 73–74.
53 Souchal, "Études sur la tapisserie," 37–39, 69.
54 Cavallo, *Medieval Tapestries*, 63.
55 Laura Weigert, *Weaving Sacred Stories: French Choir Tapestries and the Performance of Clerical Identity* (Ithaca, NY: Cornell University Press, 2004), 7.
56 Cavallo, *Medieval Tapestries*, 73.
57 Souchal, "Études sur la tapisserie," 52, 59–63, 73–79.
58 Lestocquoy, *Deux siècles*, 15.

can we point definitively to the *haute lisse* technique.[59] Nevertheless, given the evidence from 1303, it seems reasonable to assume that a number of Mahaut's Parisian purchases were *haute lisse* tapestries produced in Paris.

An entry in the records of the French royal household provides us with slightly less ambiguous evidence for the production of tapestries in Paris during the first three decades of the fourteenth century. In 1316, the household purchased from Jehan *le tapissier*, in preparation for the royal coronation the following January, ten vermilion *tapis* decorated with parrots bearing the French arms, butterflies bearing the arms of Burgundy, and trefoils (*treffles*). We can be sure that these *tapis* were tapestries rather than embroidered furnishings, since an order for a similarly decorated embroidered bedroom set was placed with a different supplier at the same time (see p. 85).[60] Nevertheless, there is no way for us to determine if the technique involved was a patterned tapestry weave (either *haute lisse* or *basse lisse*) or knotted pile; nor do we know whether or not the technique was associated with *tapiz sarrasinois*.

Records from the English royal household indicate that in the last decades of the thirteenth century and the first decades of the fourteenth, Parisian *tapis* were gaining an international reputation. The household of the English king purchased eight *tapetae* of unknown technique in Paris in 1278,[61] and by the 1330s Parisian *tapetae* had their own rubric in the English royal household accounts. Again, though, the references are too vague for us to distinguish techniques, except to say that in some cases the textiles in question were decorated.[62] Papal records from Avignon also point to numerous purchases of Parisian *tapis*.[63]

SILK TEXTILES

Our earliest evidence for the silk industry in Paris comes from the collection of guild statutes known as the *Livre des métiers*, which was first compiled sometime in the 1260s. Modern editions of those statutes indicate that there were six guilds associated with the production of silk: two guilds of silk spinners (one using large spindles, the other using small spindles); a guild of makers of silk and linen ribbon; and three different guilds of weavers: makers of silk *tissu* (cloth); makers of *drap de soie* (another term for silk cloth—the difference from *tissu* is not clear), *veluau* (velvet), and *boursserie en lice* (woven purses); and weavers of *queuvrechiers de soie* (silk head coverings).[64] In

---

59 On the purchase evidence concerning *tapis* purchased in Paris and Arras in the Artois records, see Richard, *Une petite-nièce*, 212–19. Lestocquoy (*Deux siècles*, 7–17) has drawn on Richard's discussion, but with less precision and some errors.

60 "Le premier compte de Geoffroi de Fleuri argentier du roi Philippe le Long pour les six derniers mois de l'année 1316," in *Comptes de l'argenterie des rois de France au XIVe siècle*, ed. L. Douët-D'Arcq (Paris: J. Renouard, 1851), 59–61.

61 Lysons, "Copy of a Roll of Purchases," 308.

62 London, National Archives, E 101/384/6; E 101/386/5.

63 Delort, "Note sur les achats," 232.

64 Lespinasse and Bonnardot, *Livre des métiers*, 66, 68, 70, 74, 76, 83 (titres 34, 35, 36, 38, 40, 44).

the statutes for the makers of silk *tissu* and for the weavers of silk head coverings, the nouns for the artisans who practiced the craft (*ouvrieres de tissuz*; *tesserandes de soie*) are all in the feminine—thus the working assumption is that most workers who were subject to these statutes were women. The statutes for the makers of *drap de soie*, velvet, and woven purses, by contrast, assumed a male membership. The Parisian tax assessments of the 1290s reveal a preponderance of women silk weavers: The assessments include an average of ninety-seven silk weavers per year, of whom only seven were men. Another two men were identified as makers of velvet; no women were identified as makers of velvet.[65]

Caroline Bourlet, who is working on a dissertation on the artisans of Paris, has suggested that only three of the six silk guilds—the two spinners' guilds and that of the ribbon makers—existed at the time that the *Livre des métiers* was first compiled. The other three, which constitute the solid evidence for the weaving of silk cloth in Paris, are later additions, probably dating to the 1290s.[66] An even later statute, from 1324, suggests that Paris was producing brocades of silk and gold thread.[67]

Even with a starting date of the 1290s rather than the 1260s, the presence of a silk-weaving industry in Paris was significant. Only four Italian towns are known to have preceded Paris in developing silk industries on more than a modest scale. Moreover, the statute for makers of silk *drap* and velvet constitutes our earliest written evidence for the production of velvet anywhere in Western Europe. The earliest reference to velvet production in Lucca dates from 1311.[68] Of course, regulations do not always point to actual practice. Thus, it is extremely significant that the Parisian tax assessments from the 1290s include weavers of both silk and velvet.

Drawing on the archeological evidence of a garment of woolen velvet, in which King Philip I of France was buried in 1108, and on a reference to the production of woolen velvet in Tournai in 1380, Sophie Desrosiers, who was the first scholar to highlight the significance of Paris' early velvet production, has expressed a "small doubt" as to whether the velvet that was produced in Paris in the 1290s was made of silk. She finds further reason to entertain this doubt in statute 32 (a later addition to the original statutes) of the guild of the makers of luxuriously decorated saddles, which seemed to place velvet and basan, an inferior type of leather, on an equal level.[69]

65 Archer, *Working Women*, 252. I have counted *fabricant de draps de soie, ouvriere de soie, fabricante de tissu,* and *fabricant de velours,* but not *carier de soie,* since these weavers produced small items, such as handkerchiefs. For the argument that *ouvriere de soie* meant "silk-weaver," see Archer, *Working Women,* 116–17.

66 Caroline Bourlet, "Labour Policy in Thirteenth and Beginning of Fourteenth Century Paris" (paper presentation, International Medieval Congress, Leeds, England, July 2003). Bourlet is currently preparing this paper for publication.

67 "Lettres du prévot de Paris honologuant les statuts des merciers," in *Les métiers et corporations de la ville de Paris XIVe-XVIIIe siècle,* ed. René de Lespinasse (Paris: Imprimerie Nationale, 1892), 2:245.

68 Sophie Desrosiers, "Sur l'origine d'un tissu qui à participé à la fortune de Venise: le velours de soie," in Molà, Mueller, and Zanier, *La seta in Italia,* 33, 44–45.

69 Desrosiers, "Sur l'origine," 42–45; Lespinasse and Bonnardot, *Livre des métiers,* 172 (*titre* 78, statute 32).

My own reading of the evidence favors a hypothesis that the velvets being produced in Paris in the 1290s were indeed made of silk. The velvet makers were grouped in a single guild with makers of *drap de soie*, and indeed the only fiber mentioned in the statutes for that guild is silk. As for statute 32 of the guild of makers of luxurious saddles, the text of that statute reads, "Nulz ne puet faire selle de basenne et de veluau" ("no one may make saddles of basan and velvet"). I interpret this to mean that saddlemakers were prohibited from using the two materials together on the same saddle, but not from otherwise employing those materials. Indeed, the use of basan under certain circumstances is assumed in a number of the individual statutes for the same guild.[70] We also know from account books that luxurious saddles were frequently decorated with velvet; in 1292, for instance, Count Robert of Artois commissioned a saddle that was to be decorated with his own coat of arms and velvet of silk (*veluau de soie*; this is apparently the earliest Western European reference to velvet in which the fiber—silk—is clearly identified).[71] Thus it seems that the prohibition in the statute for the Parisian saddlemakers was intended to keep the two materials separate, probably because it was thought that velvet, a luxurious textile, should not be mixed with a leather that was not considered luxurious.

Despite the solid evidence for a silk industry in late-thirteenth-century Paris, many textile historians and historians of costume continue to ignore its existence, perhaps because the evidence for the actual consumption of Parisian silks is scant.[72] Indeed, in the available printed sources to which textile historians regularly turn, there is only one solid example of silk cloth that was produced in Paris: in January 1317, on the occasion of her entry into Reims for her coronation and that of the king, Queen Jeanne of Burgundy wore a cape of cloth of gold made in Paris.[73]

Unpublished material in the English royal wardrobe accounts provides further evidence for the production of Parisian silk, and for its export in small amounts to England. Each year from 1324 to 1333, the English royal household purchased one or two pieces of Parisian silk.[74] At least half of the time, the Parisian silks had their own rubric in the margins of the accounts.[75] On those occasions when the length of the pieces is specified, they were short—thirteen and a half or fourteen and a half ells in length.[76] Over half of the descriptions indicate that the Parisian silk was striped

---

70 Lespinasse and Bonnardot, *Livre des métiers*, 169, 172 (*titre* 78, statutes 11 and 32). The mention of acceptable use of basan in statute 32 comes from the last phrase of the sentence that begins with the prohibition concerning the mixing of basan and velvet. It reads: "et ne puet border sellerie neuve de clous d'estain se [elle] n'est de basenne" ("and may not make borders of pewter nails on new saddles if the saddles are not made of basan").

71 Richard, *Une petite-nièce*, 126–27, citing Pas-de-Calais A 132.

72 See, for example, Françoise Piponnier and Perrine Mane, *Dress in the Middle Ages* (New Haven, CT: Yale University Press, 2000), 20. They assert that silk weaving did not begin in France until the fifteenth century.

73 "Pour 3 draps d'or de Paris, ouvrez ... pour faire une chappe à la royne, qu'elle ot à l'entree de Rains." "Premier compte de Geoffroi de Fleuri," 57.

74 London, National Archives, E 361/3, rot. 2, 3, 5, 9, 19, 22v; E 361/9, rot. 3, 5, 6, 10.

75 London, National Archives, E 361/3, rot. 2, 5, 9; E 361/9, rot. 3, 5.

76 London, National Archives, E 361/3 rot. 2, 5, 9.

(*radiatus*).[77] While the English accounts do not indicate that the Parisian silk contained gold or that it was a figured silk, the grouping of the Parisian silks with other silks that contained gold or with figured silks suggests that it may have been either figured, woven with gold thread, or both.[78]

EMBROIDERY

Embroidery was another major source of employment and luxury consumer goods in Paris of the late thirteenth and early fourteenth centuries. A set of statutes from the very end of the thirteenth century, which includes a list of all of the members of the guild at that time, indicates that there were ninety-four embroiderers in Paris, seventy-nine of whom were women.[79] Evidence from the French royal household accounts indicates that the local luxury market went a long way in keeping Parisian embroiderers employed. In 1316, for instance, the royal household commissioned three embroidered bedroom sets (*chambres*) for the upcoming royal coronation. One of those *chambres*—that of the queen—was supplied by Gauthier of Poullegny, whose business included both fulfilling orders for embroidered pieces and selling silk, linen, and other mercery items. The queen's *chambre* was to be made of velvet embroidered in gold with 1,321 parrots emblazoned with the arms of France and 661 butterflies bearing the queen's arms—those of Burgundy—on their wings. Interspersed among the gold parrots and butterflies were 7,000 trefoils embroidered in silver. The total outlay for this single bedroom set was over £902.[80]

Church inventories from Paris indicate that wealthy ecclesiastical institutions also fed the demand for embroidery, either through direct commissions or through gifts from aristocratic and royal households to those institutions. The 1342 inventory for the Paris church of Saint-Martin des Champs includes numerous embroidered liturgical vestments and furnishings. One alb and parament set was embroidered in gold with images from the life of St. Martin; another parament was embroidered with fleurs-de-lis and St. Martin on his horse; another alb was embroidered in gold with a man fighting a lion and two men on horseback; a cape was embroidered in silver with images of the Virgin; a bishop's miter was embroidered with images of the Nativity.[81]

---

77 London, National Archives, E 361/3, rot. 2, 3, 19, 22v; E 361/9, rot. 5, 6, 10.

78 London, National Archives, E 361/3, rot. 5: The Parisian silk is paired with *panni de Tars'*, right after *panni de turkie* and *Aresta*. Rot. 9: The rubric includes velvet, samite, *camoca*, *tars'* and Parisian silk. Rot. 22v: The Parisian silk is listed just after *panni ad aurum de Turke* and just before *panni ad aurum diaspiment'*.

79 G. B. Depping, ed., *Réglemens sur les arts et métiers de Paris rédigés au XIIIe siècle* (Paris: Impr. de Crapelet, 1837), 379–82.

80 "Premier compte de Geoffroi de Fleuri," 59–60. For Gauthier of Poullegny's activities as a merchant of mercery items, see Pas-de-Calais A 334, 28v (transcribed by Gérard et al., vol. 2).

81 L'Abbé Lebeuf, *Histoire de la ville et de tout le diocèse de Paris*, ed. Hippolyte Cocheris (Paris: A. Durand, 1867), 2:327–30.

Surviving embroidered French liturgical vestments in Sweden and France give us an idea of what these liturgical garments might have looked like. A cope completed in 1274 that apparently belonged to Archbishop Fulk of Uppsala, and is still in the cathedral there, has thirty-nine medallions embroidered with representations of martyrs in gold and silk on red silk.[82] A late-thirteenth-century cope from the abbey of Montiéramey in Champagne, which may originally have been a chasuble, has fifty embroidered quatrilobes, each enclosing a representation of a martyr, a scene from the life of a saint, or a scene from the New Testament.[83] Five contemporary fragments of a liturgical vestment, also from Montiéramey, have scenes from the lives of saints and the passion cycle. A vestment in the treasury of the basilica in Saint-Maximin in Provence, thought to have belonged to St. Louis of Toulouse and dating from the first quarter of the fourteenth century, has medallions containing scenes from the life of the Virgin and from the New Testament.[84]

Royalty, powerful aristocrats, and wealthy ecclesiastical institutions were not the only consumers of embroidery in Paris. In 1326, the Parisian bourgeois confraternity of the Pilgrims to St. James of Compostella paid to have numerous liturgical furnishings embroidered with scallops, the symbol of the pilgrimage to Compostella. A few years later they ordered altar frontals and custodials, which were also to be *coquillier*, or covered with scallops (*coquilles de St. Jacques*).[85]

Evidence from household account books and notarial registers also indicates that Parisian embroideries were commissioned for consumption outside of Paris. In 1299, Clément *le brodeur*, of Paris, delivered an embroidered vestment for the chapel of the Count of Artois.[86] In 1302, in preparation for a military campaign in Flanders, the count of Artois ordered embroidered saddles and outfits for his horses. The provenance of most of the embroideries is not specified, but the account does mention a beaver cape embroidered with gold and silk, which he bought in Paris.[87] We know as well that Mahaut of Artois placed a number of embroidery commissions with Étienne Chevalier, a Parisian embroiderer. One of those was for a set of sacerdotal vestments and liturgical furnishings for the Dominican house of Thieulloye, which she had founded. Another was for ornaments for the church of Thérouanne. Étienne

---

82 Agnes Branting and Andreas Lindblom, *Medieval Embroideries and Textiles in Sweden* (Uppsala: Almquist & Wiksells, 1932), 89–93, pl. 125–28; Agnes Geijer, *Textile Treasures of Uppsala Cathedral From Eight Centuries* (Stockholm: Almquist & Wiksell, 1964), 23–25, pl. 4–5; Regula Schorta, "Tissus et broderies," in *L'art au temps des rois maudits: Philippe le Bel et ses fils, 1285–1328* (Paris: Réunion des musées nationaux, 1998), 248.

83 Schorta, "Tissus et broderies," 249; Odile Brel-Bordaz, *Broderies d'ornements liturgiques xiiie-xive s.* (Paris: Nouvelles Editions Latines, 1982), 130–39, figs. 2–9; Pauline Johnstone, *High Fashion in the Church: The Place of Church Vestments in the History of Art From the Ninth to the Nineteenth Century* (Leeds: Maney Publishing, 2002), 52.

84 Schorta, "Tissus et broderies," 249; Brel-Bordaz, *Broderies*, 141–47, figs. 10–16; Johnstone, *High Fashion*, 52.

85 H. Bordier, "La confrérie des pèlerins de Saint-Jacques et ses archives," part 2, *Mémoires de la Société de l'histoire de Paris et de l'Ile-de-France* (1876): 357.

86 Branting and Lindblom, *Medieval Embroideries*, 93.

87 Richard, *Une petite-nièce*, 387.

also supplied an embroidered outfit for Mahaut's grandson, consisting of a coat, mantle, hood, and a sword sheath embroidered with silk and pearls.[88]

SMALL MERCERY GOODS

Paris was also known for its small luxurious textile items, especially silk almspurses and belts. A set of statutes from the very end of the thirteenth century lists 124 *faiseuses d'aumonières sarrazinoises* ("makers of Saracen almspurses"), all of whom were women.[89] Almspurses were small cloth purses that were worn on the exterior of garments, hanging from a belt. Some were made of velvet, some were embroidered with silk and gold thread, and some were made with a tapestry weave of silk and gold thread. Many of the embroidered ones depicted scenes from courtly life, including encounters between lovers.[90]

The statutes for the makers of Saracen almspurses do not indicate why these particular purses were associated with the Muslims. We know that the members of this guild used silk and gold thread, suggesting that the purses were either embroidered or tapestry-woven. Because there were precedents for silk and gold tapestry weaving in early-thirteenth-century Muslim Spain, some textile historians have suggested that Saracen almspurses were those using the tapestry weave.[91] This conjecture makes sense, given the fact that one of the early tapestry guilds in Paris made "Saracen *tapis*" (see p. 80). It is also possible that the Crusaders encountered a similar kind of luxurious purse in the Middle East: The Persian *kiseh*, for instance, was a small bag usually made of silk and worn on a belt or girdle.[92]

Household account books, vernacular literature, and manuscript illuminations indicate that members of the aristocracy made frequent purchases of almspurses, which thus provided an important source of employment.[93] Like silk belts, which were both embroidered and worked with enamels and precious metals, almspurses figured prominently in the late medieval gift economy. On the day of Queen Jeanne of Burgundy's coronation in 1317, twelve embroidered purses, six embroidered

---

88 Ibid., 89, 205, 207.

89 Depping, *Réglemens sur les arts*, 382–86.

90 For published examples, see Marie Schuette and Sigrid Müller-Christensen, *A Pictorial History of Embroidery* (New York: Praeger, 1964), pl. 214–18, XI, 221–22, and Hans Wentzel, "Almosentasche," in *Reallexikon zur deutschen Kunstgeschichte*, ed. O. Schmitt (Stuttgart: J. B. Metzler, 1937), 1:393–401. For discussion and an example of a French, possibly Parisian, almspurse in silk and gold tapestry-weave, see Rebecca Martin, *Textiles in Daily Life in the Middle Ages* (Cleveland: Cleveland Museum of Art in cooperation with Indiana University Press, 1985), 27. For references to velvet purses, see below at note 94.

91 Martin, *Textiles in Daily Life*, 27; Wadsworth Atheneum, *2000 Years of Tapestry Weaving: A Loan Exhibition* (Hartford and Baltimore, c. 1951), cat. nos. 65–67, 32–33, pl. 5.

92 "Kiseh," *Loghat-nama (Dictionnaire encyclopédique) fondé par Ali Akbar Dehkhodâ, sous la direction de Mohammad Mo`in* (Tehran: Université de Téhéran, 1946–), vol. xi, 16602. Many thanks to Sarah-Grace Heller for forwarding this reference from her colleague Richard Davis.

93 Danièle Alexandre-Bidon and Marie-Thérèse Lorcin, *Le quotidien au temps des fabliaux: Textes, images, objets* (Paris: Picard, 2003), 14, 42, 173, 224, 266–68, 274, 278–79.

velvet purses, six embroidered samite purses, sixteen other purses, and four belts embroidered with pearls were delivered to the queen.[94] She probably gave most of these items away as gifts. In November 1313, Countess Mahaut of Artois gave away nineteen almspurses and three belts during a visit from her daughter Blanche, who had married into the royal family.[95] She had made a similar distribution of purses and belts in 1307, and did so again in 1310 during a visit from the queen of Navarre, the Countess of Blois, the Countess of Namur, and Blanche of Brittanny, the widow of Philip of Artois.[96] In 1319, Mahaut gave a purse embroidered with pearls and a silk belt trimmed with gilded silver to the niece of the provost of Aire (one of the towns in the county of Artois), on the occasion of the young woman's marriage.[97]

Aristocrats and royals were not the only ones to thrive on a gift economy that frequently involved small luxurious purses and belts. In 1324, the Parisian Confraternity of the Pilgrims of St. James paid for two *aumonières* and one embroidered purse, which they gave to men who were handling a petition from the confraternity to the pope in Avignon. Since the situation probably called for bribes, one wonders what the confraternity placed inside those purses![98]

Museum curators often assume that the surviving almspurses of this period were created in Paris. Account book evidence certainly suggests that Paris was a major supplier of these luxury items. The description of two packs of goods that were confiscated from two merchants in Aix-en-Provence in 1343 includes goods from a number of places, but all of the silk purses—seventeen dozen silk and gold ones and one dozen small silk and gold ones—were from Paris.[99] Mercery of Parisian origin was also found as far afield as Naples: A record from there from 1305 includes a green silk belt embroidered with rosettes of pearls and gold, "of Paris work" *(de opere parisiensi)*.[100] Nevertheless, it is quite possible that other towns were producing embroidered silk almspurses as well. Mahaut of Artois purchased most of her almspurses in Paris, but she purchased some of them in Arras and Saint-Omer.[101] The notarial accounts of the Boni brothers of Montauban from 1340–60 include one silk purse from Paris and one "fine purse" from England.[102]

94 "Premier compte de Geoffroi de Fleuri," 66.

95 Pas-de-Calais A 316, 5v, 14v.

96 Richard, *Une petite-nièce*, 200.

97 Pas-de-Calais A 374, 22v (transcribed by Gérard et al., 3:142).

98 Bordier, "Confrérie," part 1, *Mémoires de la Société de l'histoire de Paris et de l'Ile-de-France* (1875): 200.

99 J. Billioud, "Le roi des merciers du comté de provence aux XIVe et XVe siècles," *Bulletin philologique et historique du Comité des travaux historiques et scientifiques* (1922–23): 58–59.

100 Riccardo Bevere, "Vestimenti e gioielli in uso nelle province napoletane dal xii al xvi secolo," *Archivio storico per le province napoletane* 22 (1897): 320.

101 Paris: Pas-de-Calais A 263, 18r; A 270, 25v; A 316, 20r (transcribed by Gérard et al., vol. 2); A 329, 22r (transcribed by Gérard et al., vol. 2). Arras: A 263, 18r; A 316, 14v. Saint-Omer: A 298, 15r.

102 Édouard Forestié, *Les livres de comptes des Frères Bonis, marchands montalbanais du XIVe siècle* (Paris: H. Champion, 1893), 2:437, 184. Silk purses of unspecified provenance: 1:65, 116, 174, 241; 2:22, 26, 60, 75, 272, 275, 284.

In the late thirteenth century and the first three decades of the fourteenth, Parisian textiles of an enormous variety fed the demands of royalty, popes, aristocrats, bourgeois consumers, and servants from London to Naples. It seems clear that Paris was indeed a major textile producer. My preliminary research into Northern French and English household account books and the available published records suggests that there is still much to be discovered about the quality and nature of its products and the extent of its market.

"Clothing Themselves in Acres": Apparel and Impoverishment in Medieval and Early Modern England

Margaret Rose Jaster

In *London*, the rich disdaine the poore. The Courtier the Citizen. The Citizen the Countriman. One Occupation disdaineth another. The Merchant the Retayler. The Retayler the Craftsman. The better sort of Craftsmen the baser. The Shoomaker the Cobler. The Cobler the Carman.[1]

As he pontificates against the sin of disdain in his *Christ's Teares Over Jerusalem*, first published in 1593, Thomas Nash offers us an illustration of status groups in early modern London, and his opinion of the contention between and among the groups. The groups were differentiated from one another by such characteristics as dialect and deportment, but the most accessible signifier of status in early modern English society was clothing.

Most students of medieval and early modern culture are aware that a body of legal and social texts assigned precise signifiers to various items of apparel with the goal of rendering an individual recognizable to society-at-large. These diverse texts fixed clothing as a mark of social and occupational status.

This essay will examine some of these texts in an attempt to determine how apparel was utilized in that society, both by those who sought to manipulate others through sartorial signifiers, and by those who endeavored to manipulate their own status through apparel. By focusing on one of the articulated rationales for apparel mandates, I will also demonstrate, in contrast to other scholarly speculations, that attitudes about apparel directives did not differ significantly from the medieval to the early modern period in England.

My title derives from the complaint of the protagonist in Thomas Middleton's satirical pamphlet *The Ant and the Nightingale: or, Father Hubburd's Tales*, who says that

I am grateful to the participants in the "Cloth, Clothing, and Textiles" session at the International Congress on Medieval Studies at Kalamazoo, Michigan, in May 1996 for their comments and advice on an early version of this paper. I also wish to thank Gale Owen-Crocker and Robin Netherton for their patient guidance during the revision process.

1 Thomas Nash, *Christs Teares Over Jerusalem* (London: Printed for Thomas Thorp, 1613), 142. After the initial 1593 publication, editions were published in 1594 and 1613.

the merchants catering to his landlord's sartorial extravagance are "clothing themselves in acres"—in other words, depriving the landlord, his family, and their tenants of their livelihoods.[2] Middleton treats with mordant humor the quite critical concern of early modern society with the decline of charity, and its purported replacement with high fashion. We can locate this threading of clothes and charity in the most conspicuous type of clothing text, apparel laws, as well as in texts that echo the laws; therefore, we will first examine the laws' assertion that apparel mandates were necessary to prevent the impoverishment of the realm.

The earliest apparel legislation was enacted in 1363 under Edward III; all statutes of this nature were abolished on March 25, 1604, in the first Parliament of the reign of James VI and I. For some economic historians, sumptuary legislation characterizes pre-industrial Europe, the period between the Middle Ages' very limited economic horizons and the industrial revolution's building of economic growth into people's expectations.[3] As the social structure became more complex, the strictures on apparel became more minutely detailed. Thus, the earliest Act of Apparel, which prohibited the wearing of fur or any cloth imported from outside England, Ireland, Wales, or Scotland (except for use by members of the royal family) was the shortest and least complicated of the ten major Acts of Apparel passed in this two-and-a-half-century span. So, too, as the Acts of Apparel became more specific, they were supplemented by proclamations designed to enlarge their scope in various ways.[4]

The frequent iteration of governmental mandates, especially during the reign of Elizabeth,[5] alerts us to two conditions of their existence: the population's apparent resistance to them, and the government's obvious persistence in maintaining them. While mere repetition proves the government's interest in the matter, proof of actual popular resistance is less certain, and an understanding of the motivations behind the actions of *either* group remains largely within the realm of speculation.

2 Thomas Middleton, *The Ant and the Nightingale: or Father Hubburd's Tales* (London: T. C. for Thomas Bushell, 1604), C4. I will discuss this text at length later in this essay.
3 My work is indebted to the following studies: Frances Elizabeth Baldwin, *Sumptuary Legislation and Personal Regulation in England* (Baltimore: Johns Hopkins Press, 1926); Joan R. Kent, "Social Attitudes of Members of Parliament with Special Reference to the Problem of Poverty, circa 1590–1624" (Ph.D. diss., University of London, 1971); N. B. Harte, "State Control of Dress and Social Change in Pre-Industrial England," in *Trade, Government and Economy in Pre-Industrial England: Essays Presented to F. J. Fisher*, ed. D. C. Coleman and A. H. John (London: Weidenfeld and Nicolson, 1976); and Wilfred Hooper, "The Tudor Sumptuary Laws," *English Historical Review* 30 (1915): 433–49. Like all scholars who work with Tudor legal texts, I am grateful to Paul L. Hughes and James F. Larkin, who edited *Tudor Royal Proclamations*, 3 vols. (New Haven, CT: Yale University Press, 1964–69).
4 Harte, "State Control of Dress," 134–37.
5 Although only three Acts of Apparel were successfully passed under Elizabeth I (1563, 1566, and 1571), no fewer than eight other attempts were made from 1565 to 1598; in addition, twelve Proclamations, dating from 1559 to 1597 (including three in 1562 and two in 1597), reinforced other efforts. See *The Statutes of the Realm: Printed by command of His Majesty King George the Third in pursuance of an address of the House of Commons of Great Britain, from original records and authentic manuscripts*, 9 vols. in 10 (London: G. Eyre and A. Strahan, 1810–22), vol. 4, pt. 1: 428, 494; Hughes and Larkin, *Tudor Royal Proclamations*, 2:136, 2:187, 2:192, 2:202, 2:278, 2:381, 2:417, 2:442, 2:454, 3:3, 3:174, 3:179.

Having established aristocratic concern about apparel through the repetition of dicta, we can now consider why that repetition proved necessary after the medieval period. In her comprehensive landmark study of sumptuary legislation in England, Frances Elizabeth Baldwin suggests that the increase in apparel mandates occurred because "the people of the Middle Ages took it for granted that every government had the right to check extravagance ... for the public good." She adds that "the philosophical discussion of this matter which took place in later times probably hastened the disuse of the [laws]."[6]

Most recent scholars refute Baldwin's philosophical explanation in favor of economic, constitutional, or practical causes for the failure of these mandates in either time period. This essay, which follows the work of Frank Whigham and Claire Sponsler,[7] agrees that it is much more likely that the key to the explanation for the laws' failure lies in the actions of the elite classes rather than the reactions of the subject classes. It follows that it is not the idea of intrusion into a citizen's personal life that militated against sumptuary legislation, nor is it true that those with a more urbane early modern worldview rejected the concept of sumptuary regulation while their ancestors endorsed it. On the contrary, diverse texts of the early modern period reiterate the concept, first advanced in the medieval period, that it was an individual's responsibility to curb acquisitiveness for the good of the kingdom; these texts also champion the right of the realm to encourage complicity through legislation.

Modern scholars identify various objectives behind sumptuary legislation; some motives were, in brief, economic protectionism, the preservation of the social hierarchy, and the government's attempts to curb the luxurious tendencies of its citizens for their own good and the good of the kingdom. At different times in the history of the laws, one or the other of the motives took precedence, but the most frequently iterated rationale for the laws was that a citizen's sartorial desires must be tamed in the interests of the state.

The first English sumptuary law, in 1336, is paradigmatic in this regard.[8] Edward III and his Parliament, "desiring the common welfare," dealt with dietary excesses that caused "much mischief" in the kingdom: They were an inconvenience to the rich, and the poor became "greatly impoverished" as a result of attempts to imitate their betters.[9] Even though it is unlikely that the letter of this law or its successors was ever efficiently enforced, its spirit lived on for centuries. Edward III's Parliament also initiated the second sumptuary law, which was the first Act of Apparel, in 1363.[10] It was instituted to avoid "the very great destruction and impoverishment of the land,

---

6 Baldwin, *Sumptuary Legislation*, 9.

7 Frank Whigham, *Ambition and Privilege: The Social Tropes of Elizabethan Courtesy Theory* (Berkeley: University of California Press, 1984); Claire Sponsler, "Narrating the Social Order: Medieval Clothing Laws," *CLIO* 21, no. 3 (Spring 1992): 265–83.

8 11 Edw. 3, c. 2 (1336/7), *Statutes of the Realm*, 1:280–81. Hereafter *Statutes of the Realm* will be abbreviated *SR*.

9 Ibid.; also Baldwin, *Sumptuary Legislation*, 27–28. In quotations of these laws, spelling, capitalization, and punctuation have been regularized for readability.

10 37 Edw. 3, cc. 8–14 (1363), *SR* 1:380–82.

by which cause all the wealth of the kingdom is consumed and destroyed."[11]

Although the Wars of the Roses interrupted the Parliament that convened during Edward IV's reign, the 1463 Act of Apparel noted that

> the Commons of the said realm ... do wear excessive and inordinate array [and apparel], to the great displeasure of God, and impoverishing of this realm [of England] and to the enriching of other strange realms and countries, to the final destruction of the husbandry of this said realm.[12]

Later in Edward IV's reign, Parliament blamed "the non-due execution of statutes" against excess of apparel for the fact that "the ... realm was fallen into great misery and poverty, and like to fall into greater, unless [the better remedy] be provided."[13]

The Acts of Apparel of 1510, 1515, and 1533, decreed under Henry VIII, also cite the impoverishment of the realm as justification for their existence.[14] And although the framers of the 1514 statute expressed the hope that it would "last forever," as we have seen, Elizabeth I added three new statutes, and found it necessary to fortify the Acts of Apparel with twelve proclamations. "Impoverishment of the realm," the "wasting and undoing" of estates by young heirs, and the "decay of hospitality" form part of the rationalization for the 1566, 1574, 1588, and 1597 proclamations.[15]

The revocation of sumptuary legislation in 1604 did not assuage the anxiety over this issue. James I's Proclamation of 1610,[16] which attempts to review and reconsider earlier proclamations, seems to have derived in part from a discussion in Parliament during which Francis Bacon (among others) argued that excess expenditures on apparel precipitated impoverishment in the realm.[17] Finally, Parliamentary discussions surrounding the attempt to legislate apparel in 1621 were prompted, among other reasons, by a desire to prevent gentlemen from "wasting their estates."[18]

That apparel mandates are, as Claire Sponsler suggests, actively social texts that narrate a particular view of the social order[19] explains the many reverberations of their declared motives in other texts of the period. For example, when texts such as laws, sermons, and popular pamphlets associate excess of apparel with the

---

11 Baldwin, *Sumptuary Legislation*, 47.
12 3 Edw. 4, c. 5 (1463), SR 2:399–402; Baldwin, *Sumptuary Legislation*, 101.
13 22 Edw. 4, c. 1 (1482/1483), SR 2:468.
14 1 Hen. 8, c. 14 (1510), SR 3:8; 6 Hen. 8, c. 1 (1514), SR 3:121; 7 Hen. 8, c. 6 (1515), SR 3:179; 24 Hen. 8, c. 13 (1533), SR 3:430–432; Baldwin, *Sumptuary Legislation*, 141–49.
15 Baldwin, *Sumptuary Legislation*, 214, 224, 226. In contrast to the evidence suggested by the legal texts, Felicity Heal suggests that despite profligate expenditures, hospitality in aristocratic households continued well into Elizabeth's reign. She notes that William Harrison, whose eyewitness commentaries in *A Description of England* (1588) offer colorful glimpses into Elizabethan English life, "presented the world of the noble household as though it had changed little from the medieval pattern." But she also observes that these "continuities existed with a rising chorus of laments that hospitality was dead." Felicity Heal, *Hospitality in Early Modern England* (Oxford: Clarendon Press, 1990), 91, 93.
16 James VI & I, *A Proclamation* (London: Robert Barker, 1610).
17 Kent, "Social Attitudes," 387.
18 Ibid., 405.
19 Sponsler, "Narrating the Social Order," 265.

impoverishment of the realm, these texts partake in a "shared code,"[20] which recognizes personal extravagance as detrimental to the realm.

My analysis accepts apparel mandates as part of an ideological agenda, and recognizes that claiming economic or moral motives for the institution of clothing codes must be spurious. But we must nevertheless attend to the rationales offered by the statutes themselves. However suspect, these explanations form an integral part of the medieval and early modern discourse about apparel and, more importantly, they are echoed in the texts that did the *real* work of disseminating the ideology: sermons, other homiletic texts, and pleasure reading.

The 1533 Act of Apparel, which contains the most comprehensive statement of intent, stipulates that these laws were necessary to repress

> the inordinate excess daily more and more used in the sumptuous and costly array and apparel accustomably worn in this realm, whereof hath ensued and daily do chance such sundry high and notable inconveniences as be to the great, manifest and notorious detriment of the commonweal.[21]

Echoes of the 1533 statute resonate in other texts. The government's official position can best be deduced from words from the pulpit. As attendance at church was mandatory, official homilies would have reached a huge aural audience, which would have ranged through the social scale. This audience was further extended by the publication of the homilies. As the tomes of sermons were printed in black-letter type, the type used in hornbooks of the day, the size of the potential reading audience also would have been considerable.[22]

For example, the Church of England's "An Homilie Against Excess of Apparell," included in the second tome of sermons printed for the use of their majesties' ecclesiastics, was first printed in 1562, enjoyed nine printings in 1563, and went on to have ten more reprints between 1570 and 1640. Sermons would, of course, have been preached before and after their publication; it is also notable that this particular sermon was printed and preached long after sumptuary legislation had been abrogated.

The government's frustration over the failure of sumptuary legislation is manifest from the opening section of the homily. After nodding to the laws that attempted to enforce temperance in food and drink, the author identifies his target: excess in apparel. He complains that neither God's word, nor the "the godly and necessary lawes, made of our Princes, and oft repeated, with the penalties, can bridle this detestable abuse." Our "proud curiosity" cannot be "stayed" despite the efforts of God and government.[23] Disobeying these necessary laws defies God and puts the

---

20 The term is Stephen Greenblatt's. See his "Friction and Fiction," in *Reconstructing Individualism: Autonomy, Individuality, and the Self in Western Thought*, ed. Thomas C. Heller et al. (Stanford: Stanford University Press, 1986), 47.

21 24 Hen. 8, c. 13 (1533), *SR* 3:430–2.

22 My thanks to Peter W. M. Blayney for sharing his insights on this and other issues concerning early modern printing during his seminar at the Folger Shakespeare Library.

23 *Certaine Sermons or Homilies Appointed to be Read in Churches in the Time of the Late Queene Elizabeth of Famous Memory* (London: John Brill, 1623), 102.

realm at peril. The homilist asserts that he will tell us of the moderate use of apparel, the abuse of which is causing inconveniences that increase daily.[24]

The lessons from Holy Scripture (the homilist cites Psalm 104 and St. Paul's second letter to the Colossians, among other references) sound strikingly like those of the sumptuary laws. The first, to beware of using costly apparel to tempt another to the lusts of the flesh, and the second, to heed the neglect of the soul that results from indulging the body, echo the laws' apprehension about the morally harmful effects of excesses in apparel.[25] The third and the fourth lessons are even closer to what may be read as the true spirit of sumptuary legislation. The third lesson, that apparel should be worn according to one's degree, wherever God has placed one, (and one should content oneself with this rank) is complemented by the fourth, which states that wearing clothing that is *not* ordained by one's estate will result in a diminution of charity toward one's neighbors and children, further discontent, and a wasting of revenues on inappropriate items like clothes, rather than on lands.[26] As we shall see in our analysis of Middleton's popular pamphlet, this last point highlights a vital issue in early modern England: the decline in hospitality that resulted when members of the aristocracy neglected their responsibility to their manor homes.[27]

Having established the lessons, the homilist raves about the specific sartorial excesses of the English. He seems to relish his *copia* of abuses; his minute descriptions reveal his prurient interest in the most luxurious (and prohibited) items: ornamented slippers, cauls, sweet balls, bracelets, attires of the head, slops, headbands, earrings, veils, wimples, and crisping-pins. The homilist adds that the English "are by their fantasticall devices made laughingstocks of other nations."[28]

After alluding again to "divers good and wholesome lawes" that might, if they were practiced, "serve to diminish this raging and riotous excess," the homilist focuses on the problem of women's excesses "so that none can excuse themselves, of whatever estate or condition they may be." Women are given far less leeway than men; while men had been allowed enough ornament for an "honest comeliness," a woman's ornament is her husband's virtue. This is especially so in a Christian country where his virtues will be Christian. The societal double jeopardy perpetrated on early modern women by this same Christianity is manifest in the homilist's assertion that "The ornament of a woman standeth in scarcitie of speech and apparel."[29] In addition, a woman's subjection to her husband is sufficient attire. This assertion recalls the economic motives of apparel mandates, as does the homilist's concluding

---

24 Ibid., 103.

25 Ibid.

26 Ibid., 103–4.

27 Felicity Heal understands "hospitality" in this period as deriving from the definition that operated in the ancient world, a meaning which stands in contrast to modern notions of the term. The medieval and early modern notion included the expectation that the wealthy would "feed and harbor all sorts and conditions of men" as part of their essential duty as "good housekeepers" (*Hospitality*, 2–3).

28 *Certaine Sermons or Homilies*, 105.

29 Ibid., 107.

argument: Women are causing their husbands to engage in bribery, extortion, and deceit in order to maintain their sumptuous state.

Thomas Middleton's *The Ant and the Nightingale: or, Father Hubbard's Tales*, published in 1604 (the year that sumptuary legislation was abrogated) also bemoans the impoverishment of the realm caused by excess expenditure on apparel. We are reminded of the conservative nature of all satire when Middleton employs the fable to frame his incisive criticism, while the image of the industrious ant links this text to Protestant theology.

In witty allusions to Pythagorean theories of transmigration, Middleton's ant disparages the present condition of society as he relates how he was maltreated in his several lives: He was in turn ploughman, soldier, and student. Judging by the space he devoted to each segment of the story, Middleton is most vexed at how the farmer's lot is worsened by the irresponsible excesses of his landlord's son: The ploughman's tale is almost twice the length of the soldier's tale, and almost three times the length of the student's tale.[30]

Middleton's disproportionate emphasis on the dilemma of the ploughman implies a dissatisfaction with the imminent shift from property that one does not own but holds in use (acreage) to property possessed and consumed on one's own person. As Wilfred Hooper explains, "The sons of capitalists, who had invested their money in land, were in many cases converting it back to money, and were forsaking the hospitable life of country squires to squander their patrimony in the gay round of the capital."[31]

Middleton's ant-as-farmer never had an easy life—"to be man and husband is to be a poor master of many rich cares"—but his destruction began, he says, "by the prodigall downfall" of his young landlord. Middleton sounds the satirist's nostalgic note when the ant asserts that to the days of the father, grandfather, and great-grandfather of this heir belonged "fair commons for the comfort of the poor, liberty of fishing, help of fuel by brush and underwood never denied." When the former landlord died, the bell tolled for hospitality and good housekeeping.[32] Middleton's ant laments that the failure of the aristocracy in its obligation to the poor, especially in towns and villages, and the deterioration of traditional standards of hospitality in the country, were significant problems inherited from Elizabeth, exacerbated during James' reign.[33]

Middleton addresses these dire issues with caustic humor as he imputes the heir's ruin to his craving for garish attire. The ant-ploughman yokes the images of apparel and lands in his description of the heir in London. His picture of the breeches,

---

30 As a rough measurement, in the version of *The Ant and the Nightingale* printed in Thomas Middleton, *The Works of Thomas Middleton*, 8 vols., ed. Arthur H. Bullen (Boston: Houghton Mifflin, 1886), the ploughman's tale comprises nineteen pages, the soldier's tale ten and a half pages, and the student's tale a mere seven pages.

31 Hooper, "Tudor Sumptuary Laws," 445.

32 Middleton, *Ant and the Nightingale*, C2.

33 One might suggest that conspicuous consumption displaced conspicuous charity; of course, both contribute to status display.

cloak, and spurs blends a plaintive bid for sympathy with rustic malevolence:

> his Breeches, a wonder to see, were ful as deep as the middle of winter, or the Roade way betweene London and Winchester, and so large and wide withal, that I thinke within a Twelve-month, he might very well put all his lands in them; and then you may imagine they were big enough, when they would out reach a thousand Acres

while the cloak,

> of three pounds a-yard, lined cleane through with purple Velvet, which did so dazzle our coarse Eyes, that we thought we should have bene purblind ever after ... drunk up the price of all my ploughland in very pearle, which stuck as thick upon those hangers as the white measells upon hog's-flesh.

The ant warms to his trenchant description of the extravagant heir:

> Lastly, he walked the chamber with such a pestilent gingle, that his spurs over-squeaked the lawyer, and made him reach his voice three notes above his fee; but after we had spied the rowels of his spurs, how we blest ourselves! they did so much and so far exceed the compass of our fashion that they looked more like the forerunners of wheelbarrows.

The sober message of Middleton's satire, and its sentimental privileging of land as property, cannot obscure the droll imagery of the ant-ploughman's summary:

> thus was our young Landlord accoutred in such a strange and prodigall shape, that it amounted to above two yeares' rent in apparell ... the Mercer and the Merchant, two notable Arch-tradesmen had fitted my young master in clothes, while they had clothed themselves in his Acres ... for he had not so many yards in his sute as they had yards and acres bound for the Payment.[34]

Middleton's satire is subtly inclusive; his ludicrous likeness of the profligate landlord cannot obscure his contempt for those other targets of conservative commentators: greedy lawyers, mercers, and merchants.[35] Nor can it completely obscure the seriousness of the charges against all of these transgressors whose actions so clearly endangered the stability of the realm. However, we must also be aware that Middleton's jeremiad, like those of his fellow conservatives, was "part of the stock-in-trade of the moralist."[36]

34 Middleton, *Ant and the Nightingale*, C3v, C4.

35 Apparently, there is slim probability for the young man's rehabilitation. In the one instance I found in which an attempt is made to reconvert into acreage land that had previously been transformed into lavish apparel, the outcome is predictably dismal. Sir James Cleland writes: "They have put their lands, which contained a great circuit, up into a little trunck, and hold it a point of policie to weare their lands upon their backes, that they maie see that noe wast be done by their Tennants. But alasse when they would spred abroad their gaie cloathes againe into a longe feild, or a pleasant parke, they are so shorte that they cannot reach one ridge length, & are so dubbed Sir John Had-Land, knighte of Pennilesse bench." *The Institution of a Young Nobleman* (London, 1607), 215.

36 Heal, *Hospitality*, 93.

The economic justification that excesses in apparel are impoverishing the realm, and should therefore be prohibited, provided the ideological underpinning for the texts we have just examined. While the statute of 1533 conspicuously claimed that motivation, the other texts echo its rhetoric and intent. For example, the social work of apparel codes also occurs in texts as "cultural events," incidents that contributed to the worldview of the time, but are frustratingly irreproducible today. The acts of reading, of private and public conversation, and of participation in spectacle are other such cultural events which, it can be surmised, would resonate with reiterations of the apparel laws. While we might desire to find evidence in social practices and transitions, "ideological questioning is, in the nature of its evidence, easier to describe and isolate than social transition." It is appropriate, then, to have carefully examined these prescriptive texts, even as we remain wary of them: We may never assume that even such heated arguments as presented in sumptuary legislation, governmentally conceived sermons, or conservative commentaries were directly responsible for modifying social behavior.[37]

This exploration of status issues in apparel texts has established that, in general, the circulated ideas about apparel helped to maintain the traditional social hierarchy advocated by sumptuary legislation. I have also contradicted the claims of some earlier scholars by demonstrating that the concerns of the medieval apparel codes informed cultural texts well after the medieval period, indeed, well after the laws' demise.

37 Ibid., 94.

"Ye Shall Have It Cleane": Textile Cleaning Techniques in Renaissance Europe

Drea Leed

"The first part [of this tract] deals with the clothing of people in holy orders, which are vestment and gown and alb and surplice, and how many ells of fabric one requires for them and how one refreshes the color of velvet and silk and wool fabrics which have lost their color. The second part speaks of painting silver and gold and of all colors, and of how one draws pictures upon paper, and what is required for this."[1]

Thus opens the text of the manuscript known as the Nuremberg *Kunstbuch*, written as an instructional manual for the sisters of the convent of St. Catherine's in Nuremburg, Germany. The manuscript, consisting of sixty-nine parchment folios in Gothic half-cursive, was bound into book form in the last half of the fifteenth century. It was apparently in the possession of lay sister Margaret Bindterin in 1596, the year St. Catherine's was dissolved by order of the Nuremberg council. When she died in the following year, the *Kunstbuch* was handed over to the Nuremberg Stadtbibliothek, which had earlier received the other manuscripts that had belonged to the convent.[2]

The manuscript is a wide-ranging document designed to help the nuns in the course of their daily work of making the rich liturgical vestments worn by Dominican priests, cleaning a variety of fine textiles, and painting and gilding both manuscripts and cloth. The convent's scriptorium was quite active during the last half of the fifteenth century, and it is very possible that this treatise was copied in its entirety from one or more of the books brought to the convent by the daughters of well-to-do townsfolk, or from copies of older manuscripts already in its library.

I would like to extend my thanks to the anonymous referee who shared his expertise in the field of textile cleaning chemistry. A version of this paper was presented in May 2001 at the International Congress on Medieval Studies at Kalamazoo, Michigan.

1 *Nürnberger Kunstbuch*, Nuremberg, Nürnberger Stadtbibliothek, MS cent. VI 89, 2r. For this paper, I consulted a transcription of the manuscript in Emil Ernst Ploss, *Ein Buch von Alten Farben: Technologie der Textilfarben im Mittelalter* (Heidelberg: Impuls Verlag Heinz Moos, 1962).

2 Karin Schneider, ed., *Die deutschen mittelalterlichen Handschriften*, Die Handschriften der Stadtbibliothek Nürnberg 1 (Wiesbaden: Harrassowitz, 1965), 13–15.

THE *KUNSTBUCH*'S FABRIC CARE RECIPES

The *Kunstbuch* contains a total of twelve recipes for cleaning undergarments, removing spots, and restoring the color of faded garments. Table 6.1 presents the original texts of these recipes, with translations. Although small in number, these recipes offer a glimpse into the particular issues that the sisters may have faced in repairing and cleaning their store of garments.

Although not a topic commonly addressed in the great philosophical treatises of the time, the care of fabric and textiles was a ubiquitous concern during the fifteenth and sixteenth centuries. Housewives, laundresses, and professionals in several textile-related trades all needed to know how to clean the cloth they wore and worked with on a daily basis. When one considers the value of textiles such as patterned silk velvet, which only the wealthiest could afford, it is easy to understand the attention paid to even the smallest spots and stains that found their way onto costly garments.

The recipes in the *Kunstbuch* have a slant peculiar to the needs of a convent such as St. Catherine's. It is notable that the instructions preceding those for cleaning garments are concerned with the cutting of ecclesiastical vestments from taffeta, brocade, damask, velvet, and other costly silken fabrics. Given the precious nature of these materials, it is natural that the nuns would also be interested in how these garments should be cleaned once they were made and worn. Four of the recipes in the *Kunstbuch* specifically mention silk, while the great majority of the recipes extant in other fifteenth- and sixteenth-century sources on fabric and textile cleaning rarely mention rich textiles.[3]

Green is the color most commonly named in the cleaning section of the *Kunstbuch*. The only other colors mentioned are red, brown, and pink. This preponderance of green is explained by the specialized nature of ecclesiastical dress.[4] The liturgical color palette was limited primarily to red, white, and green. Green was worn for common days and feasts of low rank.[5] The prevalence of green in the *Kunstbuch*'s

---

3 A fifteenth-century example is *Oberdeutsches Färbbüchlein*, Munich, Stadtbibliothek München, MS Cgm. 317; see transcription in Ploss, *Buch von Alten Farben*, 126–29. Four sixteenth-century comparison sources are discussed in more detail later in this article.

4 By contrast, green clothing appears to be far less common in secular inventories of the period. Some examples of German secular inventories, including some from Nuremberg, can be found in Jutta Zander-Seidel's *Textiler Hausrat: Kleidung und Haustextilien in Nürnberg von 1500–1650* (Munich: Deutscher Kunstverlag, 1990).

5 "Restatt ergo quod in diebus ferialibus et communibus uiridibus sit indumentis utendum quia uiridibus color medius est inter albedinem et nigredinem et ruborem, et specualiter inter octauam Epiphanie et Septuagesimam, et inter Pentecostem et Aduentum quando dominicale agitur officium." ("There remains, therefore, that on ferial and common days the use of green vestments because green is a color midway between white and black and red, and especially between the octave of Epiphany and Septuagesima, and between Pentecost and Advent when the Sunday office is used.") Guillaume Durand, *Rationale divinorum officiorum* (Turnhout: Brepols, 1995), 224–29. This text dates from the late thirteenth or early fourteenth century, and was a standard reference for clerical thought on liturgy in the fifteenth century. The tradition of wearing green for Mass during certain times of the year continues today. I am grateful to Thomas Izbicki for this citation and translation.

Table 6.1: Cleaning recipes from the Nuremberg *Kunstbuch*

This table shows the twelve recipes from the textile cleaning section of the Nuremberg Kunstbuch. *The original German is shown to the left; translations by the author are at the right.*

Wie man pech auß gewant pringet.	*How one gets dirt out of clothing.*
xxii. Item wiltu pech auß dem gewant pringen, so nym ein tottern von eim ey vnd zutreib den gar wol vnd streich den auf die fleck vnd reib es dar ein; piß es durchget. Darnach streich es auf die andern seiten vnd reib es auch gar wohl dar ein; so laß es trucken werden vnd nym denn ein gute seyffen vnd ein labß wasser vnd wasch es, so get es her auß.	xxii. Item if you want to get dirt out of fabric, take the yolk of an egg and beat it well and spread it on the spot and rub it in, until it goes through [the fabric]. Then spread it on the other side [of the fabric] and again rub it very well in; then let it dry, and take then good soap and a bit of water and wash it, and it will go away.
Wie man fleck auß gewant pringt.	*How one gets a spot out of clothing.*
xxiii. Item wiltu fleck auß dem gewant pringen, wie es geferbet sey, so nym erbeyß vnd sewd die, als pis die pelg abgen vnd mit dem selben waßer wasch es, so get es herauß.	xxiii. Item to get a spot out of fabric, which is colored, take peas and boil them until the coating disappears, and with the same water wash it, and it will go out.
Wie man die farb wider pringt auf seyden oder samet oder gulden tuch, das da begossen ist etc.	*How one restores the color of silk or velvet or cloth of gold, which is stained etc.*
xxiv. Item wiltu wißen, wie du farb widerpringen solt auf seyden oder auf samet oder auf gulden tuchern, das da begossen sey vnd fleck hab, so nym pachwasser vnd wasch die fleck damit vnd henck es an den luft, das die sunn nit dar an schein vnd laß trucken werden, so wirt es schon.	xxiv. Item if you want to know how you shall restore the color of silk or velvet or cloth of gold, which is wet and stained, take fresh brook-water and wash the spot therewith and hang it in the air, marking that the sun does not shine thereon, and let it dry, and it will be good.
Wie man seyden netzt, das sie pald trucken wird.	*How one works silk, to dry it faster.*
xxv. Item wiltu seiden netzen, das sie pald trucken wird, so nym ein warms prot, das erst auß dem offen get vnd laß den heyssen dunst dar ein gen; magstu es aber nit haben, so nym ein heissen stein oder ii vnd geuß ein waßer dar auf vnd last den dunst dar ein gen, so wirt sie trucken.	xxv. Item if you want to work silk, that it will soon dry, take warm bread fresh from the oven and let the heat go into [the silk]; if you do not have that, take a hot stone or two and sprinkle water thereon and let the heat go into the fabric, and it will soon dry.
Wie man die varb der grünen seiden widerpringt.	*How one restores the color of green silk.*
xxvi. Item wiltu wißen, wie man die varb der grünen seyden widerpringt, so nym weinreben vnd verprenn die zu aschen vnd mach dar auß ein kalkaß vnd wasch die fleck rein da mit vnd henck es an den luft, das die sun nit dar an schein vnd last trucken werden, so wirt es gut. Auch pringt man grün oder praün, das do wullen ist, her wider da mit.	xxvi. If you want to know how one restores the color of green silk, then take grapevines and burn them to ashes and make therefrom a lye solution and wash the stain clean therewith, and hang it up in the air; do not let the sun shine thereon and let it dry, and it will be good. One can also restore the color in green or brown wool with this.
Wie man den varb wider pringt an grünem samet.	*How one restores the color of green velvet.*
xxvii. Item wiltu farb wider pringen an grünem samet, der begossen sey von harn oder wein,	xxvii. Item if you want to restore the color of green velvet, that is stained with urine or

so nym ein kalckstein, der vnabgelescht sey
vnd zustoß den vnd leg in ein newen hafen vnd
geuß ein faulß waßer dar an vnd laß es sten auf
ein halben tag vnd necz den samet da mit vnd
hoh in an den luft, da die sunn nit hin scheint
vnd lass es trucken werden, so wirt es schon.

Wie man wagenschmir auß gewant pringt.
xxviii. Item wiltu wagenschmir auß dem
gewant pringen, so nym leym vnd thu den in
ein pfendlein vnd geuß ein waßer dar an vnd
laß es seyden, das es werd als ein muß vnd
streich es auf die fleck, doch das er das gewant
nicht prenn; so leg es an ein heiße sunnen, das
es turer werd vnd reib es den her auß, so get es
her auß.

*Wie man wider pringt grün gewant, das begossen
ist mit wein etc.*
xxix. Item wiltu grün gewant wider prengen,
das begossen sey von wein, so nym ein frischen
waidaschen vnd thu den in ein news hefelein
vnd geuß ein fauls wasser dar an vnd laß es
sten ein halben tag vnd nym den die selben
laugen vnd netz die fleck da mit vnd hencks an
den luft, das die sunn nit dar an schein vnd laß
es trucken werden, so wirt es schon.

*Wie man wider pringt farb auf rotem, prawn oder
roßin gewant, das begossen ist mit wein.*
xxx. Item wiltu wider pringen varb auf rotem,
prawn oder roßin gewant, das begossen sey
mit wein oder mit harn, so nym einen kalck,
der abgelescht sey vnd thu den in ein new
hefelein vnd geuß ein fauls waßer dar an vnd
laß es sten ii stund vnd rür es durch ein ander,
das thu drey mal vnd laß den sten ein halben
tag vnd nim selbig waßer vnd necz die fleck da
mit; sicht du, das es scharpf wil sein, so nym
des faulen waßer mer dar zu, wil es aber die
fleck nit her auß prengen, so nym des kalckes
mer, so wirt es scherpfer vnd necz die fleck
wider da mit vnd henck das an den luft, das
die sunn nit dar an scheint, so wirt es gut.

*Wie man wider pringt grün gewant, das begossen
ist mit wein.*
xxxi. Item wiltu grün gewant wider pringen,
das begossen ist mit wein oder mit harn, so
nym puchenaschen vnd mach dar auß ein
kalckas vnd wasch die fleck da mit vnd henck
es an den luft, das die sunn nit dar an schein,
so wirt es gut.

wine, take lime that is unslaked and grind it to
powder and lay it in a new cask and pour foul
water thereon and let it stand a half day, and
sprinkle it on the velvet and hang it high in
the air, that the sun does not shine thereon,
and let it dry, and it will be good.

How one gets wagon grease out of clothes.
xxviii. Item if you want to get wagon grease
out of clothing, take clay and put it in a pot
and pour water thereon, and let it boil until it
becomes like mud and paint it on the stain,
but in such a way that it does not burn the
cloth; and lay it in the hot sun until it becomes
dry and then rub it out, and it [the stain] will
go away.

*How one restores green clothing, that is stained
with wine etc.*
xxix. Item if you want to restore green
clothing, which is stained with wine, take fresh
woad ashes and put them in a new basin and
pour foul water thereon and let it stand half a
day and take then the same solution and
sprinkle the stain therewith and hang it up in
the air, that the sun does not shine thereon,
and let it dry, and it will be good.

*How one restores the color of red, brown or pink
clothing, which is stained with wine.*
xxx. Item if you want to restore the color of
red, brown or pink clothing, which is stained
with wine or urine, take slaked lime and put it
in a new basin and pour foul water thereon
and let it stand two hours and stir it together,
do this three times and let it stand a half day
and take the same water and sprinkle the stain
therewith; if you see it [the solution] is too
strong, add more foul water thereto, however
if it does not bring the stain out of the fabric,
add more chalk, then it will be stronger and
sprinkle the stain once again therewith and
hang it on high, that the sun not shine
thereon, and it will be good.

*How one restores green clothing, which is stained
with wine.*
xxxi. Item if you want to restore green
clothing, which is stained with wine or urine,
take beech ashes and make therewith a lye
solution and wash the stain therewith and
hang it in the air, that the sun not shine
thereon, and it will be good.

Wie man tintten auß gewant wescht.	*How one washes colors out of fabric.*
xxxii. Item wiltu tintten auß gewant waschen, so wasch sie mit einem frischen wein, die weil sie naß ist; lestu sie aber trucken, so get sie her auß nit. Magstu aber kein wein haben, so nym ein resche laugen, so get es her auß.	xxxii. Item if you want to wash colors out of fabric, wash it with fresh wine while the cloth is damp; if you let the cloth dry, the color will not go out. If you have no wine, take a strong lye solution and it will go out.
Wie man unterrock waschen sol.	*How one shall wash an undergown.*
xxxiii. Wiltu dy vnterrocke waschen, so nym iii metzen aschen vnd thu die in ein groß schaff vnd geuß des ersten ein heyß sydnigs waßer dar an vnd dar nach ein kaltes waßer, das das schaff vol werd vnd laß das gefallen, das es lauter werd vnd seyhe den das durch ein tuch vnd dunck die rock dar ein vnd wasch die köle, sy werden anders gelwe vnd reybt sei wol mit sewffen vmb das goller vnd vmb die ermel, vnd wo sie sweißig sind. Deucht dich aber, das der kalckas zu herb wer, so mysch den wol mit waßer oder gewß ander was an die aschen vnd misch den unter die ersten.	xxxiii. If you want to wash an undergown, take three measures of ashes and put them in a great open vessel and pour first hot boiling water thereon and then cold water so that the vessel is full and let it become strong, and sieve it then through a cloth and dunk the gown therein and wash it when cool, otherwise it will be yellow, and rub it well with soap on the collar and the sleeves, and where it is sweaty. If you think that the lye solution is too strong, mix it well with water or pour more water on the ashes and mix it with the first.

cleaning recipes serves as evidence that they were intended for an ecclesiastical context.

Of the twelve recipes listed for cleaning clothes, four specifically mention wine stains. One begins "Item if you want to restore green clothing, which is stained with wine or urine"; another, "Item if you want to restore the color of green velvet, that is stained with urine or wine." The preponderance of recipes for removing wine stains could have to do with the close and repeated proximity of ecclesiastical dress to the wine used during the ceremony of the Eucharist. Although extreme care was taken with both garments and the wine, the opportunity for staining existed. However, after wine, urine stains are most frequently mentioned; they are specifically targeted in three of the recipes. As wagon grease and dirt are the other staining substances mentioned by name, it appears that the stains in question may include those found on incoming donations. Wills of the time include numerous references to gowns, robes, and capes left to religious orders.[6] The secular textiles and items of clothing re-worked into ecclesiastical garments would need to be cleaned of existing spots and stains before being made up.

The majority of the recipes in the *Kunstbuch* are for alkaline spot-cleaning solutions (see "Alkalis," p. 111). Four are potash lye-based solutions that specify particular ashes for creating the lye: vine ashes, beech ashes, woad ashes, and common hearth ashes. Another alkali, lime, is used in both slaked (calcium hydroxide) and unslaked (calcium oxide) forms. Two of the recipes use lime as the main ingredient for refreshing

---

6 Several examples of this can be found in Samuel Tymms, *Wills and inventories from the registers of the commissary of Bury St. Edmunds and the archdeacon of Sudbury* (London: Printed for the Camden Society, 1850).

the color of clothing. A combination of unslaked lime and "foul water" is used to restore green clothing, while a recipe for slaked lime and foul water is used to refresh the color of brown, red, or pink fabric. Emil Ploss, an authority on the subject of medieval German textile coloring practices, suggests that foul water is a euphemism for urine or a urine/water solution; the ammonia content of fermented or stale urine makes it a useful alkaline cleaner. Urine also appears in other medieval dye recipes as a color fixative.[7]

One recipe specifies an adsorbent rather than an alkali: The reader is directed to remove wagon grease by rubbing clay into the fabric. The clay may be the "burned clay" mentioned in *Allerley Matkel*, a sixteenth-century cleaning manual (see "Adsorbents," p. 114).[8] It could also be fuller's earth, well known for its oil- and grease-absorbing properties. Finally, the last type of cleaning agent found in these recipes is egg yolk, a dispersing agent and emulsifier used to remove dirt.

Many of the substances referenced in sixteenth-century cleaning manuals, such as citric acid, ox gall, *alum feces*, tartar, camphor, and soapwort, are absent from the *Kunstbuch*. This does not mean that these substances were not in use in the fifteenth century; twelve recipes is too small a number to consider a truly representative sample. The book *Von manigerley ausgeprannten Wassern*, written in 1477 by Viennese professor Michael Schrick, mentions tartar and saponin-producing plants, often in combination with water and lye, as cleaning agents.

The final entry in the section of the *Kunstbuch* devoted to textile cleaning, a description of the proper way to launder an undergown, offers an informative and entertaining glimpse into washing-day in the fifteenth century (fig. 6.1):

> If you want to wash an undergown, take three measures of ashes and put them in a great open vessel and pour first hot boiling water thereon and then cold water so that the vessel is full and let it become strong, and sieve it then through a cloth and dunk the gown therein and wash it when cool, otherwise it will be yellow, and rub it well with soap on the collar and the sleeves, and where it is sweaty. If you think that the lye solution is too strong, mix it well with water or pour more water on the ashes and mix it with the first.

COMPARISON TEXTS

Examining general cleaning techniques published in the sixteenth century provides a wider context for these recipes. Four books in particular are useful for comparison.

The first is the well-known *Secretes of the Reverend Maister Alexis of Piemont*, first published in Italian in the mid-sixteenth century and quickly translated into a variety

---

7 For example, see *Innsbrucker Handschrift* (c. 1330), Innsbruck Universitätsbibliothek, Codex 355, 100v–101r: "To make a green dye, take verdigris and boil it in urine and mix alum thereto and a portion of gum arabic, and dye therewith." Ploss, *Buch von Alten Farben*, 99–100.

8 *Allerley Matkel*, 3r. For a full description of this source, see note 11.

Fig. 6.1: Washing-day in the 1530s, as illustrated in a German copy of the alchemical manual *Splendor Solis* (Berlin, Kupferstichkabinett, MS 78 D 3, 75r, detail). The image portrays several steps of the washing process. Water (or lye-water) is heated over the fire and then poured into wooden tubs. Items to be washed are immersed and scrubbed, and also are beaten with paddles to loosen dirt. Linens are either hung to dry or laid out on the grass to bleach. Photo: Kupferstichkabinett, Berlin, by permission.

of editions and volumes in German, French, and English.⁹ The edition referenced and quoted in this article dates from 1568–69 and contains more than thirty separate recipes for making soap and for solutions that purportedly removed ink, iron, grease, urine, wine, and general stains from linen, wool, silk, and cloth of gold.

The second source, *A Profitable Booke, declaring divers approved Remedies, to take out spots and staines in Silkes, Velvets, Linnen and Woollen Clothes*, was published in numerous editions between 1583 and 1605.¹⁰ It contains thirty-nine recipes specifically for cleaning stains from clothing and restoring the color to garments.

The third is a small German manual known as *Allerley Matkel* ("all sorts of spots"); the full title promises the means "to remove stains from cloth, velvet, silk, gold stuffs and clothing, these stains being of grease, oil or wine stains or any other kinds, and how to do this easily without damage, with waters or lyes as will be taught in this booklet."¹¹ Published in 1532, this is one of the earliest printed collections of textile cleaning and dyeing recipes.

The fourth book is *T Bouck va Wondre*,¹² a Dutch commonplace book in a similar vein published in 1513. It is in fact the original source for many of the recipes found in *A Profitable Booke*, and having both the original Dutch and translated English text for the same recipes has proved a useful tool for deducing synonyms for measurements and substances, as well as proving an excellent object lesson in the potential pitfalls of using sixteenth-century translated texts as primary sources.¹³

9 The English text is a translation of the French, which was a translation of the Italian original. For my transcriptions from this work, I consulted a bound compilation in the National Art Library at the Victoria and Albert Museum, catalogued as Piemontese Alessio, *Secretes; Containing Excellent Remedies Against Diverse Diseases ...* trans. Willyam Warde (London: Kyngston, 1578–80); this actually consists of three sections dated 1568, undated, and 1569, respectively. The cleaning recipes appear in the second and third parts of this multivolume work, first published in English individually as *The Seconde Parte of the Secretes of Master Alexis of Piemont* (London: Jhon Kyngston, 1560) and *The Thyrde and Last Parte of the Secretes of the Reuerende Maister Alexis of Piemount* (London: Roulande Hall, 1562) and in multiple editions thereafter.

10 The edition cited in this article is *A Profitable Booke declaring divers approved Remedies, to take out spots and staines in Silkes, Velvets, Linnen and Woollen Clothes, with divers Colours how to die Velvets and Silkes, Linnen and Woollen, Fustian and Thread ...,* trans. L[eonard] M[ascall] (London: Thomas Purfoot, 1588).

11 The full title is *Allerley Matkel und Flecken aus Gewant / Sammath / Seyden / Güldinen stücken / Kleydern zu bringen / Es seyen Schmalz flecken / blodder weyn flecken / odder wie die mögen genennt werden / Und das alles leychtlich on schaden / mit wassern odder laugen / wie es dan inn dissem Büchleyn gelert wirt / zü volbringen.* A facsimile of the original booklet, published at Meintz in 1532, is reproduced in Sidney Edelstein, "The Allerley Matkel," *Technology and Culture* 5 (1964), 297–321. After the publication of that article, another edition of the text came to light with the title *Allerley Mackel,* indicating that the "t" in the title of Edelstein's original edition was an error; see Moshe Ron, *Bibliotheca Tinctoria: Annotated Catalog of the Sidney M. Edelstein Collection in the History of Bleaching, Dyeing, Finishing, and Spot Removing* (Jerusalem: Jewish National and University Library, 1991), 29. Folio citations in this paper refer to the facsimile of the *Allerley Matkel* edition, as published on pages 301–11 of Edelstein's article. Translations are my own, based on the facsimile images; these differ slightly in style from Edelstein's.

12 Herman Frencken, ed., *T Bouck va Wondre 1513* (Roermond, Netherlands: H. Timmermans, 1934).

13 I discovered while studying the *Profitable Booke* that a large proportion of the recipes are direct translations from *T Bouck va Wondre*; later I learned that Sidney Edelstein and Hector C.

This is by no means a comprehensive list of early published sources on textile care; these four are perhaps the best known. Like all written sources of the time, they have their limitations. To begin with, both *Alexis* and *A Profitable Booke* are translations—in the case of *Alexis* more than once removed—of another text. There is no guarantee that the translator had a thorough understanding of the material being transcribed. A case in point is *A Profitable Booke*'s translation of the Dutch *wouwe* (dyer's weld) into "wood," and the Dutch *crappe van meede* (madder) into "greening weed."

Even for such untranslated sources as *T Bouck va Wondre* (which may itself be a compilation of earlier works), the efficacy of the original recipes must always be questioned. In many cases, these books may have been compiled from earlier oral or written sources of unknown validity, leading the compiler to add encouraging statements such as "For this ... hath beene wel and often prooved, and doth helpe"[14] to recipes of which he had personal experience.

The target audience for this sort of publication is another consideration. These books may have been meant to be used, or they may have been destined for casual perusal and display on the bookshelves of the well-to-do burghers and merchants who could afford such a purchase. It is an open question as to how "practical" and "profitable" these books actually were. Taking these and other cautions into account, the recipes nonetheless hint at possible approaches taken by people of the time toward cleaning their clothing.

Some of the formulas recorded in these commonplace books of the sixteenth century are general in nature, such as the recipe in *Alexis* for "A water to take all manner of spottes out of cloth of any coloure."[15] Others, like the recipe in *Allerley Matkel* describing "How one removes grease or oil spots from white cloth,"[16] target a particular type of fabric, color of fabric, or type of stain. All of the recipes, however, can be grouped into a few general types of cleaning formulas, each with numerous variations but all drawing from the same basic palette of substances and chemical interactions to achieve their effects.

Soap

Of the ingredients used for cleaning clothing and fabric, one of the most common—and familiar to the modern reader—is soap. White soap is referenced in *Allerley Matkel*, while *A Profitable Booke* specifically mentions castile soap in a recipe for cleaning silk and velvet. *Alexis* contains a number of recipes that involve soap, sometimes qualified as "white sope," "Spanish Soap," "Venice sope," or "black

Borghetty also made this connection in their translation of the *Plictho*, a sixteenth-century dyeing manual. See Sidney M. Edelstein and Hector C. Borghetty, trans., *The Plictho of Gioanventura Rosetti: Instructions in the art of the dyers which teaches the dyeing of woolen cloths, linens, cottons, and silk by the great art as well as by the common* (Cambridge, MA: MIT Press, 1969), xi.

14 *Profitable Booke*, 5.
15 *Alexis*, 2:46v.
16 *Allerley Matkel*, 3v.

soap."[17] Soap is a natural solvent for grease and oils, and as such is useful in removing them from textiles and fibers. It also functions as a surfactant, allowing water more easily to penetrate into the material being cleaned. Most of the recipes concerning soap involve the making of "soap balls" or "cakes" to use specifically for cleaning garments. Raw soap — that is, soap that has not been made into balls or incorporated with other ingredients — is not used as a sole ingredient, but is rather a base material to which other substances were added. Here are two characteristic examples, from *A Profitable Booke* and *Alexis*:

> To make a sope to take out spottes of oyle and of greace. Take of good scowring sope, and mix it finely with the sifted ashes of a vyne, of eche in like portion, then put thereunto a quantitie of the powder of burnt Allom, and also of the lyes of wine, beaten into a fine poulder, and put it thereunto, then mix and incorporate all these well together, then make thereof square brickes, or round bals ... take of warme water, and rubbe and chafe all over your spottie places, and then rub theron with your sope ball ... and so at length ye shall have it cleane forth.[18]

and

> Take a pound of white Sope of Venise, the yelkes of sixe Egges, and halfe a sponefull of beaten salte, and as much juice of Beetes as will suffice to incorporate the sayde Sope, & make therof a cleaving paste wherof you shall forme and make your balles.[19]

Alum, mentioned in four recipes for soap balls, is one of the most common additional ingredients. The gall of an ox or calf, a wetting agent, is also mentioned in four soap recipes, while egg whites or egg yolks appear in three as a dispersing or emulsifying agent. Other ingredients mentioned in recipes for soap-based cleaning products are salt, beet juice,[20] ashes, lye, saltpeter, tartar, and herbal substances used for perfumery, among them rosewater and orris root.

Soap is alkaline and somewhat harsh on silk and wool textiles. Some dyed fabrics, including kermes-dyed cloth, could not stand up to plain, undiluted soap. This fact is reflected in another passage from *Alexis*: "and if the clothe be not died in graine, putte to it a little Sope."[21] The author of *A Profitable Booke* was also aware of the dangers attendant upon using raw soap: "[T]o sope your water to much, or your clothes, is an occasion to staine both gold and silkes. A verie good way is, first to melt your sope in the licour, and then let it coole, and so to wash your clothes therin."[22]

---

17 All of these soaps are made of some form of fat combined with potassium hydroxide lye.
18 *Profitable Booke*, 2. For quotations from both this book and *Alexis*, I have transcribed the printed "u" as "v" as appropriate for such words as "have," "over," and "velvet."
19 *Alexis*, 2:45v.
20 The presence of beet juice, which itself can stain, seems strange. Some cleaning recipes specify adding red wool shavings to color a cleaning solution. It is possible the beet juice is enough to color the soap, but not enough to color any fabric.
21 *Alexis*, 2:46r. The term "died in grain" referred to the use of kermes, a highly valued red dye named for the insects from which it is derived.
22 *Profitable Booke*, 13.

This advice is followed in several recipes that use soap as one ingredient among many in a liquid cleaning solution:

> Take the Gall of an olde Oxe, and a pound of Fenigreke made in pouder, a pound and a halfe of white sope, three Flagons of strong lye, and put altogither, and seeth it on a slowe fire, until it diminishe of the halfe. Then washe what spot you wil with it, refreshing it divers tymes with cold water, and it wil take it away.[23]

Although soap recipes typically specify the making of balls or cakes, the majority of cleaning recipes of the fifteenth and sixteenth centuries are for liquid spot-cleaning solutions. Many of the finely finished silk and wool fabrics did not take kindly to immersion in hot water or energetic agitation. Therefore, the large majority of cleaning solutions are meant to be locally applied to specific stains so as not to damage the garment. This is evidenced by the ubiquitous use of such phrases as "wash the spotte with it," "wet the spot with it divers times," and "wash your spots therewith."

Alkalis

Alkaline solutions, either lye- or lime-based, are another common cleaning agent of the fifteenth and sixteenth centuries. Alkalis are best at removing stains of a fatty nature and some proteins. When applied to grease and oil stains, the saponification that occurs is an additional aid to stain removal. Lye[24] serves as the basis for a number of the recipes in these books, and each manuscript has at least one recipe describing how to make a good lye for cleaning fabric.

Here is an example from *A Profitable Booke*:

> Another good way to take out spots out of clothes with a lye. Take 3 pintes of water, and put therein halfe a pound of pot ashes, and stirre it well altogether. Let it so stand the space of foure dayes, but yee must in everie day stirre it 3 or foure times. So done, powre forth the cleere water from the ashes, and put off galles therein, then it will waxe a greene: but if you will have it a blacke, then put a little soote to soake in faire water, and put that blacke water therein. With this warmed, yee may wash your spotty places in any place of your clothes, and it will take it forth faire and cleane.[25]

In some cases an even more alkaline solution of calcium hydroxide, created by soaking unslaked lime (calcium oxide) in water, was used in lieu of a more traditional lye solution. Here it is added to an existing lye solution:

> Another means for spottes, of fatte, or Oile. Take a pound of roche Alome, and as muche fresh unsleckt lime, six unces of Alumen fecis, three pounde of white Sope

---

23 *Alexis*, 2:45v.
24 The lye referred to throughout this article is potassium carbonate ("potash") lye, rather than lye created from a sodium hydroxide or potassium hydroxide solution.
25 *Profitable Booke*, 4. "Galles" in this instance refers to oak galls, not to be confused with other references to ox gall.

cutte small, foure pound of cleere water, and lette it boile a certaine space in some vessell that is not fattie, and then straine it, and when you will occupie of it, let it be luke warme …[26]

Often, specific materials were burned for the ashes needed to make lye. "Pot ashes" and "hearth ashes" were the lowest grade; "soap ashes" were of a finer grade and were used in commercial soap manufacture, as the name suggests. Ashes of willow, beech, and vine are particularly popular in *A Profitable Booke* and *Alexis*.

In a class by itself, however, is the ash known as *alum feces*. *Alum feces* was the contemporary name for ashes created by burning wine lees (tartar).[27] In addition to being a fine and even-textured ash, *alum feces* had the additional benefit of helping to buffer the harsh action of lye (see the discussion of "Buffering agents," below). *Alum feces* was used for making a number of lye solutions:

> To take all spottes out of Crymsen Velvet. Take the ashes made of Vine twigges, and make therwith good Lye, whereof you shall take but a pynte, and put into it halfe an unce of Alumen Fecis, and let it stande a little whyle, and then strayne it.[28]

Buffering agents

During the wine-making process, solids rich in tartaric acid settle at the bottom of the wine cask. These solids, known as tartar, argol, or wine lees in contemporary sources, were a common ingredient in both lye-based and non-lye-based cleaning solutions. Tartar's acidic qualities somewhat neutralize the harshness of an alkaline solution.

The recipe that follows, found with only slight variations in *Alexis*, *A Profitable Booke*, and *Allerley Matkel*, makes reference to tartar:

> Six ounces alum feces, four ounces crude tartar, two ounces alum, one half *quintin* camphor, one half *quintin* dragon's blood, grind all together very small and mix it well together. Then take six ounces ox gall and six *bucklin* of clear water, put these things all in a kettle, let boil down a third, after which strain it through a cloth. If you cannot get the ox gall or the camphor, the water is strong enough. If you would use it, take a new woolen scrap, moisten it in the water, and rub the spot or stain with it.[29]

This recipe describes not only the use of tartar in a cleaning solution, but also a method by which cream of tartar was obtained for use in cleaning. When potash (potassium carbonate) is combined with tartaric acid in liquid solution, cream of tartar (potassium bitartrate, $C_4H_5KO_6$) is precipitated. Some precipitation occurs

---

26 *Alexis*, 2:45v.
27 *Alum feces*, known as *lume de fezza* in Italian and *alumen faecis* in Latin, was described by Cesalpino in his *De Metallicis* (Rome, 1596) as ashes of wine. Edelstein and Borghetty, *Plictho*, 188.
28 *Alexis*, 3:56v.
29 *Allerley Matkel*, 2r. The definitions of the measurements *quintin* and *bucklin* are unknown.

naturally during the winemaking process, but collecting the tartar-rich solids left over during winemaking and adding them to a solution of potassium hydroxide (lye, or potassium carbonate mixed with water) allows for a much greater amount of pure cream of tartar to be obtained. By creating a lye using *alum feces*, which is ash from burned tartar, one can sidestep the need for additional potash entirely and still create a strongly alkaline solution of lye and cream of tartar.

In *Allerley Matkel*, a recipe for removing grease spots directs the reader to take "cold lye warmed a little with wine lees and mixed well together, that it is not too hot, and use as above."[30] The tartar and its resulting precipitant cream of tartar helped to temper the harshness of the lye and brighten colors.[31]

Organic acids and sequestrants

As well as providing buffering action, the acidity of tartar and cream of tartar makes these substances useful in removing inorganic stains. They have some ability to act as sequestrants, removing metal and iron oxidation by a solubilizing action.[32]

In fifteenth and sixteenth century sources, however, the sequestrant most often mentioned is orange juice or lemon juice directly and repeatedly applied to a stain, sometimes supplemented by heat. This method is most frequently specified for linen cloth, in particular linen stained with iron rust:

> To take forth any yron moll in linnen cloth, take a chafing dish with coles, then cover the coles with a pewter dish, so let it be hote. Then lay your linnen thereon where the moll is, and with a Limon, or an Orange, but the Limon is better, to rubbe your moll therewith, and still as it dryeth in, lay the juyce thereon, and still rubbe it so til it be al cleane, and this way will have it all out. Oft prooved.[33]

Other references to lemon and orange juice specify in almost every case that the juice is particularly efficacious against ink spots.

Unlike other general cleaning solutions, which combine alkalis with wetting agents and other ingredients for maximum effectiveness, orange and lemon juice were used individually. Citric acid's ability to remove the byproducts of both ferrous and non-ferrous oxidation was known through observation though not understood chemically. Yet another recipe uses the distilled juice of wood sorrel, a source of oxalic acid, to remove grease from clothing.[34]

---

30 *Allerley Matkel*, 1v.
31 Cream of tartar is widely used as an additive to mordants and some dye baths, and is used as an agent for evening and brightening colors.
32 Cream of tartar is still an effective and often used household remedy against iron stains and fruit stains on linen.
33 *Profitable Booke*, 23.
34 The active property in wood sorrel, oxalic acid, is still used to remove stains today. In concentrated form, it is a common ingredient in commercial rust removers.

Wetting agents

Ox gall (ox bile) is a wetting agent, a substance that reduces the surface tension of water and enables it to penetrate more fully into a stain. In addition, the acidic and enzymatic action of bile, used in breaking down proteins in the stomach, is effective against grass stains, grease stains, wine stains, and other organically based stains.

When included in liquid cleaners, ox gall is always used in combination with tartar and/or lye. It is worth noting that the lye may have killed some of the ox gall's natural enzymatic action. Here is one sample recipe from *Allerley Matkel*:

> Six ox galls and as much rain water, a half pound tartar, two *loth* alum, grind it all small. Take then a drinking glass full of vinegar, put therein another half *loth* of vitriol pounded fine, boil it all down a third, and use it as aforesaid.[35]

It is also an ingredient in several recipes for washing soap found in both *Alexis* and *A Profitable Booke*:

> Take a pound of white Sope cutte very small, the gall of an Oxe, or he Goate, Alumen catinum, of eche of them an unce, the yelkes of two Egges, and a few ashes very fine, and incorporate well altogither with the sope in a morter, and so make thereof paste, wherof you shall make balles.[36]

Another wetting agent mentioned is soapwort (*Saponaria officinalis*). Soapwort contains saponin, a mildly soapy juice that can be extracted and used for cleaning. *Alexis* and *A Profitable Booke* both take advantage of soapwort's gentle cleansing properties with variations on the same recipe:

> A way to take out spots in scarlet or velvet, of what color or sorte so ever it be, not chaunging the colours. Take a hearbe called of the Surgions Saponaria, in frenche called Foullons, in English sopewort, beat them oft, and take out the juyce, and put thereof on the spottes, then let it so rest the space of one houre if it be in summer, but if it be in winter let it rest foure houres, then wash those spotty places with faire cleane water, so shall it be cleane.[37]

Adsorbents

An alternative to soap or liquid solutions was the use of an adsorbent powder sprinkled upon the stain. This method was particularly efficacious when dealing with oil and grease spots, and was less damaging to dyed fabric and delicate silks than other cleaning agents. Burnt and powdered bone were used for this purpose:

---

35 *Allerley Matkel*, 2v. The *loth* is a dry measurement of Germanic origin. The modern loth is equivalent to 0.5 oz., though a version of this recipe that appears in *Alexis* uses "ounce" in place of *loth*.
36 *Alexis*, 2:45v.
37 *Profitable Booke*, 6–7.

To make oile or grease out of a clothe of what coulore so ever it be, without any droppe of water. Take some sheepes feete, and make them very clean: then seeth them and eat them, and keepe the right bones, the which you shal barne, and make therof a cleane and fine pouder. This done heat the saide pouder, and lay it uppon the spotte, and let it remaine in the Sunne, and when you see that the pouder beginneth to waxe black, take it by and by off, and put other freshe uppon it, and do this so often that you see the pouder no more blacke, and then the spotte will be gone, and the coulore of the cloth not perished.[38]

Fuller's earth, also known today as diatomaceous earth, was another prevalent adsorbent mentioned in sixteenth-century recipes:

Another good way to take foorth spottes of greace out of any woollen or linnen. Take first a little fayre water, all to weate and rubbe therewith the said greacie spots. Then take a quantitye of walkers claye, called Fallers earth, and rub a little therewith your spottes all over.[39]

Fuller's earth also appears as an ingredient in liquid cleaning solutions of the time:

How to sponge woollen clothes. Take a quart of faire water, and let it be heat luke warme on the fire, then take a quantitie of walkers clay and all to crush it therein, then let it stand until it be clere, then poure that water into another potte, and set it on the fire againe, till it begin to seeth: then take of Venice sope, or other good sope, and put thereof into the sayd water, in stirring it well all about, then take it of the fire and all hote, sponge or occupie therewith at your pleasure.[40]

Similarly adsorbent minerals appear in other recipes, among them "Earthen pots bruised,"[41] "burned clay,"[42] and "olde claye of some oven."[43]

Dispersants

Fuller's earth and powdered bone were not the only substances used for removing grease or stains by direct application. Egg white is applied in combination with alcohol to remove spots from velvet in a recipe from *Alexis*:

To take spottes out of white Silke or Velvet, in Greene or Crimsen Velvet. Take strong Aqua vite of three distillings, and wette the spotte with it up and downe: Then take the white of an newe layde egge, and sprede it uppon the spotte, and so sette it in the Sunne to dry.[44]

---

38 *Alexis*, 2:47v.
39 *Profitable Booke*, 2.
40 *Profitable Booke*, 10–11.
41 *Alexis*, 3:54r.
42 *Allerley Matkel*, 3r.
43 *Alexis*, 3:55v.
44 *Alexis*, 2:46r.

The addition of egg white to an alcohol solvent aided in dispersing dirt and keeping it in suspension.[45] Egg whites, egg yolks, and eggs entire were also used as a binding ingredient in three separate recipes for soap in *Alexis* and *A Profitable Booke*.

Other agents

Another food-based remedy for stained cloth, found in *Allerley Matkel*, is equally simple. Peas are boiled in water, in which the stained fabric is soaked. The fabric is then rinsed in fresh water. The specific action or agent in this case is not clear. Edelstein suggested that the peas formed a starch-based solution that functioned as an emulsifier.[46] It is also possible that the starch from the peas would help to absorb the grease or oil from the fabric.

Other components of cleaning recipes also have dubious or unknown efficacy. Among these are camphor, which may serve as a solvent, but whose cleaning properties are uncertain. Another is dragon's blood, a maroon-colored resin obtained from the *Calamus draco* tree; it is possible that the aluminum resinates in dragon's blood act as a solvent, adsorbent, or coloring agent.[47] Mushroom juice is mentioned in this simple recipe for cleaning veils: "To remove various stains from silken veils. Take juice of chanterelles, soak the stains therein for two hours, wash it then with clear water and let it dry."[48] A similar recipe in *A Profitable Booke* describes washing gowns or garments with water in which beets have been boiled; another instructs the reader to boil strawberries in water. Several herbs of unknown effect also appear in the recipes. *A Profitable Booke* contains a cleaning recipe involving gentian (*Gentiana officinalis*), *Alexis* and *Allerley Matkel* both contain variations on a recipe for cleaning cloth of gold that involves cinquefoil (*Potentilla* family), and *Alexis* has another recipe that incorporates celandine (*Chelidonium majus*) into a soapy, lye-based solution:

> To take all spottes out of Crymsen Velvet. Take the ashes made of Vine twigges, and make therwith good Lye, whereof you shall take but a pynte, and put into it halfe an unce of Alumen Fecis, and let it stande a little whyle, and then strayne it. This done, take a dragme of Alome, halfe a Dragme of Spanish Sope, and half a Dragme of soft Sope, a quarter of a Dragme of common salt, and a quarter of salt Armoniake, halfe a quarter of the juyce of Celondine, a quarter of the Gall of a Calfe. Put all together and strayne it thorowe a linnen cloth. And when you wyll occupie of the sayde water, take flocks or shearings of Scarlett, and a little Brasill small, seeth al that a little in the sayde water, and then strayne it thorowe a linnen cloth, and you shal have a fayre water, which wyll take the spottes out of any lyke Crymsen colour. And what colour soever

45 Egg white is an excellent medium for maintaining small particles in suspension. For this reason, among others, it was a popular medium for pigments in medieval and Renaissance painting.

46 Edelstein, "Allerley Matkel," 315.

47 Dragon's blood was used for medicinal purposes and as a colorant in medieval times. Edelstein suggests in "Allerley Matkel" (4) that it may act as an adsorbent.

48 *Allerley Matkel*, 3r.

your cloth be of, that hath the spottes, the same coloure flockes, or shearing must you take. Notwithstanding if it be not redde, you must leave out your Brasill.[49]

Dyes and coloring agents

The above recipe also serves as an example of a process which has since faded into disuse: that of incorporating coloring agents into the cleaning solution itself.[50] As well as being difficult to wash, many textiles of the time were colored with dyes less colorfast than their modern counterparts. Several measures were taken to prevent bright colors from fading. This recipe from *A Profitable Booke* addresses a number of common concerns:

> A good way to washe a shirt, and save the Gold or silke thereon, from stayning. Take a new shirt first of all afore it bee ever weat, and lay the coller and ruffes or silke in pisse somewhat warme half an houre space, then take it forth, and then wash it in hote scalding liquor, or seeth it, and it shall never stayne the silke. If ye have not pisse, yee may take grounds of strong beere or ale, and let the silke lye therin the night before ye doe wash it. And this hath been oft prooved verie true. But alwayes ye must foresee, that ye hange not your clothes in the hote sunne after they be washt, but laye another cloth thereon betwixt the Sunne and it, or else the Sunne will chaunge both Golde, Silver and Silke. Therefore it is better to hang them in some place of shade after their washing, if ye can. Also to sope your water to much, or your clothes is an occasion to staine both gold and silkes. A verie good way is, first to melt your sope in the licour, and then let it coole, and so to wash your clothes therein.[51]

Some dyestuffs required more care than others. The active principals in madder (*Rubia tinctorum*) and brazilwood (*Caesalpinia sappan*), alizarin and brazilein respectively, change color when exposed to strongly alkaline solutions. Adding the shearings of scarlet (the fuzz sheared from scarlet fabric during the textile finishing process) and other red dyestuffs to the alkaline "good Lye" of the aforementioned recipe aids in retaining a more uniform red color during the spot-cleaning process.

In some cases, the solution itself was colored; in others, fabric that matched the color of the stained cloth was dipped in the solution and rubbed on a stain, to obtain the same effect:

> A water to take all manner of spottes out of cloth of any coloure ... putte into it three unces of Aqua vite of three distillings, and so keepe it in some vessell of Glasse untill you will occupie it. And if the spotte be in Skarlet, take a corner of the same clothe, and wette it in the sayd water, and rubbe well twise or thrise the spotte, and then

49 *Alexis*, 3:56v. A recipe identical in content is also found in the *Allerley Matkel*, 3r.
50 The "Scarlett" mentioned in the recipe was a fine quality wool that was dyed red or purple. A discussion of the dual nature of scarlet as a fabric and a color can be found in John H. Munro, "The Medieval Scarlet and the Economics of Sartorial Splendour," in *Textiles, Towns and Trade: Essays in the Economic History of Late-Medieval England and the Low Countries* (Brookfield, VT: Variorum, 1994), 13–70.
51 *Profitable Booke*, 13–14.

washe it againe with cleare water, and it wil goe out. The like may you doe in all sortes of coloured cloth, in taking a little of the like coloured clothe, or other that is nigh unto the colour, wetting it and rubbing it as is aforsaid, and it shalbe done.[52]

Other recipes in these collections dealt primarily with restoring a garment to its original color or refreshing and brightening garments. These are not quite as involved as full-fledged dye recipes, but utilize the same materials and processes found in recipes for both cleaning and coloring garments. A lye or alcoholic solution was frequently the base. Either fabric, organic dyestuffs, or mineral pigments of the color desired were soaked in the solution for anywhere from a few hours to a few weeks, as in this recipe:

> To restore the lost color to a garment. Take one pound of crushed willow ashes and pour four *mass* of water thereon. Let it stand a night, and then pour off the lye and take two ox galls and a handful of dried birch leaves, mix them together in the lye and let it boil together a half hour or until the leaves sink to the bottom. Let it cool; then, whichever color you would restore, add wool shearings dyed that color to the lye and boil it again and let it stand fourteen days or longer. The lye will take the color from the wool. Then pour it off and wash the cloth therein that you wish to renew. In this way the color returns again to the cloth.[53]

THE *KUNSTBUCH* IN CONTEXT

There can be no doubt, after examining the scientific materials and processes involved, that the *Kunstbuch* recipes did work. They were discovered through generations of observation and experimentation rather than through modern chemical analysis, but nevertheless the author or authors of these cleaning solutions had a practical if superficial understanding of what worked and what did not, and why.

Medieval recipes of this kind cast a fragmentary illumination on other aspects of the authors' cultural milieu. The number of spot cleaners as opposed to immersive solutions reveals much about the innate value of fabric and the dyes used to color it. The types of stains discussed were the result of common daily activities, and the raw materials for cleansers were for the most part byproducts of everyday life as well. One cannot say how long these simple remedies for spots and stains existed before being written down. One can detect in the *Kunstbuch* a long tradition of orally transmitted home remedies, variations upon which existed throughout Nuremberg and Europe itself for decades and centuries beforehand.

The handful of recipes encountered in this manuscript were noted down side by side with recipes for paints, instructions for making glass, and measurements for

---

52 *Alexis*, 2:46v–47r.
53 *Allerley Matkel*, 2r. The literal English translation of the German word *mass* (or *maß*) is "measure." In a similar recipe in the English translation of the *Alexis*, the quantity is translated as one pint. The German dictionary *Duden Universalwörterbuch* states that the modern *maß* is equal to 1.94 quarts.

cutting albs and surplices. This miscellaneous format is echoed in such contemporary manuscripts as the *Oberdeutsches Färbbüchlein*[54] as well as in the earlier *Innsbrucker Handschrift*.[55]

It is these delightfully wide-ranging fifteenth-century manuscripts like the Nuremberg *Kunstbuch* that served as primary sources for the comprehensive recipe compilations printed in the sixteenth century. The recipes in the *Kunstbuch* may have been recorded by the sisters of St. Catherine's based upon their experience with ecclesiastical garments, or may have been transcribed from earlier secular sources. Regardless, the similarity between the recipes in the *Kunstbuch* and those in later sixteenth-century commonplace books is clear. It is reflected in the ingredients and cleaning techniques used, as well as in the way the later recipes reside cheek by jowl with fascinating and unrelated tips on making dogs dance, curing the plague, and making roses bloom in the dead of winter. In such marvelous company, it is natural for the recipes themselves to become vested with more authority and significance than their homely antecedents of the previous century. They become wonders and secrets, passed back and forth between publications and across national borders until their original source and context are forgotten.

A truly mature understanding of these recipes and how they worked can be attained only by experimentation and chemical analysis, and my hope is that this survey of techniques and formulas provides others a starting place from which to pursue a more practical, in-depth study of textile cleaning chemistry in Renaissance Europe.

---

54 Ploss, *Buch von Alten Farben*, 126–29.
55 Anonymous, *Innsbrucker Handschrift*.

Fleas, Fur, and Fashion: *Zibellini* as Luxury Accessories of the Renaissance

Tawny Sherrill

Perhaps one of the most curious fashions of all time is the luxury fur piece of the late fifteenth and sixteenth century. In its simplest form, this was the pelt of a marten or sable worn draped over the wearer's shoulders or arm, or carried in the hand. At its most extravagant, the animal's skin featured a jeweled head, and often paws, of gold or crystal, and the whole was generally attached by a ring on the muzzle to a chain and worn on a girdle.[1]

The first known mention of this luxurious item occurs in 1467 in the inventory of Charles the Bold, Duke of Burgundy: "a marten for putting around the neck, the head and feet of gold with ruby eyes, with diamonds on the muzzle and paws;"[2] but no pictorial evidence exists as early as this citation, and no other written or visual examples appear until a Milanese document, dated February 1489, records an ungarnished sable worn by Isabella d'Aragon, Duchess

A version of this paper was presented in May 2004 at the International Congress on Medieval Studies at Kalamazoo, Michigan. My work on this subject is dedicated to the memory of Professor Diane Martel, who showed me the way.

1 My interest in these objects began in 1992 with the portrait of *An Unknown Elizabethan Woman*, c. 1595, attributed to Sir William Segar (Ferens Art Gallery, Kingston upon Hull). Preliminary investigation led me to Yvonne Hackenbroch's *Renaissance Jewellery* (London: Sotheby, 1979) as well as a number of articles: John Hunt, "Jeweled Neck Furs and 'Flohpelze,'" *Pantheon* 21 (May 1963): 150–57; R. H. Randall, Jr., "A Mannerist Jewel," *Apollo* 87 (1968): 177–78; Günther Schiedlausky, "Zum Sogenannten Flohpelz," *Pantheon* 30 (November–December 1972): 469–80; and Francis Weiss, "Bejewelled Fur Tippets—and the Palatine Fashion," *Costume* 4 (1970): 37–43. At the end of Weiss' article are listed thirty-one portraits and sculptures that depict women wearing these furs. My own hunt for images began with that list; my current list numbers more than sixty women and includes a cameo, plates in a sixteenth-century costume book, plates in an album of costume illustrations, leaves in an *Album Amicorum*, and a fresco series. Surely, in time, even more will come to light.

2 Hunt, "Jeweled Neck Furs," 156. I have been unable to independently corroborate this inventory entry. In any event, the marten in Charles' inventory appears to be something of an oddity, as no further Burgundian examples have come to light. Even assuming that others might exist, it seems clear that the fashion never evolved or developed to any significant degree in Burgundy.

of Milan.[3] (A summary of documentary references to these items follows this article.)

In terms of the fashion's development, both the visual and the written record suggest a northern Italian origin for *zibellini*—that is, sables—as the Italians referred to them.[4] The vogue began with simple, ungarnished pelts, as noted in a document of 1490 in which Isabella d'Este writes to Giorgio Brognolo, her agent in Venice, "Wishing for a beautiful sable lining for a *sbernia*, we would like you to buy eighty pelts of the most excellent quality, even if you should look everywhere in Venice, and see if you can find us one to be held by hand, with the bone in the head, as we wrote to you earlier, even if it should cost 10 *ducati*, as long as it is beautiful, we don't mind the cost."[5]

It seems likely that this is the same pelt that Isabella ordered as part of the wardrobe she assembled to attend the January 1491 wedding of her younger sister, Beatrice, to Ludovico Sforza, Duke of Milan—a wardrobe that included eight ells of the finest quality crimson satin and a gold belt engraved with the crest of her husband's family, the Gonzagas.[6] Clearly, an ostentatious appearance was intended: Isabella originally proposed arriving with an entourage of 114, transported by ninety horses. It was only when the groom protested that he lacked the accommodations for a party that size that the numbers were reduced to fifty people and thirty horses.[7]

To my knowledge, the first known depiction of a marten or sable pelt worn as a fashion accessory appears draped over the crossed hands of Beatrice d'Este on her tomb effigy (Certosa, Pavia), which dates to about 1497. She is depicted in the clothing she wore to mark the birth of her son Ercole in 1493.[8]

It is often difficult, if not impossible, to determine the origin of any fashion with any degree of certainty; however, the familial connection among the sisters Beatrice and Isabella d'Este and their cousin Isabella d'Aragon[9] certainly points toward these three women as the originators of this style. As no less an authority than Jacqueline Herald has noted, the Este sisters "enter the history books as two of the most innovative ladies of fashion."[10] Beatrice, in particular, was recognized as particularly

---

3 Paola Venturelli, *Gioielli e Gioiellieri Milanesi: Storia, Arte, Moda: 1450–1630* (Milan: Silvana, 1996), 138. My thanks to Beatrice Carswell for translation of this source and all other translations of non-English sources throughout this paper.

4 On rare occasions, the term *martore* (marten) is used.

5 Clifford M. Brown with Anna Maria Lorenzoni, *Isabella d'Este and Lorenzo da Pavia: Documents for the History of Art and Culture in Renaissance Mantua* (Geneva: Librarie Droz, 1982), 253; Daniela Pizzagalli, *La Signora del Rinascimento: Vita e Splendori di Isabella d'Este alla Corte di Mantova* (Milan: Rizzoli, 2001), 50. A *sbernia* was a cloak in the Spanish fashion.

6 George R. Marek, *The Bed and the Throne: The life of Isabella d'Este* (New York: Harper, 1976), 46. Although Marek interprets the single pelt as "a whole skin, head and claws included, which could be used for a muff," it should be noted that the original text (quoted in the previous paragraph) makes no mention of such an intended use.

7 Ibid., 46.

8 Jacqueline Herald, *Renaissance Dress in Italy 1400–1500* (London: Bell & Hyman, 1981), 142; based on a description of her dress in a letter written to her sister, Isabella, by Bernardino de Prosperi on that occasion. Ercole was later called Massimilliano.

9 Isabella d'Aragon was the daughter of Alphonse d'Aragon, who was the brother of Eleonore d'Aragon, mother to Beatrice and Isabella d'Este.

10 Herald, *Renaissance Dress*, 138.

inventive. A contemporary, Francesco Muralto, described her as *novarum vestium inventrix* (inventor of new fashion).[11] It seems that her inventiveness was, in part at least, intended to create a dramatic effect. Consider her entry into Ferrara in 1493, an occasion upon which she wore a gown embroidered with the towers of the port of Genoa, a motif that referred to the dominion of Milan over Genoa; the towers appeared on each sleeve as well as on the bodice front and back.[12] This sort of calculated effect, as well as Isabella d'Este's *zibellino*, will be further discussed later in this article.

Whatever the origins of the jeweled fur piece, by 1501, the dowry inventory of Paola Gonzaga, Countess of Mesocco, in Milan records "a *zibellino* with nails and the snout of gilded silver" and "a *zibellino* to carry at the side furnished with silver."[13] Combined with the previously mentioned examples, this firmly sets the fashion's origins in northern Italy.

Silver gave way to gold, as evidenced by an entry of January 19, 1516, in Lucrezia Borgia's inventory of jewels: "A sable with a head of beaten gold with a ring in its mouth attached to a chain of gold."[14] Ultimately, some of the creatures also featured gold paws. It is not until 1537 that we have visual representation of one of these precious objects, in Titian's portrait of Isabella d'Este's daughter, Eleonora Gonzaga, Duchess of Urbino (Uffizi Gallery, Florence).

The written record indicates that heads and paws were also made of crystal, as can be seen in the list of objects on offer by the Saracchi brothers' workshop in Milan, which specialized in crystal objects. A letter to Albrecht V of Bavaria in 1573 regarding terms of service states, "And I will also make small things such as pendants, pine cones, acorns [beads], belts, *zibellino* head, aglets and other things like the samples I sent you."[15] Although crystal heads survive, I know of none in portraiture.[16] As

---

11 Franciscus Muraltus, *Annalia Francisci Muralti: I.U.D. patricii comensis*, ed. Petro Aloisio Doninio (Milan: Cura et impensis Aloisii Daelli Novocomensis, 1861), 54. This is a transcription of Muralto's original manuscript, a history covering the years 1492–1519.

12 Herald, *Renaissance Dress*, 186.

13 Venturelli, *Glossario e Documenti per la Gioielleria Milanese: 1459–1631* (Milan: Nuova Italia, 1999), 159–60; Venturelli, *Gioielli e Gioiellieri Milanesi*, 138. The first of these is probably the same object referred to by Rosita Levi Pisetzky, *Storia del Costume in Italia* (Milan: Istituto Editoriale Italiano, 1964), 3:104, n. 235, as being in a sixteenth-century inventory: "a *zibellino* with the nails and the snout/muzzle of gilded silver."

14 Hackenbroch, *Renaissance Jewellery*, 387. Lucrezia was the wife of Alfonso d'Este, brother to Isabella and Beatrice.

15 Rudolf Distelberger, "Die Sarachi-Werkstatt und Annibale Fontana," *Jahrbuch der Kunsthistorischen Sammlungen in Wien* 71 (1975): 95–164, at 162; also cited in Anna Somers Cocks and Charles Truman, *Renaissance Jewels, Gold Boxes, and Objets de Vertu* (New York: Vendome, 1984), 70.

16 One crystal head (with crystal paws) is in a private collection; it is illustrated in Schiedlausky, "Zum Sogenannten Flohpelz," 474. Another, now mounted on a gold-plated dog's body as a decorative object, is in the Museo Lázaro, Madrid; for a specific discussion of this object, see Georges Salmann, "Une Bonbonnière qui n'en Était Pas Une," *Connaissance des Arts* 283 (September 1975): 90–91. Two others were at one time in the Thyssen-Bornemisza Collection, Lugano, Switzerland. I have been unable to ascertain their current location following a relocation of part of this collection to Madrid.

noted in the inventory of Mary, Queen of Scots, heads were also made of jet,[17] but it seems that none of these survive, nor do they appear in the visual record.

Although jet and crystal would seem to be lesser quality materials, these items were no less sumptuously embellished. One owned by Mary appears to be one of the first-ever *faux* furs. It is listed in an inventory of 1561: "Two ermines—one with a gold head enameled in white and a chain of black and white and the other of plush silk with a head of jet covered in gold and a chain enameled in black."[18] Her 1566 inventory includes "an ermine garnished with a head of jet garnished with three rubies and two diamonds, two ruby eyes, and two pearls at the ears/the four gold paws enameled in white."[19] A surviving crystal head is embellished with a collar and muzzle of *champlevé* enameled gold set with table-cut rubies, with cabochon rubies for the eyes.[20]

By the early sixteenth century, the *zibellino* had become one of the most prestigious and sought-after accessories of its day, as evidenced by the visual record of the unembellished pelts in portraiture, most notably Parmigianino's so-called *Antea* (mid–1530s, Galleria Nazionale di Capodimonte, Naples) and Raphael's *Giovanna d'Aragon* (c. 1518, Louvre, Paris), as well as a portrait of Isabella d'Este herself (surviving as a copy by Peter Paul Rubens, c. 1605, after Titian's now-lost original of the 1520s, Kunsthistorisches Museum, Vienna). The pelts appear also in the period's wildly popular costume books, including Cesare Vecellio's *Habiti Antichi et Moderni di Tutto il Mondo* of 1598, which depicts them in the illustrations of "Costume of Venetian Women about 1530" and "A Young Married Woman of Padua" at the time that Henry III of France visited Venice in 1574 (fig. 7.1).[21] Vecellio notes that Paduan women were noted for the elegance of their attire.[22]

The fact that a number of illustrations by foreign travelers show women wearing

17 Joseph Robertson, ed., *Inventaires de la Royne Descosse Douairiere de France: Catalogues of the Jewels, Dresses, Furniture, Books, and Paintings of Mary Queen of Scots: 1556–1569* (Edinburgh: Bannatyne Club, 1863). These items are included in a number of documents in this source, referenced specifically below.

18 Ibid., 12. The silk one appears to be the same item identified in the 1566 inventory as a marten (*martre*), 109.

19 Ibid., 108–9. This inventory includes "testimony" in the Queen's own hand in the margin: a listing of the recipients of these items in the event of the Mary's death. This is a particularly poignant document as the impending birth of her son necessitated preparations for the possibility of her death in childbirth.

20 Cocks, *Renaissance Jewels*, 70–71. This head, once in the Thyssen-Bornemisza Collection, is one of those cited in note 16. The table cut was a style of gem cutting popular through the sixteenth century and into the seventeenth century. It gave a stone a flat, table-shaped surface—the advantages of faceting having not yet been realized.

21 Cesare Vecellio, *Habiti Antichi et Moderni di Tutto il Mondo* (Venice: Appresso i Sessa, 1598), 74v, 158v. At this time, Padua was a part of Venetian territory. The king's visit was an occasion of great pomp and ceremony. Venetian women were allowed—even encouraged—to display their most luxurious dress, disregarding sumptuary laws. Vecellio noted, "To these women it was conceded that they can dress and ornament themselves as it pleases them the most, which they cannot do at other times. So it was when King Henry III, King of France, was brought ... to a superb and marvelous spectacle" (101r).

22 Ibid., 158r.

Fig. 7.1: A Venetian woman wears a *zibellino* draped over her shoulders in the plate "Costume of Venetian Women about 1530" from Cesare Vecellio's *Habiti Antichi et Moderni di Tutto il Mondo*, 1598, author's collection.

Gentildona Padvana.

Fig. 7.2: A Paduan woman carries a *zibellino* over her right arm, from the *Album Amicorum* of a German soldier, 1595, Los Angeles County Museum of Art (gift of the 1991 Collectors Committee, M.91.71.60). Photo: Copyright © 2005 Museum Associates/ LACMA, by permission.

these objects adds to the evidence that the fashion became relatively widespread in northern Italy. For example, *zibellini* appear in images depicting "A Bolognese Gentlewoman," "A Paduan Lady," and "A Paduan Courtesan" in the 1595 *Album Amicorum* of a German soldier in the Los Angeles County Museum of Art (fig. 7.2).[23] Similarly, "A Noble Wife of Bologna" and "A Lady of Cremona" are both pictured wearing bejeweled pelts in Niclauss Kippell's c. 1588 collection of costume images, now in the Walters Art Museum, Baltimore.[24]

Initially worn by northern Italian women, the fashion quickly spread. By the third decade of the sixteenth century, *zibellini* appear in non-Italian documents. A French invoice of 1529 states, "To Pierre Gedoyn, a jeweler residing in Paris, as payment for the gold and the fashioning of a marten with its four paws that he arranged in a natural fashion on the back of a very beautiful marten pelt, for the eyes he used two rubies; for the gold, 40 l. 18 s., for the two rubies, 8 l., for the marten, 30 s., for the fashioning, 30 l."[25] From about 1530, the wardrobe account of Isabel of Portugal lists "two martens ... fastened together and trimmed with feet, forepaws, and head of gold for Her Majesty's [neck]."[26]

It should be noted that there exist a very few mentions of these pelts in pairs, including the pair just cited, although to my knowledge no visual record of such survives. However, there is today in the German National Museum in Nuremberg a decorative object that can only be described as a knickknack; it is a gilded bronze piece created in the seventeenth century, consisting of two beasts of fantasy. The two crystal heads of the beasts are identical—very clearly recycled from a pair of *zibellini*.[27]

By the mid-sixteenth century, jeweled fur pieces appear in non-Italian portraits, such as that of Isabel of Valois in Spain (c. 1604–8, Juan Pantoja de la Cruz, after an original by Sofonisba Anguissola, Museo del Prado, Madrid) and Hans Mielich's *Portrait of Anna of Austria* (1556, Kunsthistorisches Museum), in which she holds the fur that is also illustrated in Mielich's pictorial inventory of her jewels (illumination

23 The *Album Amicorum* ("Book of Friends," or, in German, *Stammbuch*) was something of an autograph album. Beginning in the mid-sixteenth century, German students would collect signatures and greetings from those they met throughout their travels. A typical page might contain a formal greeting (often in Latin) to the book's owner and the signator's heraldic device or a small picture. See M. A. E. Nickson, *Early Autograph Albums in the British Museum* (Oxford: Oxford University Press, 1970). For a specific discussion of costume in *Alba Amicorum*, see J. L. Nevinson, "Illustrations of Costume in the *Alba Amicorum*," *Archaeologia* 106 (1979): 167–76.

24 Walters Art Gallery, MS W.477, 24r and 27r. Kippell (or Keppell) was probably German as well. The images, in tempera on paper, are bound in an album and depict Italians from all walks of life. On December 30, 1608, Kippell presented the album to Beat Hagenbach of Basel as a New Year's gift. For a discussion of this album, see Lilian M. C. Randall, "'Happy New Year, 1609!' Italian Costume Studies by Niclauss Keppell," *The Walters Art Gallery Bulletin* 33, no. 4 (January 1981), 1–4.

25 Hunt, "Jeweled Neck Furs," 151–52. The original invoice, written in French, is today in the National Archives in Paris.

26 Ruth Matilda Anderson, *Hispanic Costume: 1480–1530* (New York: Hispanic Society of America, 1979), 245.

27 Schiedlausky, "Zum Sogenannten Flohpelz," 245. Assuming the identification as *zibellini*, this pair brings the total number of extant crystal heads to six.

on vellum, 1550–55, Bayerisches National Museum, Munich).[28]

For the most part, the fashion appears to have reached Britain slightly later. Mary, Queen of Scots, brought no less than eight jeweled fur pieces with her when she returned to Scotland from France in 1561, as evidenced by her inventory, which includes, in part:

> A head of a marten garnished with rubies, diamonds and sapphires with two pearls / the four paws the same. One ruby is missing from the head.... A head of a marten in crystal, garnished with turquoise around the four paws the same.... An ermine with a head of gold enameled in white and a chain of white and black, garnished with rubies, diamonds and pearls with the paws the same.... Another ermine with a head of black jet covered in gold and a black enameled chain.... Another ermine, the gold head enameled black.... A marten garnished with a gold head with rubies, diamonds and pearls.... Another ermine without garnish.... A chain and a white marten garnished with forty-seven gold paternosters and forty-seven *entredeux a jour*.[29]

It seems that her cousin Elizabeth had to wait until 1584 to receive hers as a New Year's gift from the Earl of Leicester. It is cited in the New Year Gift Roll: "Sable Skynne the hed and fourre featte of gold fully furnyshed with Dyamondes and Rubyes of sundry sortes."[30]

Jewelers' pattern books must have added to the fashion's dissemination. In 1562 Erasmus Hornick published designs for a jeweled head and paws in Nuremberg.[31] Surviving illustrations for use by goldsmiths further indicate the fashion's widespread appeal. Examples of these include a watercolor of a marten's head, top and bottom, attributed to Jan Collaert (c. 1570–80, Akademie der Bildenden Künste, Vienna) and an anonymous pencil drawing of a design for the paws and head (c. 1580, Staatliche Museum, Berlin).[32]

---

28 This image is reproduced in Hackenbroch, *Renaissance Jewellery*, 142, and Weiss, "Bejewelled Fur Tippets," 39. It should be noted that this illustration is often identified as a pair of *zibellini*, when, in fact, it simply includes images of the object (including the pelt) from both above and below.

29 Robertson, *Inventaires de la Royne*, 84–85, 89. In this case, the term "paternosters" appears to refer to individual beads. Ronald W. Lightbown notes that "by the fifteenth century [paternosters] could also simply mean beads, at any rate in France." Lightbown, *Mediaeval European Jewellery with a Catalogue of the Collection in the Victoria & Albert Museum* (London: Victoria & Albert Museum, 1992), 346. (My thanks to Chris Laning for suggesting this reading.) Although I am unable to provide a translation for *entredeux a jour*, it seems likely, given the use of the term *entredeux* (insertion) and the fact that these items occur in numbers equal to the paternosters, that the term refers to objects inserted between the beads.

30 Weiss, "Bejewelled Fur Tippets," 38; Hackenbroch, *Renaissance Jewellery*, 409. There is what appears to be an isolated reference to two jeweled fur pieces in a 1547 inventory of the goods of Henry VIII (noted later in this article). However, *zibellini* also appear later in English portraits. Examples include *Frances Sidney, Countess of Sussex*, c. 1570–75, by an unknown artist, at Sidney Sussex College, Cambridge; *Portrait of an Unknown Woman*, c. 1595, attributed to William Segar, in the collection of the Ferens Art Gallery, Kingston upon Hull; and a family portrait in a private collection, c. 1605, of which I have seen only details.

31 Hackenbroch, *Renaissance Jewellery*, 142; Weiss, "Bejewelled Fur Tippets," 39.

32 Schiedlausky, "Zum Sogenannten Flohpelz," 470.

Within Italy, *zibellini* became targets of sumptuary laws. On March 7, 1545, in Bologna, legislation directed toward women decreed: "In order to avoid any superfluous costs and to get used to some ornaments honest and proper, it is ordained and ordered that regarding *zibellini* and fans, they cannot make heads, or handles, or other ornaments in gold, silver, pearls, or jewels but it is tolerated that they can be attached with a gold chain if the said chain does not exceed between 15 and 20 *scudi* and not more."[33]

Clearly, compliance was an issue, because by October 31 of that same year, the statute had been amended: "Except that it is permitted to who wants it, to wear *zibellini* with gold heads and a gold chain and have fans with gold handles, also with a gold chain without pearls or gems of any sort. But it is encouraged that the gentlewomen content themselves with the first ordinance rather than to use this new license."[34] Additionally, *zibellini* with gold heads were allowed only to Bolognese women who had been married a minimum of two years.[35]

By 1565, noblewomen of Milan were restricted from wearing "pearls or any kind of jewels on the ... headdress, not at the belt, not on a handle, not in heads or on collars of a *zibellino* ..."[36] Legislation in Cesena in 1575 left no doubt regarding the ban on this excessively luxurious fashion: "*Zibellini, lupo cerviero* [lynx], marten and other pelts that are whole or ornamented with the heads in gold or silver or without and the same for the fan with handles, to all women of any status or condition even if their husbands want it, no matter who, it is forbidden, it is prohibited and forbidden."[37]

It is perhaps not surprising that so much governmental attention was paid to these seemingly innocuous objects. By the middle of the sixteenth century, the *zibellino* was costlier than cloth of gold; forty pelts were valued at more than 1,000 gold *scudi*.[38] The embellishment lavished on them was equally precious: In the 1573 Milanese inventory of Maddalena Riva, a gold collar for a *zibellino* is valued at 20 lire, while a diamond in a gold ring is valued at only 4.5 lire.[39]

Throughout the fashion's lifespan, *zibellini* were luxury items, limited almost exclusively to those who could afford such extravagance. With the notable exception of a gilded copper head in the Musée de Cluny, Paris, there is no surviving evidence, either written or visual, that indicates that lesser quality versions existed or that the fashion ever trickled down to the lower classes.

Jewelers must have lavished every skill on these objects. A Venetian example from c. 1550–60 in the Walters Art Museum (fig. 7.3) is gold, set with table-cut rubies and

33 Maria Giuseppina Muzzarelli, *La Legislazione Suntuaria: Secoli XIII–XVI: Emilia Romagna* (Rome: Ministero per I Beni e le Attività Culturali, 2002), 184.
34 Ibid., n. 176.
35 Corrado Ricci, *Figure e Fantasmi: 64 Incisioni Fuori Testo* (Milan: Ulrico Hoepli, 1931), 182.
36 Venturelli, *Glossario e Documenti*, 165; Venturelli, *Gioielli e Gioiellieri Milanesi*, 138.
37 Muzzarelli, *La Legislazione Suntuaria*, 359. A number of sources have stated that wolf skins were also worn in the manner of *zibellini*; it seems likely that this is a misreading of the sixteenth-century Italian term for lynx: *lupo cerviero*.
38 Venturelli, *Gioielli e Gioiellieri Milanesi*, 137.
39 Ibid., 137–38.

Fig. 7.3: A marten's head of enameled gold with rubies and pearls, a red movable tongue, and white teeth; Italian, c. 1550–60. Photo: The Walters Art Museum, Baltimore, by permission.

seed pearls and heavily enameled. On either side of the snout are holes that still contain remnants of the natural whiskers of a marten. Combined with the fact that the enameled red tongue moves, it must have been a rather lively object in its day.

The written record suggests even more extravagant luxury: The 1547 inventory of Henry VIII describes a coffer containing two pelts:

> Item oon other Coofer ... one other sable skinne with a hedde of golde conteineng in it a Clocke with a Coller of golde enameled blacke set with foure Diamoundes and foure Rubies and with two perles hanginge at the Eares [like earrings] and two Rubies in the eyes the same skinne also hauing feete of golde the Clawes thereof being Saphires two of them being broken and with a Diamounde vppon the Clocke ... oon other like Sableskinne withe a hedde of golde musled garneshed and set with foure Emerades iiij Turquises vj Rubies ij Diamoundes and v peerles with iiij feete of golde echie sett withe a Turquesse the tonge being a Rubie.[40]

40 David Starkey, ed. *The Inventory of King Henry VIII: Society of Antiquaries MS 129 and British Library MS Harley 1419* (London: Harvey Miller, 1998), 430. These items are followed by "Item one paier of Sables for the Necke" and "Item twoo paier of Sables for the necke with blacke vellat." The inclusion of these items in the king's inventory have led a number of authors to conclude that *zibellini* were also a male fashion (the lack of visual evidence to the contrary); however, the fact that they appear to be the same pair as that listed in "Parcell of the Quenes Juelles" (94–95) helps cement their place in the female realm. (Unfortunately, I am unable to identify the specific queen, who is identified only as "the late Quene.")

Fig. 7.4: A fashionable Italian woman wears a jeweled fur piece over her right shoulder in *A Thirty-year-old Noblewoman*, c. 1570, by Giovanni Battista Moroni. Photo: Accademia Carrara di Belle Arti, Bergamo, by permission.

Margherita of Savoy also owned a marten with a gold head set with a clock—not to mention gold paws set with "many diamonds and lots of rubies."[41] One was known to exist with a whistle in its mouth,[42] and a drawing made by Giulio Romano in the 1530s, recognized as a design for a *zibellino* head, suggests a wolf (Musée de Besançon).[43]

41 Levi Pisetzky, *Storia del Costume*, 3:104, n. 238.
42 Schiedlausky, "Zum Sogenannten Flohpelz," 478.
43 Hackenbroch (*Renaissance Jewellery*, plate 51) identifies this as being in the collection of the Musée de Besançon. Giulio Romano was the court painter for Federigo Gonzaga, in Mantua.

While the vogue appears to have begun with a simple pelt attached to the girdle, evolving to the heavily jeweled objects of the mid-century, it is interesting to note that the fashion for the ungarnished fur continued alongside the jeweled versions throughout the century, as evidenced by a number of portraits. As an example, consider two paintings of Italian women painted by Giovanni Battista Moroni around 1570: A portrait of Angelica Agliardi de Nicolinis (Musée Condé, Chantilly) shows an ungarnished pelt, while *A Thirty-year-old Noblewoman* (fig. 7.4, Accademia Carrara di Belle Arti, Bergamo) shows one with a gold head.

Also, although marten and sable were the most common fur choices, ermine[44] and, to a lesser degree, lynx were also used. In Lavinia Fontana's 1584 *Portrait of the Gozzadini Family* (Pinacoteca Nazionale, Bologna), Ginevra, the sister at left, is shown with a *zibellino* attached by an elaborate gold chain to her girdle. Its gold head sports drop pearl earrings that match her own (although the *zibellino's* earrings include the added touch of red—presumably silk—bows). At right, her sister Laudomia is depicted with a lynx pelt, draped across her lap. The lynx is also featured in Isabella d'Este's portrait by Titian (c. 1534–36, Kunsthistorisches Museum). This may relate to the blindfold lynx, which was an *impresa* of the house of Este.

In the nineteenth century, these fur pieces came to be known as *Flohpelz*, or flea pelts, a term coined by Wendelin Boeheim in his 1894 biography of Philippine Welser.[45] Boeheim claimed that the furs were meant to attract fleas away from the body of the wearer, the concept being that the pests would leave a human body, attracted by the fur of the dead animal. They could then be shaken off the pelt. However, in their time, the Italians simply referred to them as *zibellini*. And in non-Italian inventories as diverse as those of Mary, Queen of Scots (see p. 128); Henry VIII of England (see p. 130); Archduke Maximilian (later Kaiser Maximilian II) of Germany;[46] and Philip II of Spain[47] they are listed simply as sables, martens, or

44 I have often been questioned about the possible connection between these pelts and the animal in Leonardo's painting, *The Lady with the Ermine* (sometimes referred to La Belle Feroniere). It is ironic to note that the subject in that work is now accepted to be Cecilia Gallerani, the mistress of Ludovico Sforza, Beatrice d'Este's husband, and the woman for whom he postponed his marriage.

45 Schiedlausky, "Zum Sogenannten Flohpelz," 478. Elspeth Veale, in her article "On So-Called 'Flea Furs,'" *Costume* 28 (1994): 10–13, notes that "Max Boehn made use of the inventory and biography [of Philippine Welser] ... in his eight-volume history, *Das Beiwerk der Mode* (Munich, 1908–25), and must have found 'Flohpelz' a convenient term to use. As his volumes were translated into English by Joan Joshua and published between 1932 and 1935 under the title *Modes and Manners*, the term has received wide currency in English" (10–11).

46 Schiedlausky, "Zum Sogenannten Flohpelz," 470. An inventory between 1550 and 1557 lists a sable "with a golden head and decorated with precious stones."

47 Priscilla E. Muller, *Jewels in Spain: 1500–1800* (New York: Hispanic Society of America, 1972), 103. A 1550 entry lists five martens with gold heads and paws, precious stones embellishing the heads. Muller also cites an entry at the time of his death in 1598, as follows: "A jeweled dull (*mate*) gold marten's head with four matching claws contained in a brass-latched, partly gilded small box lined with white and crimson satin. ... 'Frutas' [fruit] ornamented the head, its white, vermilion and other colored enamels studded with fifteen table emeralds of assorted sizes and cuts, six rubies, twenty-eight smaller diamonds and twelve pearl units. Mounted in its neck were six additional emeralds and in each claw was an emerald,

ermines, as the case may be. Even Shakespeare, a man who never missed an opportunity to ridicule the superficial excesses of society, makes no reference these furs in relation to fleas, although fleas are mentioned no less than seven times in his works.[48]

Although there appears to be no contemporary evidence to support this function, the myth has persisted to the present day, in costume and art history texts as well as in museums and on their Web sites, which present a face of authority to the public at large. Consider the text that accompanies Bartolomeo Veneto's *Lady Playing a Lute* (c. 1530) on the Web site of the J. Paul Getty Museum in Los Angeles: "A fur piece is draped over her left arm. Worn by high-ranking women in the 1500s, such furs were thought to keep away fleas."[49] The notable exception to the acceptance of this theory has been modern Italian costume and art historians; to them, the objects are *zibellini da mano*—sables for the hand—perhaps taken from early-sixteenth-century documents such as the aforementioned dowry inventory of Paola Gonzaga of 1501: "a *zibellino* to carry at the side furnished with silver."

The common sense of anyone who has ever owned a dog or cat would argue against the idea that fleas would leave the warmth of a living body and trudge through the multiple layers that constituted sixteenth-century dress to avail themselves of a dead fur, but disproving a myth requires something more than common sense. An effort to debunk this theory resulted in an extended correspondence with Dr. Michael Dryden, Professor of Veterinary Parasitology at Kansas State University, a man widely recognized as the world's leading authority on fleas. Dr. Dryden confirmed what common sense suggests: Fleas are attracted not to fur, but to the warmth of a living body, one within which blood flows. He indicated that he has observed "fleas leaving, within minutes, a host that has died or even has become hypothermic."[50] Further, he noted that when a "wad" of fur is placed in a container with a group of fleas, they will prefer the fur over the smooth surface: "This is a natural thigmotaxic response. However, if the hair is not warm, they will then jump off.... It must be remembered that the fleas will in no way be 'attracted' to the hair."[51]

a ruby and a diamond. The mouth held a ring with small gold fastening link (*assiilla*)." Philip was the son of Isabel of Portugal; it is possible that these were originally her property.

48 I am grateful to Geitel Winakor and Jane Farrell-Beck for suggesting this line of inquiry.

49 http://www.getty.edu/art/collections/objects/o772.html (accessed November 27, 2005). The Getty is not alone in this assertion. Consider also the description of *Portrait of a Couple* (c. 1580–1585, attributed to Lavinia Fontana) at the Cleveland Museum of Art's Web site: "The woman holds the skin of a marten (similar to a sable), which attracted fleas away from the body and clothing." http://www.clevelandart.org/Explore/artistwork.asp?searchText=lavinia+fontana (accessed November 27, 2005).

50 E-mail correspondence, May 26, 2000.

51 Ibid. The Chinese had long understood the concept of fleas being attracted to warmth, employing flea traps: At bedtime, a hollow piece of bamboo or ivory was warmed and passed between the sheets to attract the vermin; the trap, with its offensive cargo, was then tossed into a pail of water. Although trade with China had long accounted for a portion of Italian commerce, one might argue that this contraption or concept was unknown to Italians.

Zibellini were fashionable accessories for virtually the entire sixteenth century. It could hardly have taken contemporary sophisticates a hundred years to recognize the failure of these objects—if indeed they had originally been designed to be the world's most glamorous flea collars. But if not flea pelts, then what? Perhaps like so much other fashion, simply whimsy run amok … but perhaps something more.

In the sixteenth century, sables, martens, ermines, and even skunks were lumped together, somewhat indiscriminately, under the heading of "weasels," which had long been associated with childbirth.[52] Contemporary bestiaries indicate that the female weasel conceived through the ear and gave birth through the mouth.[53] This may be an association with the myth of Galanthis, related by Ovid in his *Metamorphosis*: As the result of an affair with the god Jupiter, the mortal Alcmena became pregnant. Jupiter's wife, Juno, sent Lucina, the goddess of childbirth, in the form of an old hag, to hinder the labor. Lucina sat at Alcmena's door, "holding her own knees shut with her fingers interlaced like a trellis."[54] Galanthis, Alcmena's maidservant, foiled Lucina's scheme by announcing the birth of her mistress' child. The surprised Lucina changed position, whereupon Alcmena successfully delivered Hercules. In a fit of spite, Lucina turned Galanthis into a weasel, cursing her to give birth through her mouth, "just as her deceitful words gave birth to Hercules."[55]

There may be an additional association of *zibellini* with the Annunciation, which is based on the aforementioned misconception relating to members of the weasel family: The belief that the animals conceived through the ear and gave birth through the mouth was seen as a parallel to Christ's conception through the ear of the Virgin by the words of God spoken by His angel.[56] The Walters Art Museum's head (fig. 7.3) is a prime example of both the mythological and the religious associations. The

52 In fact, this association continued well into the seventeenth century, as can be seen in a series of letters from Dowager Grand Duchess Cristina de' Medici to her daughter, Caterina de' Medici, Duchess of Mantua, posted by the Medici Archive Project. On April 13, 1617, when "it is believed that Caterina is in an early stage of pregnancy … Cristina … sends her a 'belt made from a Polish animal' (probably a marten or ermine) to be 'worn directly on the skin,' together with a 'pregnant rock' on loan from Grand Duchess Maria Maddalena d'Austria, who claims that it has helped with the births of her children"; see vol. 6110, fol. 16, entry 6874, online at http://www.medici.org/hum/topics/topicreports/CostumeandDress_1Page131.html. The belt is mentioned again in two subsequent letters, dated April 28, 1617 (vol. 6110, fol. 343, entry 7037), and September 27, 1617 (vol. 6110, fol. 43, entry 6883), online at http://www.medici.org/hum/topics/topicreports/CostumeandDress_1Page133.html and http://www.medici.org/hum/topics/topicreports/CostumeandDress_1Page132.html respectively (all accessed November 27, 2005).

53 T. H. White, *The Bestiary: A Book of Beasts: Being a Translation from a Latin Bestiary of the Twelfth Century* (1954; repr., New York: Cambridge University Press, 1960), 92–93. However, White also indicates that "on the other hand, others declare that they conceive by mouth and give birth by ears." Jacqueline Marie Musacchio notes this explanation was proffered by "the anonymous authors of various Medieval and Renaissance bestiaries," in "Weasels and Pregnancy in Renaissance Italy," *Renaissance Studies* 15, no. 2 (Summer 2001): 173–87, at 181.

54 White, *The Bestiary*, 92–93.

55 Musacchio, "Weasels and Pregnancy," 180–81.

56 Randall, "A Mannerist Jewel," 177–78; see this article for a further discussion of this specific object.

ears are oversized; the mouth is open; and, as has been noted many times, the white dove across the upper snout serves as a reference to the Annunciation.[57]

It is at this point that we return to the Este sisters. Devices and mottoes held an "extraordinarily dramatic and narrative power"[58] in fifteenth-century Italy. In much the same vein as the embroidered Genoese towers, it seems entirely plausible that Beatrice's display of the "weasel" pelt on the birth of her son was a consciously dramatic reference to his name, Ercole (Hercules).[59]

The name of Beatrice's and Isabella's father was Ercole also. It is, perhaps, from him that Beatrice inherited her flair for the dramatic. He was known to encourage an association with Hercules. His palace in Ferrara included numerous depictions of the hero, among them two bronze statues of Hercules set on columns on the courtyard's staircase,[60] a gilded statue holding a shield adorned with the ducal coat of arms,[61] and a set of four Hercules wall hangings.[62] A fresco of Hercules adorned a wall in his villa in Belriguardo.[63] Perhaps most charming of all were the sugar sculptures created for celebrations, in the shapes of the Columns of Hercules and Hercules killing the dragon.[64] Given Ercole's conscious references to Hercules, it seems not unlikely that on an occasion as important as her sister's wedding—a celebration at which she would be expected to represent her family—Isabella herself would provide a visual, fashionable allusion to the father of the bride.[65] That she might have appropriated the fashion for her own purposes from her cousin's use of it two years earlier seems also not unlikely.

Zibellini are represented in portraits in which they can be seen as a reference to pregnancy or childbearing, such as that of the Countess Livia da Porto Thiene and her daughter, by Paolo Veronese (c. 1551, Walters Art Museum). The large form of the Countess and her gesture toward her abdomen indicate her pregnancy. As originally hung, she would have directed her gaze toward the pendant portrait of her husband, Count Giuseppe da Porto, one of the most influential men in Vicenza, shown with their oldest son. Her bejeweled marten figures prominently in the composition.

Parmigianino's *Portrait of Camilla Gonzaga, Countess of Secondo, with her Three Sons* (c. 1537–39, Museo del Prado) is an even more impressive depiction of a dynasty in

57 One must wonder about the implications for this reference in light of the *zibellino* worn by the previously mentioned Paduan courtesan.

58 Herald, *Renaissance Dress*, 188.

59 My thanks to Julia Miller for her help with the Ercole connection. Musacchio has suggested that the pelt on Beatrice's tomb effigy also may serve as a reminder of the cause of her death; she died in childbirth in 1497 ("Weasels and Pregnancy," 186).

60 Thomas Tuohy, *Herculean Ferrara: Ercole d'Este, 1471–1505, and the Invention of a Ducal Capital* (Cambridge: Cambridge University Press, 1996), 69.

61 Ibid., 106.

62 Ibid., 226.

63 Alison Cole, *Virtue and Magnificence: Art of the Italian Renaissance Courts* (New York: Abrams, 1995), 274.

64 Tuohy, *Herculean Ferrara*, 273–74.

65 Such an allusion parallels Isabella's reference to her husband by use of the Gonzaga family crest engraved on her gold belt, as mentioned previously.

the making. Camilla's *zibellino*, with its head of gold, is draped over her left shoulder. Her husband, a famous soldier, in the service at different times of Charles V and Duke Cosimo de' Medici, appears in the pendant portrait (also at the Museo del Prado). *Zibellini* figure again in a cameo of Cosimo de' Medici, his wife Eleonora of Toledo, and their children, in which Eleonora wears a pelt draped over her shoulders[66] (fig. 7.5; c. 1557–62, Museo degli Argenti, Palazzo Pitti, Florence), and in a family group portrait by Giovanni Antonio Fasolo, in which the mother wears an unembellished fur draped over her left shoulder (1558, Fine Arts Museums of San Francisco).

Caroline Murphy has made much of the lynx and jeweled sable in the previously mentioned *Portrait of the Gozzadini Family* by Lavinia Fontana. She notes that although Laudomia's father Ulisse Gozzadini purchased for her a *zibellino* with a metal head and gold chain when she married Camillo Gozzadini in 1569, the fact that Laudomia is depicted in this work with a lynx is intended to send a message, as is Ginevra's *zibellino*.[67] This family portrait was commissioned by Laudomia Gozzadini in 1584. Script on the painting's back indicates the identities of the sitters and their status. The woman at left is identified as "Ginevra Goz[z]adini, who died at the age of 28 on the 15th day of March 1581."[68] Before her death, Ginevra gave birth six times, bearing three sons who survived infanthood. Certainly, her *zibellino* can be seen as an allusion to her childbearing success. Laudomia herself, remaining barren, enjoyed no such success. Murphy has suggested that her lynx conveys another message.

The lynx was associated with chaste behavior. Pliny advised sprinkling its ashes onto women to restrain lustful desire. Murphy suggests that the lynx's "connotation with tempered conduct made the lynx fur suitable for older matrons, while the *zibellino*, as a fertility symbol, was for younger wives."[69] She goes on to suggest that an

---

66 C. 1559–60; given the date and the fact that Eleonora died in 1562, this is apparently not the same object mentioned in a document from Cosimo to Isidoro da Montauto, dated January 3, 1566, in which Cosimo authorizes payment for the acquisition of a jeweled head for a sable fur: "paid according to this mandate to Bernardo Vecchietti for the gold head of a *zibellino* bejeweled with rubies, diamonds and pearls bought from him, for this piece" from the Medici Archive Project (vol. 225, fol. 66, entry 1232), online at http://www.medici.org/hum/topics/topicreports/CostumeandDress_1Page97.html (accessed November 27, 2005). The latter may, however, be the object listed in an inventory of February 7, 1586, of the jewels of Cosimo's second wife, Camilla Martelli, which she consigned to their daughter Virginia: "A *zibellino* head in gold which also has three rubies, one diamond, a star of diamonds with six pearls, twenty-three pearls, a *quore* [heart?] of diamonds and rubies in the mouth of this head," Maria Sframeli and Irene Cotta, *I Gioielli dei Medici: Dal Vero e in Ritratto* (Livorno: Sillabe, 2003), 202. This may coincide with Virginia's marriage to Caesare d'Este, Duke of Modena, on February 6, 1586. Although Cosimo and Camilla were married March 29, 1570, their relationship must have begun by at least 1567, as Camilla gave birth to their daughter Virginia on May 29, 1568.

67 Caroline P. Murphy, *Lavinia Fontana: A Painter and her Patrons in Sixteenth-century Bologna* (New Haven: Yale University Press, 2003), 127, 209 n. 103.

68 Ibid., 117; "According to the language used, the wording must have been placed there on the instructions of [Laudomia] herself."

69 Ibid., 127.

Fig. 7.5: Eleonora of Toledo wears a *zibellino* over her shoulders in a cameo by Giovanni Antonio de' Rossi depicting Cosimo I de' Medici and his family, c. 1557–62 (detail). Photo: Museo degli Argenti, Palazzo Pitti, Florence, by permission.

additional attribute of the lynx, unusually sharp vision, is a reference to Laudomia as a sharp-eyed woman, one who had been witness over the years to a family saga of "manipulation, fear, greed, deception, anger, envy, frustration and adultery" and who sees clearly all that goes on around her.[70]

These messages (along with others in the portrait) may, in fact, have been Laudomia's intent. No documentation is known to either support or dispute that

70 Ibid., 120.

possibility. But whether the messages would have been clear to a contemporary viewer or simply too complex to read seems debatable.

However, *zibellini* are depicted in bridal portraits, such as Lavinia Fontana's *Portrait of a Young Noblewoman* (c. 1580–84, National Museum of Women in the Arts, Washington, D.C.)—marriage, of course being the natural prelude to childbirth— and in a rare example of a couple, also attributed to Lavinia Fontana (c. 1580–85, Cleveland Museum of Art), which seems likely to be a marriage portrait. They were popular as wedding gifts, often listed in gift rolls, including that of the niece of the doge in 1525 Venice: "a heavy silver casket containing a lovely *zibellin* [sic], a small stuffed animal with a covering made for its head to which is attached a gold chain."[71] Beyond that, they appear frequently in dowry inventories throughout the century, further cementing their contemporary connection to marriage and childbirth.

Perhaps the most beautiful surviving illustration of *zibellini* is in the *Salotto delle Dame*, in the Palazzo Martinengo in Brescia.[72] The frescoes by Moretto da Brescia depict eight women, two per wall. We know that three walls were completed by 1543, when the room was a part of the celebration of the marriage of Girolamo Martinengo to Eleonora Gonzaga, Duchess of Sabbioneta, on February 4 of that year,[73] giving these images a connection to childbirth also—albeit in a slightly less straightforward way. Of the two women on each wall, one sports a *zibellino*. The women have been identified as members of both the Gonzaga and Martinengo families: among them, Eleonora and her sister, Giulia, the Countess of Fondi; Girolamo's three sisters; the second wife of Girolamo's father; and the wife of a subsequent son. However, today, we are unable to identify the women individually, although a figure on one wall is presumed to be Giulia Gonzaga.[74]

It is always dangerous to ascribe too much meaning to "fashion." In Lavinia Fontana's *Visit of the Queen of Sheba to Solomon* (c. 1598–1600, National Gallery of Ireland), a jeweled sable head rests among other treasures on a tray held by an attendant. Again, Caroline Murphy examines this work, assigning a significance to the head that depends on a complex series of conclusions that include such well-made points as the identification of the Queen of Sheba as Eleonora de Medici on her way to an important family wedding.[75] Murphy contends that *zibellini* were "probably held to be fertility charms."[76] We must consider, however, that by the date of this painting, whatever message these objects had initially conveyed would surely have been diluted, at least to some degree, by their role in luxurious, fashionable dress. Günther Schiedlausky has noted the head's prominent position on the tray as simply an indication of the high value associated with these objects.[77] Whatever the

---

71 Stella Mary Newton, *The Dress of the Venetians: 1495–1525* (Aldershot: Scolar Press, 1988), 111.
72 Sometimes referred to as the Palazzo Salvadego.
73 Pier Virgilio, *Alessandro Bonvicino: Il Moretto da Brescia* (Brescia: La Scuola, 1988), 450.
74 Gian Alberto Dell'Acqua, *Alessandro Bonvicino, il Moretto* (Bologna: Nuova Alfa, 1988), 240.
75 Murphy, *Lavinia Fontana*, 106–10.
76 Ibid., 109.
77 Schiedlausky, "Zum Sogenannten Flohpelz," 471.

public perception of this image, clearly *zibellini* continued to be perceived as suitable—and desirable—wedding gifts.

Much has been made of Lorenzo Lotto's *Portrait of Lucina Brembati* (c. 1518, Accademia Carrara di Belle Arti, Bergamo), citing the inclusion of the moon and a marten, as well as the placement of her hand on her belly, as indications of a pregnancy late in life. David Brown, however, has argued—in my opinion quite convincingly—against that assumption, noting, among other points, that we have no information about a late pregnancy for Lucina and that the resting of the right hand on the belly is a common gesture in portraiture.[78]

Having lost the context within which the seemingly endless parade of portraits of unknown Italian women was created, we can never know in every example what meaning, if any, their *zibellini* were meant to convey. The jeweled fur pieces in self-portraits of Sofonisba Anguissola (1559, private collection, Milan) and Marietta Robusti[79] (c. 1553–55, Kunsthistorisches Museum) lend an air of mystery and elegance; but, in the end, they raise more questions than they answer. For example, might the fact that Marietta Robusti's husband was a jeweler account for her depiction with this extravagant object?

In Giulio Campi's *Game of Chess* (c. 1530–34, Museo Civico d'Arte Antica e Palazzo Madama, Turin), the central female figure wears an ungarnished sable pelt over her right shoulder, attached to her girdle by a heavy gold chain. The image makes no apparent reference to either marriage or childbirth.[80] It seems fair to say that, as with so many features of dress that were originally intended to communicate information regarding the wearer's status or condition, as the century wore on many women coveted *zibellini* purely as luxurious, fashionable accessories.

Jeweled fur pieces are depicted on fashionable ladies as late as the final decade of the sixteenth century. They appear then to have fallen abruptly out of favor, which was, no doubt, due to the inevitable passing of fashion. The development of the rose cut for gems in the early seventeenth century enabled jewelers to release more of a stone's brilliance than ever before—and rendered much earlier jewelry passé. Surely this accounts for the scarcity of surviving *zibellini*. Like so much other sixteenth-century jewelry, they must have been dismantled, their precious materials recycled in a more fashionable mode.

---

78 David Alan Brown, *Lorenzo Lotto: Rediscovered Master of the Renaissance* (Washington: National Gallery of Art, 1997), 115–16.

79 The museum currently considers this to have been painted by her father, Tintoretto; in either case, the sitter is identified as Marietta Robusti.

80 In fairness, however, the meaning of this work is still under debate. One less popular theory proposes the theme of "Mars succumbing to Venus in a Neoplatonic contest possibly alluding to a marriage"; Andrea Bayer, *Painters of Reality: The Legacy of Leonardo and Caravaggio in Lombardy* (New York: Yale University Press, 2004), 164–65, referencing Giulio Bora, "Giulio Campi," in *I Campi: Cultura Artistica Cremonese del Cinquecento*, ed. Mina Gregori (Milan: Electa, 1985), 127–44. Although Bora suggests that the symbolism in this work supports it as a depiction of marriage (134), he makes no mention of the *zibellino* in any context.

Zibellini may be destined to remain something of an enigma. Fashion by its very nature is ephemeral and whimsical—resistant to even the most systematic, sympathetic scholarly inquiry. While it seems safe to say that *zibellini* were very probably recognized by contemporary Italians as being an allusion to childbirth, it seems as likely that over time, like so much of human finery, they lost a strict adherence to their original reference. What we can say with certainty is that, like all good fashion, they served absolutely no practical purpose and yet, even today, speak eloquently of the time in which they were worn.

Table 7.1: *Zibellini* in contemporary documents

This compilation of contemporary references to zibellini is a work in progress; additions are welcome and can be sent to tsherril@csulb.edu; please use "zibellini" in the subject line. Direct quotations are given where available; other references are paraphrases or descriptive citations by earlier historians. Locations are noted if known and not already apparent from the entry. Each entry is keyed to a source in the reference list following. In cases of multiple sources for an entry, the first listed is the source of the quotation (where present) and/or the most complete. I am indebted to Beatrice Carswell for translations of non-English sources. — TS

1467—Inventory of Charles the Bold, Duke of Burgundy:

"a marten for putting around the neck, the head and feet of gold with ruby eyes, with diamonds on the muzzle and paws." (Hunt, 151, 156 n. 2)

1489, February (Milan)—Document records Isabella of Aragon, Duchess of Milan, wearing "the zibellino in front of the eyes and the mouth seems to be crying." (Venturelli, *Gioielli*, 138; my translator and I are both confused by this translation)

1490, November 12 (Mantua)—Isabella d'Este writes to Giorgio Brognolo, her husband's agent in Venice:

"Wishing for a beautiful sable lining for a *sbernia*, we would like you to buy eighty pelts of the most excellent quality, even if you should look everywhere in Venice, and see if you can find us one to be held by hand, with the bone in the head, as we wrote to you earlier, even if it should cost ten *ducati*, as long as it is beautiful, we don't mind the cost." (Brown and Lorenzoni, 253; Pizzagalli, 50; Chesne Dauphine Griffo, 268)

Note: Although Chesne Dauphine Griffo provides an abbreviated reference, it is this source that indicates the exact date. It seems likely that this is the same sable skin that Isabella ordered as part of the wardrobe she assembled to attend the wedding of her sister Beatrice: "The Venetian agent was bade to buy eighty perfect sable skins as lining for a *sbernia*, and if he could manage to get a whole skin, head and claws included, which could be used for a muff [probably a misunderstanding by the author], so much the better." (Marek, 46)

1500s (Milan)—Undated inventory of objects of the property of the Trivulzio family:

"A head of a *gibellino* [zibellino] of gold with a value of 80 *scudi*." (Venturelli, *Glossario*, 158)

1501 (Milan)—Dowry inventory of Paola Gonzaga, Countess of Mesocco, wife of Gian Nicolò Trivulzio, Count of Mesocco:

"A *zibellino* with nails and the snout of gilded silver.
"A *zibellino* to carry at the side furnished with silver." (Venturelli, *Glossario*, 159–60; Levi Pisetzky, 104 n. 235)

1507, October 18 (Mantua)—Isabella d'Este writes to Taddeo Albano, her banker and factotum, in Venice, for a *zibellino* "to carry in the hand." (Brown and Lorenzoni, 254 n. 6)

1511, February 12 (Venice)—Taddeo Albano writes to Isabella d'Este regarding his inability to procure a lynx skin she has asked for:

"It seems to be that it is already the cold season ... in any event, for this winter we cannot do much." (Brown, 375 n. 17)

1512, January 15 (Mantua)—Isabella d'Este writes to Taddeo Albano:

"We have written regarding your responses that you were going, if you could, to send me this lynx of sixteen *ducati* on approval [consignment], if you haven't done that we would like you to do it at all costs. And if you cannot get it on approval, then buy me one of the most beautiful that you can find intact and send it by this vessel with the two altarpieces of Our

Lady …" (Brown, 375 n. 17)

1512, February 12 (Venice)—Taddeo Albano responds to Isabella d'Este's letter of January 1512:

"Of the lynx, I do not see any way to accommodate Your Excellency because, in truth, there is none of the quality that you would like, nor intact as you require/request. The few that are available are in the hands of one merchant and he sells them at his guise [in the way he likes] and they are all open and not intact." (Brown and Lorenzoni, 253; Brown, 375 n. 17)

1515, November 12 (Mantua)—Isabella d'Este writes to Zoan Angelo Vismara for a *zibellino* "to carry on the person proper." (Brown and Lorenzoni, 254 n. 6)

1516, January 19 (Ferrara)—Lucrezia Borgia's inventory of jewels:

"A sable with a head of beaten gold with a ring in its mouth attached to a chain of gold with a hook at the other end." (Bellonci, 563; Hackenbroch, 387)

Note: Although Hackenbroch includes this entry in its original Italian (387), within the text (14) she translates: "a marten fur with golden head and claws, with a ring through its mouth with a chain for attachment to a belt." It should be noted that the inventory identifies the fur as sable and makes no mention of claws.

1516, October 1 (Mantua)—Isabella d'Este again writes to Zoan Angelo Vismara for a *zibellino* "to carry on the person proper." (Brown and Lorenzoni, 254 n. 6)

1525 (Venice)—Paolo Contarini marries Viena, the niece of the doge, Andrea Gritti; the wedding party notes a gift from Paolo Cappello:

"a heavy silver casket containing a lovely *zibellin*, a small stuffed animal with a covering made for its head to which is attached a gold chain." (Newton, 111; Levi Pisetzky, 104; Chesne Dauphine Griffo, 268)

Note: Newton indicates that the giver of the gift was Bernardo Capello; Levi Pisetzky identifies him as Paolo Cappello. Newton notes that the first entertainment associated with the wedding was on January 16, 1525. Both sources draw on Marino Sanudo's diaries for this.

1529—A document accompanying payment:

"To Pierre Gedoyn, a jeweler residing in Paris, as payment for the gold and the fashioning of a marten with its four paws that he arranged in a natural fashion on the back of a very beautiful marten pelt, for the eyes he used two rubies; for the gold, 40 l. 18 s., for the two rubies, 8 l., for the marten, 30 s., for the fashioning, 30 l." (Hunt, 152)

1529–38 (Spain)—Isabel of Portugal's wardrobe account:

"two martens were fastened together and trimmed with feet, forepaws, and head of gold for Her Majesty's *rostro* (face or rather neck)." (Anderson, 245)

1545 (Bologna)—Sumptuary legislation restricts *zibellini* with gold heads and embellishment to women married a minimum of two years. (Ricci, 182)

1545, March 7 (Bologna)—Sumptuary legislation:

"In order to avoid any superfluous costs and to get used to in some ornaments some honest and decent/proper, it is ordained and ordered that regarding *zibellini* and fans, they cannot make heads, or handles, or other ornaments in gold, silver, pearls, or jewels but it is tolerated that they can be attached with a gold chain if the said chain does not exceed between fifteen and twenty *scudi* and not more." (Muzzarelli, 184)

1545, October 31 (Bologna)—Sumptuary legislation, revision in reference to that of March 7, 1545:

"Except that it is permitted to who wants it, to wear *zibellini* with gold heads and a gold chain and have fans with gold handles, also with a gold chain without pearls or gems of any sort. But it is encouraged that the gentlewomen content themselves with the first ordinance rather than to use this new license." (Muzzarelli, 184 n. 176)

1547, April 11 (Westminster)—Inventory of Henry VIII: "Parcell of the Quenes Juelles and other stuff which came from the late Admyralles howse of Sudeley in the Countie of Glocestre":

"Item a lytle square Coofer couered with nedell worke having in the same two sables skynnes with a heade of golde being a clocke in eche eye a rocke rubie & about the coler three small table rubies and iij small table dyamoundes with <iiij> fete of golde." (Starkey, 96)

1547, September 14 (Westminster)—Inventory of Henry VIII: "Stuff in Tholde Juelhous at Westminster in the Chardge of James Rufforth":

"Item in the same coffre one Sable skynne with a hedd of golde conteyning in yt a clocke with a coller of gold enameled blacke sett with iiij diamountes and foure rubies and with twoo perles hanging at the eares and twoo rubies in the yees, the same skynne having allso feete of golde, the claws thereof being saphyres, two of theym being brokin, with a dyamount uppon the clocke.

"Item one other like sable skynne with a hedd of golde musled garnished and sett with foure Emerades foure turquesses vj rubies twoo dyamountes and v perles with foure feete of golde eche sett with a turques the tonge being a rubye." (Starkey, 256; first entry, Veale, 145)

Note: These items are followed by "Item one paier of Sables for the Necke" and "Item twoo paier of Sables for the necke with blacke vellat."

1547, September 16—Inventory of Henry VIII: "Stuffe Receaued by James Rufforthe of Edmunde Pigeon the xvj[th] of Septembre anno Regni Regis Edwardi xj[th] primo":

"Item oon other Coofer with five Timbre of Sables and xxiiij skinnes one other sable skinne with a hedde of golde conteineng in it a Clocke with a Coller of golde enameled blacke set with foure Diamoundes and foure Rubies and with two perles hanginge at the Eares and two Rubies in the eyes the same skinne also hauing feete of golde the Clawes thereof being Saphires two of them being broken and with a Diamounde vppon the Clocke.

"Item oon other like Sableskinne withe a hedde of golde musled garneshed and set with foure Emerades iiij Turquises vj Rubies ij Diamoundes and v peerles with iiij feete of golde echie sett withe a Turquesse the tonge being a Rubie." (Starkey, 430)

1549 (Modena)—Sumptuary legislation:

"Thirdly, it is commanded that it is forbidden regarding the *zibellini* and the fans, it is forbidden to wear heads, handles and other ornaments in gold, silver, pearls, precious stones and enamel, but it is allowed to wear a gold chain between ten and fifteen *scudi* in value but not more." (Muzzarelli, 403)

1550 (Brussels)—Inventory of Philip II, while prince, lists five martens with gold heads and paws, precious stones embellishing the heads. (Muller, 103)

Note: possibly those of his mother, Isabel of Portugal.

1550 (Reggio Emilia)—Sumptuary legislation:

"Also, it is conceded that they can wear *zibellini* and lynx with a gold head without enamel that do not exceed fifteen *scudi* in price and with chains that do not exceed ten *scudi* in value, the same goes with the fans without handles and the other ornaments of gold and silver." (Muzzarelli, 629 n. 95)

1550, March 7 (Reggio Emilia)—Sumptuary legislation:

Regarding married women: "It is prohibited to carry/wear *zibellini* and lynx but it is permitted to have fans without handles or other ornaments of gold or silver except the chains mentioned above." (Muzzarelli, 629)

1550, March 20 (Reggio Emilia)—Sumptuary legislation:

> "It is conceded that she can wear the *zibellini* and lynx if they do not exceed fifteen *scudi* and without enamel; similarly she is permitted fans without handles and other ornaments of gold and silver and chains to the *zibellini* that do not exceed ten *scudi*." (Muzzarelli, 629 n. 95)

c. 1550–55—The Hans Mielich pictorial inventory of the jewels of Anna of Austria, wife of Albrecht V, Archduke of Bavaria, includes a jeweled fur piece, which she also wears in her portrait of 1565 by Mielich. (Cocks, 70; Hunt, plate 6; Hackenbroch, plates 360A–B)

1550–57 (Germany)—An inventory of Archduke Maximilian (later Kaiser Maximilian II) lists a sable "with a golden head and decorated with precious stones." (Schiedlausky, 470)

1553—Inventory of Westminster Palace, made on the death of Edward VI:

> "One sable skin with a head of gold, muffled (?muzzled), garnished and set with four emeralds, four turquoises, six rubies, two diamonds, and four pearls; four feet of gold, each set with a turquoise; the tongue being a ruby. One sable skin with a head of gold, containing in it a clock, with a collar of gold, enameled black, set with four diamonds, and four rubies, and two pearls hanging at the ears, and two rubies in the ears, the same skin also having feet of gold, the claws thereof being sapphires, two of them being broken, and with a diamond upon the clock." (Hunt, 156 n. 11)

Note: Hunt suggests that the two probably belonged to his father, Henry VIII; indeed they appear to be the objects listed in both of Henry's September 1547 inventories (above).

1553 (Bologna)—Sumptuary legislation, revision:

> "Except that it is permitted to who wants it to wear *zibellini* with gold heads and a gold chain and have fans with gold handles, also with a gold chain without pearls or gems of any sort." (Muzzarelli, 184 n. 176)

1559—Inventory of Philip II, Spain:

> "a marten's head of black-enameled hammered gold with three diamonds, three rubies and six large pearls." (Muller, 103)

1559, April 12 (Forlì)—Sumptuary legislation:

> "It is forbidden to women of whatever sort [to] wear necklaces around the arms [bracelets], handles or other things or belts of any sort, or *zibellini*, or pendants, or rings, or earrings, or headdress [*brette*] ..." (Muzzarelli, 334)

1561—Inventory of Mary, Queen of Scots:

> "A marten's head garnished with two pearls and several small rubies and sapphires—the four paws the same.
>
> "Two ermines—one with a gold head enameled in white and a chain of black and white and the other of plush silk with a head of jet covered in gold and a chain enameled in black." (Robertson, 12)

1561, February—Inventory of Mary, Queen of Scots:

> "A head of a marten garnished with rubies, diamonds and sapphires with two pearls / the four paws the same. One ruby is missing from the head.
>
> "A head of a marten in crystal, garnished with turquoise around the four paws the same.
>
> "An ermine with a head of gold enameled in white and a chain of white and black, garnished with rubies, diamonds and pearls with the paws the same.
>
> "Another ermine with a head of black jet covered in gold and a black enameled chain.
>
> "Another ermine, the gold head enameled black.

"A marten garnished with a gold head with rubies, diamonds and pearls.

"Another ermine without garnish.

"A chain and a white marten garnished with forty-seven gold paternosters and forty-seven *entredeux a jour.*" (Robertson, 84–85, 89)

1562 (Nuremberg)—An engraving by Erasmus Hornick, probably part of a pattern-book or a series of pattern plates, shows a design for a zibellino head and paw. (Hackenbroch, plate 142)

1562—In the inventory of the possessions of William Herbert, Earl of Pembroke, as part of a listing of the Countess' jewels:

"A Sabelles heade with xxj^{ti} Diamondes and a ringe with a rubie in his mouthe and with x^{ti} sparkes of Diamondes with iiij^{vr} clawes of gold and diamondes therein and a Cheine hanginge at it." (Victoria and Albert, 132)

1563 (Modena)—Sumptuary legislation:

"To the women it is forbidden to wear gold belts or of any other material or ornaments with the exception of plain silk or of things of minor value. And thus it is forbidden to attach to the belt *zibellini* with heads and feet and fans with handles of gold, with pearls or jewels real or false or any other adornment mentioned above." (Muzzarelli, 409)

1563 (Bologna)—*Libro di ricordi d'Ulisse Gozzadini* records that Ulisse Gozzadini purchases a *zibellino* for Faustina Guidotti when she marries his nephew, Fabritio. (Murphy, 209 n. 104)

1564 (Modena)—Sumptuary legislation:

"Women cannot wear on the belt *zibellini* which have head or feet nor fans which have handles of gold nor any other thing of gold or jewels or pearls which are attached to those *zibellini* and fans. The same applies to the muff." (Muzzarelli, 415)

1565, November 20 (Milan)—Sumptuary legislation:

"The noble women … cannot wear pearls or any kind of jewels on the leather headdress, not at the belt, not on a handle, not in heads or on collars of a *zibellino*, not on handles of fans, nor in any other form except in rings, as long as these are not of excessive price and no more than three." (Venturelli, *Glossario*, 165; Venturelli, *Gioielli*, 138)

1566, January 3 (Florence)—Cosimo I de' Medici authorizes payment to Bernardo Vecchietti for the acquisition of a jeweled head for a sable fur:

"paid according to this mandate to Bernardo Vecchietti for the gold head of a *zibellino* bejeweled with rubies, diamonds and pearls bought from him, for this piece …" (Medici Archive Project)

Note: Cosimo married Camilla Martelli on March 29, 1570, although their daughter Virginia was born on May 29, 1568, which puts the beginning of their relationship sometime in 1567, at the latest. Perhaps this object was ordered for Camilla. It may also be the same head cited below in the document of February 7, 1586.

1566, May and June—Inventory of Mary, Queen of Scots, listed under "Martes" (that is, "martens"):

"To Madame de Martigues: A lynx garnished with a head of a marten of crystal *acoustree* gilded with red enamel garnished with xxj turquoises and four paws also of crystal each paw garnished with three turquoises / and one chain containing twenty-four xiiij paternoster beads.

"To Madame d'Arguilles: A marten garnished with a gold head and a collar garnished with ii rubies in settings and two diamonds in the two eyes and two pearl pendants in the ears and four paws of gold.

"To Madame de Mar: A white marten garnished with a gold head garnished with sixteen rubies, five diamonds and two sapphires / two pearl pendants at the ears / four paws each garnished with five rubies and one diamond.

"To Madame de Mora: A marten *jaulne* garnished with a gold head garnished with eight rubies, five diamonds, two pendants at the ears enameled in red, a gold chain garnished with viij pieces total and eight *esseu* partition/insertion and four gold paws enameled in white.

"To Madame d'Hatel: An ermine garnished with a head of jet garnished with three rubies and two diamonds, two ruby eyes and two pearls at the ears / the four gold paws enameled in white.

"To Madame de Leuinston: Another ermine garnished with a head enameled in white and speckled with black/ a chain enameled in black and white / the four paws the same.

"An ermine without garnish.

"To Ien Stuart: A silky plush [marten] garnished with a head of gold garnished in jet with a gold chain enameled in black / the four paws the same." (Robertson, 108–9; I am unable to provide a translation for *acoustree, jaulne,* or *esseu*)

1568, April 12 (Bologna)—Sumptuary legislation:

"Regarding the *zibellini* and the fans, the heads and the handles of gold with a gold chain, there is an express prohibition to any of these above mentioned necklaces, bracelets or heads of *zibellini* any pearls, any jewels or other similar things, real or false." (Muzzarelli, 217)

1569 (Bologna)—Ulisse Gozzadini purchases a *zibellino* with a metal head and gold chain, for his daughter Laudomia when she marries Camillo Gozzadini. (Murphy, 127, 209 n. 103)

1569, July 12 (Bologna)—The ledgers of Camillo Gozzadini:

"Mr. Annibal bought a *zibellino* from Mr. Giovanni Battista Varotaro for thirty-eight *ducati*, and it was furnished by Mr. Paolo Emillio Allè, jeweler." (Gozzadini, 3; Hackenbroch, 388; it should be noted that Hackenbroch gives a date of June 20, citing Gozzadini as her source)

1569, September 6 (Bologna)—The ledgers of Camillo Gozzadini:

"Mr. Annibal bought a chain for the *zibellino* and the fan, the chain was weighing twenty-four and a half *ducati* of gold, and the manufacture is another three and a half *ducati*, totaling twenty-eight ducati of *gold*, and it was sold by Mr. Paolo Emillio Allè.

"Annibale bought a gold and enameled head for the *zibellino* from Mr Pavolo Emillio Allè, jeweler for the price of twenty-nine *ducati*. (Gozzadini, 3–4; Fortunati Pietrantonio, 187; Levi Pisetzky, 104; Hackenbroch, 388; Hackenbroch dates this June 20 and gives a price of twenty *ducati* for the enameled head)

1569, December 14 (Milan)—Jacopo Acerbi deposits some jewels with Agosto Foppa:

"a *zibellino* with four paws of gold and the head with three rubies and two [blue stones] and six pearls." (Venturelli, *Glossario,* 167; Venturelli, *Gioielli,* 138)

1570, July 3 and 5 (Bologna)—Sumptuary legislation:

"It is forbidden that the women at the same time wear *bonegratie, zibellini,* lynx, or fans, but only one of these at a time; the *bonegratie* cannot be embroidered or in any way or fashion have gold or silver or jewels in it; at the same time it is declared that in the heads of the *zibellini* or the handles of the fans even though they be made out of gold, the same going for the chains, they cannot have jewels or real enamel." (Muzzarelli, 220)

Note: Muzzarelli's glossary translates *bonegratie* as "feminine ornament for finery or gala" (702).

1572, September 15 (Milan)—Inventory of the goods of the late Count Giulio Cesare Borromeo:

"A collar for a *zibellino.*

"The head of a *zibellino* with one diamond and one emerald and one ruby on the collar and three pearls and the head fully encrusted with diamonds with the eyes and teeth of diamonds.

"A *zibellino* head all of gold with two earrings/pendants at the ears." (Venturelli, *Glossario*, 169)

1572, October 31–November 1 (Bologna)—Sumptuary legislation:

"It is forbidden to the women to wear the *buone gratie* or muff in gold, silver, embroidered with pearls or any other thing prohibited above also meant to include the *zibellini*, the lynx, the fans to which, however, it is considered that they can wear the head and the handles out of gold and the chains also out of gold without any other jewels or other precious stones as above." (Muzzarelli, 224–25)

Note: The identical passage was repeated in legislation of April 6–7 and 9 (Muzzarelli, 239). The term *buone gratie* is apparently an alternate spelling of *bonegratie*.

1573 (Milan)—Inventory of Maddalena Riva mentions "a collar for the gold *zibellino*" weighing approximately ten *denari*, valued at twenty lire. (Venturelli, *Gioielli*, 137–38)

1573—A list of objects on offer written by the Saracchi brothers of Milan to Albrecht V of Bavaria, as part of their terms of service:

"And I will also make small things such as pendants, pine cones, acorns [beads], belts, *zibellino* head, aglets and other things like the samples I sent you." (Distelberger, 162; Cocks, 70)

1573, November 16 (Milan)—A letter from Prospero Visconti, a Wittelsbach agent in Italy, to Duchess Renata of Monaco:

"I send you the head of a *zibellino* [stamped with lapis lazuli] and two pairs of earrings." (Hackenbroch, 30; Levi Pisetzky, 104; Venturelli, *Gioielli*, 191)

Note: Levi Pisetzky dates this document to November 18 and 19; both authors cite the same source.

1574, March 12 (Faenza)—Sumptuary legislation:

"We ordain, and testify and expressly command that no lady can wear a belt, handle or bracelets of gold, of enamel, amber paste, of musk or other perfumes, *zibellini* and fans, but the ladies are only permitted in the winter to wear a muff lined with fur, as long as it is not *zibellino* and that it is in no way embroidered with silk nor finished with gold or silver, whether hammered or spun." (Muzzarelli, 546–47)

1575, February 16 (Cesena)—Sumptuary legislation:

"*Zibellini*, lynx, marten, or polecat and other pelts that are whole or ornamented with the heads in gold or silver or without and the same for the fan with handles, to all women of any status or condition even if their husbands want it, no matter who, it is forbidden, it is prohibited and forbidden." (Muzzarelli, 359)

1576—On the occasion of her marriage to Giacomo Buoncompagni, the Duke of Urbino offers to Costanza Sforza, the Contessa di Santa Fiora: "a *zibellino* head bejeweled of two to three thousand *scudi*." (Levi Pisetzky, 104 n. 240)

Note: Although no date is given in this source, the wedding date of February 5, 1576, appears in the De Carné online geneaology at http://a.decarne.free.fr/gencar/dat194.htm (accessed November 27, 2005).

1578, May 19 (Milan)—Inventory of the property of Count Teodoro, known as Giovanni Giacomo Trivulzio, died December 14, 1577:

"A head of a *zibellino* of gold with diamonds and two rubies with four paws and three large pearls, 200 *scudi*." (Venturelli, *Glossario*, 172)

1578, September 19 (Milan)—Inventory of the personal effects of the late Teodoro Trivulzio, sent to and accepted by his wife, the Contessa Ottavia Marliano; among the jewels:

"A head of a *zibellino* of gold with five diamonds and two rubies and four paws with three large pearls, 200 *scudi*." (Venturelli, *Glossario*, 173; Venturelli, *Gioielli*, 138)

Note: This is clearly the same object mentioned in the Count's inventory of May 19, 1578 (above).

1579–80—A document in which Duke Ludwig III of Wüttemberg paid Wolf Mair of Nuremberg, "a jeweler and goldsmith," 500 gulden for a sable head decorated with emeralds, rubies, and diamonds and 625 gulden for another such head also decorated with precious stones. (Schiedlausky, 469)

1584, May 30 (Cesena)—Sumptuary legislation:

> "*Zibellini*, lynx and other entire pelts with the head of gold and silver cannot exceed three *scudi* in value." (Muzzarelli, 356)

1584–85—New Year Gift Roll, Earl of Leicester presents to Elizabeth I:

> "A sable skynne the hedd and fourre feet of gold fully garnished with dyamonds and Rubyes of sundry sortes." (Weiss, 38; Hackenbroch, 407)

1585 (Spain)—From the effects of Isabel of Valois, given to the Infanta Catalina Micaela:

> "a marten's skin, its head holding forty-one diamonds and small ruby eyes." (Muller, 103)

1585 (Munich)—The dowry of Princess of Jacobe von Baden when she wed Prince Johann Wilhelm von Jülich-Cleve-Berg includes five jeweled fur pieces. (Schiedlausky, 470–71)

1586—Inventory of Mary, Queen of Scots:

> "A Martien, the Head and Feet being of gold, and the Neck sett with Diamonds and Rubies.

> "A hermine, with feet and head of gold, the neck and eyes sett with rubies and Diamonds." (Hunt, 156 n. 5a)

1586, February 7 (Florence)—An inventory of jewels of Camilla Martelli consigned to her daughter Virginia:

> "A *zibellino* head in gold which also has three rubies, one diamond, a star of diamonds with six pearls, twenty-three pearls a *quore* [heart?] of diamonds and rubies in the mouth of this head." (Sframeli, 202)

Note: Virginia married Caesare d'Este, Duke of Modena, on February 6, 1586; perhaps there is an association with that event.

1591, August 14 (Florence)—Inventory of jewels and gold of Grand Duke Ferdinando Medici of Tuscany:

> "A *zibellino* head in gold with enamel of many colors and stones in bezels as well as pearls and first around the collar:
> Six emeralds of new stone/rock in table-cut
> Twelve pearls which separate the emeralds in pairs on the bridle/harness that skims the head
> Twelve rubies in low table-cut
> On the head to the point of the nose
> Nine emeralds of new stone and diverse sizes
> Two rubies on the band that goes towards the ears
> On the band on the left side of the head
> Two emeralds of stone in table-cut
> Seven rubies in table-cut
> On the band on the right side
> Two emeralds of new stone in table-cut
> Seven rubies in table-cut
> On the part underneath the throat
> Seven emeralds of bigger size of new stone
> A gold ring enameled in the mouth to which the chain was attached
> Paws of a *zibellino*

Four paws of gold for said *zibellino* with two emeralds and one ruby in table-cut for each"
(Sframeli, 209; abbreviated reference in Hackenbroch, 30)

1594 (Rimini)—Sumptuary legislation:

"The muff of whichever pelt even those forbidden for the garments [above] and covered
with simple silk without any kind of ornaments of gold, silver or silk, but expressly is
forbidden the *zibellino* with gold as well as simple and the same goes for the lynx." (Muzzarelli,
674 n. 26)

1597 (Germany)—Inventory on the death of Princess of Jacobe von Baden lists five jeweled fur
pieces, of which the most splendid, valued at 206 *Reichstaler*, was identical to one mentioned in her
dowry of 1585. (Schiedlausky, 470)

1598, October 12 (Spain)—Inventory following the death of Philip II:

"A head of a marten with four paws; all of matte gold, enameled in white, rose and other
colors, with some fruit; on the head it has fifteen emeralds of diverse styles and sizes, all
table-cut, and on the collar six other emeralds—small square table-cut, all of good color and
greenness and twelve *asientos* of pearls *nectos* and on the whole head twenty-eight small
diamonds of various sizes, square table-cut, and six rubies, bigger than the diamonds; and in
the mouth a ring with a link of gold and in the four paws set in each one of them one emerald
and one ruby and one diamond, next to each other, all square table-cut; the weight of the
aforementioned head and paws ... three ounces and six eighths and a half; in one small box
lined half in white satin and half in crimson, partly gilded, with six latches of brass; with
complete value of one thousand and one hundred and twenty and seven *ducados*." (Sánchez
Cantón, 230; Muller, 103; I am unable to provide a plausible translation for *asientos* or
nectos)

1634—Inventory of Lettice Knollys, Countess of Leicester:

"One sabee, with guilded head and clawes." (Hunt, 156 n. 13)

Note: Hunt suggests that "this may have been an old treasure of the family"; however, it seems
more likely that this object actually belonged to the Countess, who was born about 1541 and died
December 25, 1634. It is interesting to note that Lettice was a cousin to Elizabeth I and in 1578
married Robert Dudley, the Earl of Leicester—who gave Elizabeth a jeweled sable as a New Year
gift, 1584–85 (see entry above).

No date—Inventory of Margherita of Savoy:

"a head of a marten and the four paws where there are many diamonds and lots of rubies
and a clock inside." (Levi Pisetzky, 104 n. 238)

Note: Margherita of Savoy (1589–June 26, 1655) was the daughter of the Infanta Catalina Micaela
(see 1585 entry) and the wife of Francesco III Gonzaga, Duke of Mantua (1586–1612).

REFERENCES

Anderson, Ruth Matilda. *Hispanic Costume: 1480–1530*. New York: Hispanic Society of America,
1979.

Bellonci, Maria. *Lucrezia Borgia: La Sua Vita ei Suoi Tempi*. Milan: A. Mondadori, 1960.

Brown, Clifford Malcolm. "'Una Testa de Platone Antica con la Punta dil Naso di Cera': Unpublished
Negotiations between Isabella d'Este and Niccolo and Giovanni Bellini." *Art Bulletin* 51, no. 41
(December 1969): 372–77.

Brown, Clifford M., and Anna Maria Lorenzoni. *Isabella d'Este and Lorenzo da Pavia: Documents for
the History of Art and Culture in Renaissance Mantua*. Geneva: Librarie Droz, 1982.

Chesne Dauphiné Griffo, Giuliana. "Cronache di moda illustri: Marin Sanudo e le vesti veneziane
tra Quattro e Cinquecento." In *Il Costume Nell'Età del Rinascimento*, ed. Dora Liscia Bemporad,

259–72. Florence: Edifir, 1988.

Cocks, Anna Somers, and Charles Truman. *Renaissance Jewels, Gold Boxes, and Objets de Vertu*. New York: Vendome, 1984.

Distelberger, Rudolf. "Die Sarachi-Werkstatt und Annibale Fontana." *Jahrbuch der Kunsthistorischen Sammlungen in Wien* 71 (1975): 95–164.

Fortunati Pietrantonio, Vera. *Lavinia Fontana, 1552–1614*. Milan: Electa, 1994.

Gozzadini, Giovanni. "Di Alcuni Gioielli Notati in un Libro di Ricordi del Secolo XVI." *Atti e Memorie: Deputazione di Storia Patria per le Provincie di Romagna*, ser. 3, vol. 1 (1883): 1–16.

Hackenbroch, Yvonne. *Renaissance Jewellery*. London: Sotheby, 1979.

Hunt, John. "Jewelled Neck Furs and 'Flohpelze.'" *Pantheon* 21 (May 1963): 150–57.

Levi Pisetzky, Rosita. *Storia del Costume in Italia*, vol. 3. Milan: Istituto Editorale Italiano, 1964.

Marek, George Richard. *The Bed and the Throne: The Life of Isabella d'Este*. New York: Harper & Row, 1976.

The Medici Archive Project, vol. 225, fol. 66, Archivio di Stato di Firenze, Mediceo del Principato, entry 1232; available online at http://www.medici.org/hum/topics/topicreports/Costume andDress_1Page97.html (accessed November 27, 2005).

Muller, Priscilla Elkow. *Jewels in Spain: 1500–1800*. New York: Hispanic Society of America, 1972.

Murphy, Caroline P. *Lavinia Fontana: A Painter and her Patrons in Sixteenth-century Bologna*. New Haven: Yale University Press, 2003.

Muzzarelli, Maria Giuseppina. *La Legislazione Suntuaria: Secoli XIII–XVI: Emilia Romagna*. Rome: Ministero per I Beni e le Attività Cuturali, 2002.

Newton, Stella Mary. *The Dress of the Venetians: 1495–1525*. Aldershot: Scolar Press, 1988.

Pizzagalli, Daniela. *La Signora del Rinascimento: Vita e Splendori di Isabella d'Este alla Corte di Mantova*. Milan: Rizzoli, 2001.

Ricci, Corrado. *Figure e Fantasmi: 64 Incisioni Fuori Testo*. Milan: Ulrico Hoepli, 1931.

Robertson, Joseph, ed. *Inventaires de la Royne Descosse Douairiere de France: Catalogues of the Jewels, Dresses, Furniture, Books, and Paintings of Mary Queen of Scots: 1556–1569*. Edinburgh: Bannatyne Club, 1863.

Sánchez Cantón, F. J. *Inventarios Reales: Bienes Muebles que Pertenecieron a Felipe II*, vol. 1. Madrid: Real Academia de la Historia, 1959.

Schiedlausky, Günther. "Zum Sogenannten Flohpelz." *Pantheon* 30 (November/December 1972): 469–80.

Sframeli, Maria, and Irene Cotta. *I Gioielli dei Medici: Dal Vero e in Ritratto*. Livorno: Sillabe, 2003.

Starkey, David, ed. *The Inventory of King Henry VIII: Society of Antiquaries MS 129 and British Library MS Harley 1419*. London: Harvey Miller, 1998.

Venturelli, Paola. *Gioielli e Gioiellieri Milanesi: Storia, Arte, Moda: 1450–1630*. Milan: Silvana, 1996.

———. *Glossario e Documenti per la Gioielleria Milanese: 1459–1631*. Milan: Nuova Italia, 1999.

Veale, Elspeth M. *The English Fur Trade in the Later Middle Ages*. Oxford: Clarendon Press, 1966.

Victoria and Albert Museum. *Princely Magnificence: Court Jewels of the Renaissance, 1500–1630*. London: Debrett's, 1980.

Weiss, Francis. "Bejewelled Fur Tippets—and the Palatine Fashion." *Costume* 4 (1970): 37–43.

The Matron Goes to the Masque: The Dual Identity of the English Embroidered Jacket

Danielle Nunn-Weinberg

The dawn of the seventeenth century was a time of transition, in art as well as life, from the rigid and stately societal model of the late Elizabethan period to the less formal and more relaxed culture of the Stuart reign. This change is apparent in a group of portraits in which the sitter is wearing a distinctive item of clothing: a highly embellished, embroidered jacket. The depictions of the jackets are stylistically consistent with extant examples, and in one case, a portrait depicts a known surviving garment.[1]

A surprising number of these embroidered upper-body garments (which modern scholars also call bodices or doublets as well as jackets) have survived. The style of these garments is conspicuous and unique to England, with origins in the sixteenth century and the culture revolving around Queen Elizabeth (1558–1603). The jackets became established in their distinct form during the early seventeenth century in the climate of the court of King James I of England (1603–25).

Also surviving are nearly one hundred portraits showing these jackets in wear. Images of women[2] wearing these garments fall into two main categories: the respectable domestic portrait, and the socially significant depiction of the jacket as masque-dress.[3] Participation in the court masque was a coveted social signifier that

I would like to thank the following people for providing advice and encouragement as I researched and wrote this paper: Dr. Michelle Nordtorp-Madson, Dr. Susan V. Webster, Dr. Mireille Lee, Dr. Gale Owen-Crocker, Robin Netherton, the anonymous referee, and Michael Nunn-Weinberg. I am also grateful for the invaluable assistance from Charles Lister of Boughton House and Jennifer Lister of the Museum of London. An abbreviated version of this paper was presented in July 2004 at the International Medieval Congress at Leeds, England.

1 Margaret Laton's jacket and portrait (fig. 8.2); see discussion on pages 160–61.

2 Although some portraits show men wearing embroidered jackets, these are rare; out of nearly one hundred portraits depicting these garments, only four sitters were male. Because the jackets share the same features regardless of the sex of the wearer, these images are included in the following discussion of color and embellishment of the jackets as seen in portraits. However, the male portraits are excluded from the subsequent analysis of the jacket's role in female fashion over time.

3 The masque was a form of amateur entertainment popular at court and among the English nobility during the later sixteenth century and the first half of the seventeenth century. It originally consisted of dancing and acting in a dumb show, the performers being masked and habited in character.

Fig. 8.1: *Elizabeth Vernon,* Countess of Southampton, unknown artist, 1600, Boughton House, Northamptonshire, England. Photo: The Duke of Buccleuch and Queensberry, by permission.

was limited to a very wealthy, privileged few—those fortunate to be in royal favor.

This paper will examine the styles of jackets in the visual renderings along with the extant examples, and will establish a relationship between this type of clothing and the social milieu in which it would have been worn. The portrait of Elizabeth Vernon, Countess of Southampton (fig. 8.1, 1600, artist unknown), belonging to the collection of the Duke of Buccleuch and Queensberry, will be used as a case study for identifying the masque-type portrait. It will be demonstrated that representations of these embroidered jackets in masque situations are signifiers of high status, indicating membership in the inner elite circles around the courts of Queen Elizabeth I and later James I.

IMAGES OF JACKETS AND EXTANT EXAMPLES

The depiction of this item of clothing in visual media appears to be limited to painting. For this study, I identified ninety-six separate paintings that represent embroidered jackets.[4] Portrait miniatures form the largest category of these paintings, with a total of thirty-eight.[5] The next most common type of painting is the full-length portrait, of which there are twenty-four. There are twenty-three half-length and three-quarter-length portraits. Of the remaining paintings, seven are what I will call "pseudo-miniatures," or paintings with a specific *trompe l'oeil* effect: In these artworks, a rectangular or square canvas contains a portrait painted as if it were a miniature, with the oval "window" painted in.[6] The remaining four paintings are best described as portrait busts.

Seventy-nine of the ninety-six jackets are depicted as having a white or very light-colored ground fabric, while seventeen have a colored ground. Unfortunately, many of the paintings were accessible for this analysis only as black-and-white reproductions, so it was not possible to identify the colors used. In a few of these cases, a written description of the colors accompanied the reproductions. For example, one portrait thought to be of Frances Howard, Countess of Essex, is described by Lionel Cust as displaying a purple satin bodice,[7] while a portrait of Elizabeth, Lady Tanfield,

---

4 This number cannot be considered exhaustive. It does include every applicable image on display in several art museums as well as those available in nearly two hundred books pertaining to costuming and associated arts such as embroidery, compilations of paintings by various sixteenth- and seventeenth-century artists, art exhibition catalogues, and published portrait collections.

5 Daphne Foskett defines a miniature as follows: "The size of a miniature may vary from one as small as a thumb nail, to one as large as twelve inches or more, but it may not be larger than can be held in the hand." Foskett, *British Portrait Miniatures* (London: Methuen and Co., 1963), 2.

6 This type of painting, although larger than an actual miniature, is noticeably smaller than the other types of paintings studied for this paper. For example, the Elizabeth Vernon "pseudo-miniature" is less than two feet high by one and one-half feet wide. These depictions also follow miniature-painting conventions in pose and background, further strengthening the association.

7 Lionel Cust, "Marcus Gheeraerts," in *The Annual Volume of the Walpole Society* 3 (1913–14): 33.

Fig. 8.2: Jacket worn by Margaret Laton, c. 1610, altered c. 1620, Victoria and Albert Museum, London (T.228-1994), shown alongside the portrait of Margaret Laton attributed to Marcus Gheeraerts the Younger, 1620-22 (E.214-1994). Photo: Victoria and Albert Museum, by permission.

apparently shows a green bodice embroidered in silver.[8]

Seventy-six of the paintings contain representations of polychrome needle-worked ornamentation. The remaining twenty paintings have monochrome embroidery, although the difficulty remains in discerning which color was used in some of these.[9] In a few of the cases the embroidery was clearly metallic; all-metallic needlework is classified in this study as monochrome, due to the difficulty in distinguishing between depictions of gold, silver, and silver-gilt work.

There are very few surviving garments from this period that can be identified conclusively with portraits. Janet Arnold mentions only three examples from approximately the same time period: Margaret Laton's embroidered jacket of c. 1610 (fig. 8.2), Sir Richard Cotton's slashed satin suit of 1618, and Jane Lambarde's

8 Ibid., 43.
9 For monochrome embroidery of this period, the three most popular colors were black, red, and blue, which contrast well with the white linen usually employed as a ground. Donald King and Santina Levey, *The Victoria & Albert Museum's Textile Collection: Embroidery in Britain from 1200 to 1750* (London: V&A Publications, 1993), 16.

velvet mantle.[10] Arnold describes the precision of the artist's recording of the garments in these cases as "almost photographic in quality."[11] Although this is likely to be the exception rather than the rule for the images studied for this paper, it does give one hope that works attributed to Marcus Gheeraerts the Younger, which include the Jane Lambarde and Margaret Laton portraits, can be held to contain a reasonable degree of veracity and precision. While no evidence of portrait and extant clothing combinations exist for other artists of the time, such as Nicholas Hilliard, Isaac Oliver, and William Larkin, their reputation for quality and fine workmanship allows the possibility that the images bear more than a passing resemblance to any actual garments portrayed.

For this study, I examined seven extant examples of embellished jackets: four at the Victoria and Albert Museum, London (which also has four other jackets in its collection), and three at the Museum of London.[12] In addition to these, I am aware of three jackets at the Gallery of Costume at Platt Hall, Manchester; three at the Museum of Costume, Bath; and one each at the Burrell Collection, Glasgow, the Boston Museum of Fine Art, and the Metropolitan Museum of Art, New York. A jacket at the Ulster Museum in Belfast was destroyed in a 1976 bombing. Certainly other examples have survived; the number in private collections is unknown.[13]

All of the extant jackets examined are constructed of a white or off-white linen,[14]

10 Janet Arnold, "Jane Lambarde's Mantle," *Costume* 14 (1980): 56. The mantle was a foreign fashion that consisted of a rectangle of fabric worn wrapped around the body. References to mantles appear in Queen Elizabeth's wardrobe accounts during the sixteenth century, although the garment seems not to be depicted in women's portraits until after 1600. Jane Lambarde's portrait (which also shows a jacket) is undated, although the Company of Drapers, which owns the portrait, has labeled it as 1620. Arnold discusses evidence for possible dates in the 1620s and 1630s. Based on such details as the neckline shape, sleeve length, and hairstyle, I would propose a dating of the late 1620s.

11 Ibid.

12 One additional jacket at the Museum of London, made of black silk and gold brocade on white fabric, was excluded from this study because it was not embroidered and because it is of a later style, from about the 1640s. Hereafter the Museum of London will be abbreviated as MoL, and the Victoria and Albert Museum as V&A.

13 Images of some of these jackets appear in the following sources: Janet Arnold, *Patterns of Fashion: The Cut and Construction of Clothes for Men and Women c1560–1620* (London: Macmillan, 1985), 51 (jackets from Bath, Glasgow, and a private collection); Janet Arnold, *Queen Elizabeth's Wardrobe Unlock'd* (Leeds, UK: W. S. Maney & Sons, 1988), 144 (one from the V&A); George Wingfield Digby, *Elizabethan Embroidery* (London: Faber and Faber, 1963), 174–77 (the Boston jacket and three from the V&A); Zillah Halls, *Women's Costume 1600–1750* (London: Her Majesty's Stationery Office, 1970), 9–10 (one from the MoL); Avril Hart and Susan North, *Historical Fashion in Detail: the 17th and 18th Centuries* (London: V&A Publications, 1998), 6, 17, 19, 25, 75, 149, 151 (seven from the V&A); Karen Hearn, *Dynasties: Painting in Tudor and Jacobean England 1530–1630* (New York: Rizzoli, 1995), 44 (one from the V&A); Andrew Moore and Christopher Garibaldi, eds., *Flower Power: The Meaning of Flowers in Art* (London: Philip Wilson, 2003) 34, 35 (one from the V&A).

14 Discoloration of the ground textile is more pronounced in some cases, in particular the so-called Falklands jacket at the V&A (T.80-1924) and a jacket from the MoL collection (A 7594). Both of these jackets are embroidered in monochrome black silk. The change in the ground textile could derive from multiple sources, including overexposure to light or a chemical reaction between the linen ground textile and the mordant used to dye the silk; however, an expert would need to be consulted to confirm the cause of the severe discoloration.

with the exception of one that is salmon pink silk laid over coarse white linen.[15] All of the jackets fasten in the front, and nearly all are embellished with silk thread, metal thread, or both, with two exceptions: one jacket embroidered in red wool,[16] and another embroidered in an unknown black fiber.[17] The jackets are very consistent in general cut and construction, with the exception of one A-line garment.[18] The majority of the jackets are constructed in a form-fitting style with triangular gussets inserted at the lower edge to allow the garment to fit smoothly over the hips and skirts. Nearly all of the jackets are constructed with high, round necklines, with or without some sort of collar.[19] It is interesting that (aside from the A-line jacket, which has a V-neckline) the two jackets with lower necklines owe this difference to later alterations.[20] The significance of the neckline height is the fact that all the jackets in

15 The pink silk jacket (V&A 179-1900) was embellished with blue silk couched in a scrolling pattern.

16 This jacket (V&A T.124-1938) is problematic because it was crudely altered at a later date. The embellishment, done in wool, is of the type that would be called "crewel-work."

17 This jacket is part of the MoL collection and has no apparent accession number. Halls states in *Women's Costume* (31) that the jacket is embroidered in black silk; however, I find this unlikely. There is no discoloration of the linen fabric or disintegration of the embroidery, and the black thread lacks the subtle luster of silk. Upon close examination, the thread has a slightly fuzzy and fibrous appearance but is not tightly twisted. The hairy nature of the fiber appears identical to that of V&A T.124-1938, which is known to be worked in wool, suggesting that the thread in the London jacket is wool as well. Microscopic examination of the textile is necessary to confirm the fiber identification.

18 This jacket (V&A CIRC.541-1923) is a creamy white A-line linen garment ornamented with scrolling polychrome silk floral embroidery. The shape of this jacket is unusual, bearing more resemblance to the Elizabeth Vernon portrait than to others such as the Margaret Laton jacket. It is this particular garment that Susan North suggested might have been worn for pregnancy; see Karen Hearn, *Marcus Gheeraerts II: Elizabethan Artist in Focus* (London: Tate Publishing, 2002), 44. However, the center front of the garment is shorter than both the back and sides, which is counterintuitive to accommodating a pregnant belly. The jacket is clearly front-opening; however, it is impossible to determine the original fastening method because modern blue silk ribbon ties have been added.

19 Most of the examples of jackets with collars actually had an unstiffened or very lightly stiffened half-collar. These semicircular collars sit at the back of the neckline and extend only as far as the top shoulder seams. The reason for the use of a half-collar instead of a full collar is unknown at this time, and no scholarly publications consulted in the course of this study address this issue.

20 One of the two garments with lowered necklines is the previously mentioned crewel-work jacket (V&A T.124-1938). The second one (V&A 1359-1900) was displayed at the Sheffield (UK) Millennium Galleries in a 2003 exhibition titled *Flower Power: The Meaning of Flowers in Art*. Although I was unable to examine this jacket up close, it was still very clear that the garment had been altered. The embroidery over most of the garment flowed smoothly over various seams (including the gussets) with no break in the pattern. However, there were insertions under each arm and in the shoulder straps, with an obvious discontinuity in the embroidery pattern, indicating that these were not part of the original jacket design. At the hem, cuffs, and center front opening, it was clear that the embroidery stopped abruptly at the edge of the garment so that no decorative needlework was performed in an area that would not be seen. At the neckline, however, the embroidery continued visibly on the inside of the garment, disappearing into the rolled hem. This indicates that the neckline was lowered after the garment was originally constructed.

their original states were of the high-necked variety typical of one specific type of image, the domestic portrait. These portraits, which depict women wearing these embroidered jackets in a domestic situation, give the viewer an impression of informality, a noticeable change from the formal dress of other portraits from this time period.[21] These "informal" portraits are radically different from both earlier Elizabethan and contemporary portrait conventions.

FOLLOWING FASHION IN PORTRAITURE

Out of the vast numbers of English portraits surviving from the end of the sixteenth century and the beginning of the seventeenth century, a small portion depict women wearing embroidered jackets. However, there are enough to provide a reasonable variety of images from which to derive a stylistic timeline.[22]

The ten portraits showing garments that could be categorized as early versions of the English embroidered jacket were all painted before 1600. The clothing portrayed in these images from the last quarter of the sixteenth century is very stiff and formal, usually containing the following features: low square necklines, elongated bodices, heavy and elaborate jewelry, great French farthingales, exaggerated ruffs, and large bombasted sleeves, also known as trunk-sleeves.[23] The fashionable hairstyles rise tall above the forehead with a French hood in back or with a jeweled headdress of some variety on top. The alternative, more sober style in hairdressing is the lace-edged coif over hair with the volume toward the sides rather than straight up, and usually topped with a hat. These rigid court fashions are in marked contrast to styles that begin to appear in the portraits of around 1600, such as mantles, metallic fringes, and loose, flowing hair.[24]

---

21 Interestingly, authors who discuss these embroidered jackets typically refer to them as informal wear. However, none of them gives a reason for this classification. For examples, see Arnold, *Queen Elizabeth's Wardrobe Unlock'd*, 145, and Jane Ashelford, *The Art of Dress: Clothes and Society 1500–1914* (London: National Trust Enterprises, 1996), 64.

22 When all of the images with an ascribed date were laid out in chronological order, it became obvious that the dates attributed to several of the paintings were incorrect, since distinct trends in clothing and hairstyles were unmistakable. None of the apparently misdated portraits had any concrete date indicators such as a date on the canvas or association with a known event such as a wedding. (Although archaism is always a possibility in portraiture, it was unlikely in the studied examples; in archaized portraits, some details such as hairstyle, hem, waist, or sleeve length typically reflect the artist's contemporary aesthetics and expose the inconsistencies of dating.) Because of their questionable dating, these few images were not included in the following analysis of jacket style development over time. The thirteen images without ascribed dates were also excluded, as were the four male portraits.

23 The French farthingale was a padded roll worn at the hips, under the gown, to extend the skirts away from the body. The ruff was an article of neckwear, often of starched linen, arranged in horizontal flutings and standing out all around the neck. Trunk-sleeves were large and cannon-shaped, tapering from shoulder to wrist.

24 These are all characteristics of English masque-dress, which will be addressed in more detail below.

Fig. 8.3: *Lucy Harrington, Countess of Bedford, as a "Power of Juno" in Ben Jonson's Masque "Hymenaei,"* painting attributed to John de Critz, 1606. Photo: By kind permission of His Grace the Duke of Bedford and the Trustees of the Bedford Estates.

The contemporary court fashions of women's garments, described above, are present in a less ostentatious manner in the 1596 narrative portrait of Sir Henry Unton.[25] What is particularly useful about this image is the fact that it also includes a scene of a masque performance, showing several women wearing the style of masque-dress of that time.[26] Their masque costumes, which include embroidered jackets, bear a striking resemblance to the type of clothing Elizabeth Vernon, Countess of Southampton, wears in her full-length portrait (fig. 8.1), suggesting that the portrait's accepted date of 1600 is probably correct. Also from around 1600, and also showing embroidered jackets in a similar masque-type or allegorical context, are Marcus Gheeraerts' *Lady in Persian Dress*[27] and his *Rainbow Portrait* of Queen Elizabeth,[28] as well as three miniatures of women in obvious masque-dress. These are the only paintings of the studied group dated prior to 1610 in which mantles are worn.

Among the images collected were three nearly identical paintings of a woman in masque costume attributed to John de Critz the Elder and his studio (fig. 8.3).[29] Two of these portraits are clearly labeled as being of Lucy Harrington, Countess of Bedford; the third is almost certainly of the same woman. The image has long been identified as showing Lucy Harrington costumed as a "Power of Juno" in Ben Jonson's 1606 masque *Hymenaei*.[30] Although all three depictions include embroidered jackets, these differ greatly from the other jackets shown in portraits of the time; the jackets in these images are sleeveless, with an open inverted V shape in front.[31] Although these images were of little use in the analysis of the evolution and style of women's embroidered jackets, they were useful for itemizing masque-dress iconography.

One of the first depictions of a lady wearing an embroidered jacket in the style of the extant garments is a 1607 portrait of an unknown lady.[32] She wears a polychrome

25 Artist unknown, National Portrait Gallery, London, catalog no. NPG 710. An online exploration of the scenes in this portrait is available as a link from http://www.mape.org.uk/activities/unton/index.htm (accessed November 27, 2005). This portrait is the only one in the study group to include more than one representation of a jacket. Because the jackets pictured were identical in style, I counted this painting as a single jacket image for the purposes of this study.

26 Jane Ashelford, "Female Masque Dress in Late Sixteenth-Century England," *Costume* 12 (1978): 43. Ashelford makes specific reference to the use of blonde wigs as part of masque dress in the Unton portrait.

27 This painting, also called *Lady in Fancy Dress* or simply *Unknown Lady*, is currently on display in Hampton Court Palace, part of Her Majesty's collection.

28 At Hatfield House, Hertfordshire, England.

29 The portrait in figure 8.3 is in the collection of the Duke of Bedford; one of the others is in the collection of Capt. R. G. W. Berkeley, and the third is in an unnamed private collection.

30 The Countess of Bedford (Lucy Harrington's title) is listed under the "Masquers" section for this masque; see Stephen Orgel and Roy Strong, *Inigo Jones: The theatre of the Stuart Court; including the complete designs for productions at court, for the most part in the collection of the Duke of Devonshire, together with their texts and historical documentation* (Berkeley: University of California Press, 1973), 1:105.

31 There is no apparent evolution of a distinct style of sleeveless embroidered jackets in either the visual record or any extant garment.

32 This anonymous painting, in the collection of the Honorable Michael Astor, is reproduced in Graham Reynolds, *Costume of the Western World: Elizabethan and Jacobean* (London: Harrap, 1951), 175.

embroidered jacket with clearly depicted hip gussets over a full petticoat.[33] Unlike the extant garments, her jacket's neckline is scooped, but filled in by a lace partlet with a rebato-style collar (a kind of stiff collar worn by both sexes from about 1590–1630), the earliest such collar to appear in the group of jacket portraits. Despite the partlet, one can see that the jacket is worn over another dark-colored garment with a higher neckline. The sleeves on her jacket are full-length, though more fitted than the examples from the previous decade. Over her jacket and petticoat she wears a loose gown with hanging sleeves and abundant jewelry.[34] A lace-trimmed, polychrome coif (whose embroidery apparently matches the jacket) is worn over hair arranged in an exaggerated puffed fashion over each ear.

It was during the middle of the second decade of the seventeenth century that these garments reached the apex of their popularity, judging from the frequency of representations. Thirty-four images are dated in the range from 1610–15 inclusive, with the larger portion of these from around 1615. The jacket images from 1610–15 are predominately miniatures. Nearly all of these portraits depict women with low scoop-neckline jackets, the lace edge of their smocks[35] folded over the jacket neckline, their hair loose about their shoulders, a few pieces of jewelry, and a mantle draped over the left arm or shoulder. Only two portraits and one miniature from this period depict women in high-necked jackets. These three exceptions, which also show covered hairstyles, plainly belong to the "domestic women" category of jacket images rather than the masque type, which is where all the others from this period can be placed.

The ten artworks dated from 1616–20 are more varied than those in the previous period, ranging from miniatures to full-length portraits to pseudo-miniatures and half-lengths. During this time, necklines reach their lowest point. Most of the women wear either a loose gown or mantle over their jackets and petticoats and, again, most also have their hair loose or uncovered. The ladies who are depicted wearing the less-revealing garments also have respectable coiffures in one form or another. It is at this time that sleeves become shorter, until they resemble a modern three-quarter-length sleeve more than the earlier trunk-sleeve.

After 1620, the number of jacket images decreases dramatically, with only seven paintings in this group. At this time, the jacket is no longer depicted in miniature portraits. One painting is from the early 1630s (see below). The others are dated to the first half of the 1620s, and in nearly all of these, the waistline is conspicuously raised to an unnatural level. It does not appear as though the garments themselves are cut in that fashion; instead, another garment, usually a petticoat or apron, is worn over the jacket to give the illusion of an elevated waistline. The Margaret Laton jacket and associated portrait (fig. 8.2) provide a perfect example: The portrait,

---

33 The petticoat was a skirt or underskirt, usually richly decorated and intended to be seen.

34 The loose gown, an A-line style, was usually worn as an outer layer, either for warmth, during pregnancy, or for informal housewear. However, when made out of rich textiles and ornamented, it could also be worn at court.

35 The smock, also called a shift or chemise, was the female undergarment, typically of linen.

which is dated 1620–22, displays an elevated waistline. However, the jacket itself, which dates from c. 1610–15, is the customary hip-length garment and is constructed with a normal waistline. All but one of the images from this decade display the features of the domestic portraits of women: covered heads, neckwear of some variety, and a loose gown worn over the ensemble.

There is only one portrait dated to the early 1630s, that of Elizabeth Craven,[36] and the clothing style seems to have changed little from the previous decade. The most notable difference is that the waistline has returned to its normal location and the jacket is again being worn over the top of the skirt. The sleeves are still not full-length, but they are longer than those of the 1615–20 period. The jacket, which has a white or off-white ground with polychrome embroidery, is a high-necked style worn open at the neck so that the red lining is visible, with the smock collar worn folded over it. The hairstyle is the truly different aspect of the painting. For the first time, the hair is worn with small soft curls framing the face rather than swept back. A red ribbon holds the rest of the hair away from her face.

When one looks at the entire period of the representation of these unusual garments in the visual record, the differences between the two types of portrait are easily distinguished. The portraits framed in the domestic sphere span the entire period from the end of the sixteenth century to the early 1630s, while the images in the second genre, which depict the stylized masque-dress of the social elite of the English court, occur within a much shorter time frame. The first clearly recognizable portrayal of the embroidered jackets in masque context appears in 1596 in Sir Henry Unton's narrative portrait, and the end of this socially significant fashion in portraiture occurs by 1620.

THE ROLE OF MASQUES IN THE ENGLISH COURT c. 1600

As the sixteenth century drew to a close, masques, which had been lavishly performed throughout the century, became the most stylish and sumptuous form of entertainment in the English court. According to Arnold, the English masque was inspired by the Italian *intermedi* and the French *ballet de cour*.[37] These court spectacles have been interpreted as allegories in praise of the monarchy, presenting wise and gracious rulers who set to right the confusions and difficulties that lesser beings created.[38] However, this is a superficial view at best. Marion Wynne-Davies discusses the fact that the court entertainments may originally have been designed "to support the status quo, a paean of praise for the monarchy and his or her court," but that in

---

36 This portrait is held in the Powis Castle collection and is reproduced in Ashelford, *The Art of Dress*, 65, fig. 48.

37 Janet Arnold, "Costumes for Masques and Other Entertainments," *Historical Dance: The Journal of the Dolmetsch Historical Dance Society* 3, no. 2 (1993): 11.

38 William Gaunt, *Court Painting in England from Tudor to Victorian Times* (London: Constable and Co., 1980), 62.

actuality they "rarely succumbed to this function."[39]

Despite their frivolous appearance, these theatrical displays played an important role in the Jacobean court, as stated most succinctly by Wynne-Davies:

> The court masque was a collective cultural construct which allowed the women of the court, and specifically the Queen, access to a politically resonant discourse. Their penetration into this exclusively masculine field disrupted the court, for the Queen's masque not only challenged the gendered preserves of authorship but questioned the legitimacy of absolute male power as symbolized by the Stuart King.[40]

Thus, it is through these gaps between the ideal and the actual that the female voice was able to "escape, so that that the tensions in the masque often became those of gender, replete with political as well as sexual signification."[41]

The lavish masques were not simply theatrical spectacles, but were intricately linked to court protocol. In order to maintain the separation between the courtiers and the paid actors, the actors were given all the speaking roles, clearly separating the noble amateurs and the common professionals. By contrast, dancing in the masque was acceptable for a gentleman or lady because dancing was a prerequisite court skill for all lords and ladies. Ben Jonson and Inigo Jones helped to further this division by separating the masque into two parts: the first, called the "anti-masque," was performed by the professional actors and usually represented the corrupt and chaotic world, which would then be overcome by the courtly virtues of the masquers who performed the second part, the "masque."[42]

Many of the great literary talents from the period, including famous authors such as Jonson as well as lesser-known writers such as James Shirley and Samuel Daniel, wrote masques to be performed by royalty and scores of the court's luminaries.[43] In many cases, the major roles were assigned to the various lords and ladies in the actual script.[44]

Because the roles the court elite played were non-speaking parts, the costumes had to speak for the participants.[45] To this end, many masque authors clearly outlined the specifics of the costumes needed for each performance, either through sketches, such as those produced by Inigo Jones, or by written description.

---

39 Marion Wynne-Davies, "The Queen's Masque: Renaissance women and the seventeenth-century court masque," in *Gloriana's Face: Women, Public and Private, in the English Renaissance* (Detroit: Wayne State University Press, 1992), 82.

40 Ibid., 80.

41 Ibid., 82.

42 Arnold, "Costumes for Masques," 11.

43 Ashelford, "Female Masque Dress," 40; David Norbrook, "The Reformation of the Masque," in *The Court Masque*, ed. David Lindley (Manchester: Manchester University Press, 1984), 94, 96.

44 Orgel and Strong, *Inigo Jones*, 1:92. For example, for his *Masque of Blackness*, Ben Jonson enumerates the following ladies and their roles: "The Queen, Countess of Bedford, Lady Herbert, Countess of Derby, Lady Rich, Countess of Suffolk, Lady Bevill, Lady Effingham, Lady Elizabeth Howard, Lady Susan de Vere, Lady Wroth, and Lady Walsingham."

45 Wynne-Davies, "The Queen's Masque," 82.

Jane Ashelford claims that masque-dress was distinguished in part because it bore little relation to the fashionable dress of the time.[46] Arnold, however, directly contradicts this assertion in her discussion of masque-dress in a particular portrait, claiming that "the costume is, in fact, an adaptation of ordinary fashionable dress."[47]

In any case, there is a distinct difference between costumes worn for a masque performance and clothing worn on more pedestrian occasions. Due to the masques' usual staging location in candlelit halls or gardens, effective visibility was of primary consideration.[48] For this reason, the costumes were usually made of metallic textiles, such as tinsel and cloth of silver.[49] Metallic trimmings, such as gold tassels, silver lace, gilt bells, metal-thread embroidery, and fringes of diverse styles were used to reflect the candlelight in an indoor setting, or the sunlight or torchlight used to illuminate a garden setting.[50] The extensive use of metalwork in the costumes would most likely set the masquers apart, maintaining the visual distinction between audience and performer.

These opulent displays were popular because of their scenery and rich costumes, and also because they allowed a select, elite few the opportunity to participate. It is obvious from both the textual sources and the visual record that participation in the masque was exclusive. It was limited to the most favored elite of the court, usually the same small circle of people, such as Lady Arabella Stuart; Lucy Harrington, Countess of Bedford; and Frances Howard, Countess of Essex. These ladies appear in many different portraits wearing masque-dress, and repeatedly have their names entered in the lists of participants for the various masques.[51] The elite nature of the masque is supported by various surviving accounts that enumerate the financial obligations associated with production of a masque, whether hosted by royal or noble personages.[52] Clearly these activities were the province of the wealthy elite only. The broader populace would have been unable to afford to participate in such a production and most likely would have had little contact with this specific form of court theatre except for what they saw in popular plays like those of Shakespeare. Consequently, the embroidered jackets depicted in a masque context could be viewed as symbols of the pinnacle of financial achievement, social success, and popularity.

46 Ashelford, "Female Masque Dress," 40.

47 Arnold, "Costumes for Masques," 12. The portrait referred to is of an unknown lady wearing masque costume by an unknown artist. It is located in the Bristol City Museum and Art Gallery.

48 Ashelford, "Female Masque Dress," 42.

49 Tinsel, or *tynsell*, was made to glitter by the interweaving or brocading of gold or silver metallic thread or by overlaying with a thin coating of gold or silver. Cloth of silver was woven with a warp of colored silk and a weft of silver metallic thread.

50 Ashelford, "Female Masque Dress," 42.

51 Orgel and Strong, *Inigo Jones*, 1:89, 92, 105, 131, 191, 193, 383.

52 Orgel and Strong provide both partial and complete itemized lists of expenses for many of the masques they discuss in *Inigo Jones*. Specifically, they quote a letter from Vincent to Benson: "It cost the King betweene 4. and 5000li to execute the Queen's fancye" (1:89–90). Some other examples can be found on the following pages: 1:105, 122–23, 131, 191–92, 229–30, 277–78, 313–16, 363–64, 369–70, 383–84.

VISUAL SYMBOLISM

Any discussion of masques and the visual language used to represent these court spectacles must address the symbolism used in painted depictions of the masques and their participants. It is also important to enumerate various masque-costuming practices that did not enter mainstream fashion. The English masque traditions were inspired by other cultures, in particular that of Italy. Of particular note is the description of ideal nymphs, laid out by Leone de'Sommi in *Quattro dialoghi in material di rappresentazione sceniche*, written at the Mantua court between 1565 and 1566:

> They should wear feminine *camicie*,[53] embroidered and varied in style but always sleeved. ... They should be girded with coloured silk to make them puff out a little and appear to be very light and airy and they should be short, so that they do not reach the ankle. ... Over their chemise they should wear a sumptuous mantle which passes round one hip and is gathered up on the opposite shoulder. Their coiffure should be blond and, in some cases, allowed to fall over the shoulders with a garland round the head, alternatively it can be held by a golden filet tied across the forehead.[54]

In almost all of the full-length portraits with women in apparent masque-dress, the skirts are ankle-length or shorter and are usually trimmed with a metallic fringe or lace. Stella Mary Newton comments on the masque context of fringe, making reference to various masque and theatrical costumes being "bordered at the hem with gold fringe."[55] Ashelford also cites contemporary descriptions of masque costumes that specifically mention metallic fringe (in particular on the skirts).[56] This feature would scintillate in any light source used in staging masques.

The shortened skirts depicted on the ladies in masque-dress draw attention to the shoes. In almost every case they are elaborate jeweled or embroidered works of art in their own right, usually with large decorative rosettes, which were worn by both men and women in this period.

The jeweled embellishments on the footwear, when visible, were frequently echoed in the sitter's jewelry. Pearls can be seen displayed on clothing and in jewelry in almost every female portrait from the late sixteenth and early seventeenth centuries. Pearls also have a recognizable connection to masque, and are specifically noted in Ben Jonson's description of the costumes for his *Masque of Blackness*:

> The attire of [the] Masquers was alike, in all, without difference: the colours, azure and silver; (their hayre thicke and curled upright in tresses like Pyramids), but returned on the top with a scroll and antique dressing of feathers and jewels interlaced with ropes of pearle. And, for the front, eare, neck, and wrists, the ornament was of the most choise and orient pearle; best setting off from the black.[57]

53 Italian for smock or chemise.
54 Stella Mary Newton, *Renaissance Theatre Costume and the Sense of the Historic Past* (New York: Theatre Arts Books, 1975), 213.
55 Ibid., 224.
56 Ashelford, "Female Masque Dress," 42–43.
57 Arnold, "Costumes for Masques," 11.

One cannot assume the appearance of masque-dress in a portrait simply because a sitter is wearing pearls, as pearls were sought after by every woman. However, depictions that can be labeled as masque costumes because of various other visual symbols will usually show that pearls were worn.

Masque coiffures in portraits typically featured hair worn loose about the shoulders, with or without an elaborate headdress, which could range from a chaplet of flowers to a crown or even a towering arrangement of gilded scrollwork, jewels, and feathers much like Jonson described. These coiffures were markedly different from ordinary hairdressing practices both inside and outside the English court. In portraits of respectable women (and some not so respectable) wearing garments other than embroidered jackets, there are specific and distinct hairstyles and headdresses that were acceptable fashion for any foray outside the home or contact with people other than family members. None of these hairstyles featured hair loose about the shoulders. A large number of the portraits that depict the sitter wearing an embroidered jacket also show the women sporting such fashionable coiffures. However, thirty-seven of the jacket portraits depict women with their hair worn down around their shoulders, and in twelve of these the sitter wears some sort of headdress or ornament. Many of these portraits show other masque-dress features as well.

Another feature common but not restricted to masque-dress was the wearing of a mantle. These large rectangles of rich cloth were worn draped around the body and typically tied at one shoulder. Both the portraits and Inigo Jones' masque-costume drawings depict women wearing these garments in the masque context. Newton notes that the mantle, a frequent fixture in masque and theatrical costuming, served as a shorthand visual reference to "antique" times.[58] The repeated visual representation of women wearing mantles with apparent masque costumes is logical when one considers the fact that many of the court masques whose records survive are set during the classical period.

The background or setting of a portrait can also give the viewer clues to the masque context. Strong tells us: "The garden was a setting for masques and alfresco entertainments, for philosophical contemplation and melancholy meditation."[59] The *Portrait of a Lady of the Hampden Family* (fig. 8.4) serves as an example of the import of the garden setting. The lady wears a hip-length embroidered jacket and an embroidered petticoat with a silver fringe at the hem. The petticoat is folded over and pinned to the French farthingale to form a flounce, below the jacket hem, making the skirt short enough for dancing. Over the jacket and petticoat she wears a peach-colored silk mantle, edged in pearls, silver lace, and silver fringe, and her hair hangs loose about her shoulders, crowned with a jeweled floral chaplet. She is depicted outside on a terrace with palm trees, overlooking a well-ordered Jacobean garden. In all the portraits depicting women wearing embroidered jackets, it is only the ones with distinct masque connotations that portray outdoor scenery and gardens. The depiction of outdoor settings only in portraits portraying masque-dress confirms Strong's association

---

58 Newton, *Renaissance Theatre Costume*, 212.
59 Roy Strong, *The Renaissance Garden in England* (London: Michael Joseph, 1975), 11.

Fig. 8.4: *Portrait of a Lady of the Hampden Family,* unknown artist, early 1600s, Museum of Art, Rhode Island School of Design (No. 42.283, gift of Miss Lucy T. Aldrich). Photo: Museum of Art, Rhode Island School of Design, by permission.

between masques and gardens and is a useful visual signifier of masque-costume.

In contrast to the many images with clear masque connotations and symbolism, there are portraits of women wearing embroidered jackets who are definitely not depicted in masque-dress. The women in these paintings, such as Marcus Gheeraerts' portrait of Mary Throckmorton, Lady Scudamore (fig. 8.5), represent respectable wealthy women. These women are shown with their hair covered by a traditional hat or coif, or arranged in a decorous but stylish hairstyle. Many of these ladies are depicted with a loose gown over their jacket and petticoat, as well as some sort of neckwear such as a ruff or rebato, and in some cases, gloves. All of the high-necked variations of the jacket are represented in this type of portrait, although the height and style of the neckline does change with time, in keeping with fashion. These images all clearly depict the subject indoors, usually with some sort of furniture or other indicator of the somewhat relaxed atmosphere of the household sphere.

It is significant that it is only in this second, domestic type of portrait that multiple figures are recorded. In these cases, the woman wearing an embroidered jacket is accompanied by her children; none of the studied images includes the husband. This multiplicity of sitters stands in direct contrast to the masque genre of portraits, wherein the women are all represented in solitary splendor.

In summary, there are features distinct to each of the two types of portraits depicting the embroidered jackets. The representations of masque-dress can be identified by the presence of most or all of the following signifiers: shortened skirts, elaborate footwear, a low neckline, a wig (especially blonde), hair worn loose about the shoulders with or without a fanciful headdress, a mantle fastened on one shoulder, and an outdoor setting. The portraits set in the domestic sphere contain a number of specific characteristics: a loose gown instead of mantle worn over the jacket, a conservative neckline, hair arranged in a fashionable coiffure, and a setting containing furniture indicating the domestic domain. The domestic portrait can also encompass multiple sitters such as the woman's children, while the portraits with masque imagery focus on a single figure.

ELIZABETH VERNON'S MASQUE COSTUME: A CASE STUDY

The portrait of Elizabeth Vernon, Countess of Southampton (fig. 8.1) is a visually striking image that bears little resemblance to the other jacket portraits in this study. This anomalous image is rife with subtle meaning, much of which, I believe, is conveyed through Elizabeth Vernon's previously unidentified masque-dress. The depiction of Elizabeth clad in masque-dress created a deliberate statement concerning her place in late Elizabethan culture, as well as offering social and political criticism.[60]

60 There is little surviving information about Elizabeth Vernon, the Countess of Southampton. She was born in January of 1573 to Elizabeth Devereux (died 1583) and Sir John Vernon of Hodnet in Shropshire. By the mid-1590s Elizabeth had been orphaned and preferred to the queen's service as a maid of honor by her first cousin, the Earl of Essex. It was in the closed

On first encountering the painting, the viewer immediately registers the sitter's partially dressed state and the intimate dressing-room setting. She stands beside her dressing table, combing her hair, while her pet dog lies on a cushion near her feet. Despite the signs that may suggest boudoir paintings to a modern audience, this image cannot be dismissed as merely a risqué and titillating Elizabethan painting. Even though this is one of the earliest apparent examples of a noble lady deliberately recorded in dishabille as a formal portrait,[61] it is not unique. Isaac Oliver's portrait of Frances Howard, the Countess of Essex,[62] depicts its subject with a gaping embroidered jacket, standing behind a lace-covered table with a jewelry box and a double-ended whisk or bristle brush. The embroidered jackets, the free-flowing locks, the pearl jewelry, and the presence of a table with a jewelry box on it are the only common elements between the two portraits. If the waistline is any indication, the Oliver portrait was painted at least 20 years later than that of Elizabeth Vernon, which was executed c. 1600.

In order to explain the unusual setting of the Elizabeth Vernon portrait, one must begin with Cesare Ripa's *Iconologia*, published in 1593, specifically his image of Pride. Pride, or vanity, is iconographically represented by a richly dressed woman, draped in jewels, primping in front of a mirror.[63] In the Elizabeth Vernon portrait, Elizabeth is combing her hair, and yet there is no visible mirror inside the frame. Instead, she gazes out of the painting in such a way that she makes eye contact with the viewer. This allows the observer to connect with the representation of Elizabeth and act as her "mirror." Although she does not wear an excessive amount of jewelry, there are numerous beautiful and valuable pieces clearly displayed on the table. She wears a richly embroidered jacket and an embroidered petticoat, and she displays a great deal of silver fringe and spangles. She also wears mules (shoes without heels), which are covered in a large number of pearls. A velvet, ermine-lined, jeweled garment is draped on gold-embroidered cushions nearby, above which hangs a ruff and an object composed of gold, jewels, and pearls. Taken as a whole, this painting can easily be understood to represent "pride" or vanity according to Ripa's iconography.

world of the English court that Elizabeth Vernon met Henry Wriothesley, the third Earl of Southampton, one of the queen's favorites and rival to Essex. Southampton immediately fell in love with the "faire Mistress Vernon" and decided to join his fate to Essex's. They became best friends and he subsequently referred to himself as "the other self of his friend." A. L. Rowse and G. B. Harrison, *Queen Elizabeth and Her Subjects* (London: George Allen & Unwin, 1935), 103; Gerald Massey, *The Secret Drama of Shakespeare's Sonnets Unfolded with the Characters Identified* (1872; repr., New York: AMS Press, 1973), 56.

61 This statement deliberately excludes women of the lower classes or of a profession that calls into doubt their morals. This statement also excludes ancient examples such as Greco-Roman figures of Aphrodite/Venus.

62 Given Elizabeth's family relations, it is interesting that the only portrait which at all resembles this one is of Frances, the Countess of Essex. However, I am unable to attach any special significance to this relationship at this time.

63 Cesare Ripa, *Baroque and Rococo Pictorial Imagery: The 1758–60 Hertel Edition of Ripa's 'Iconologia,'* trans. Edward A. Maser (New York: Dover Publications, 1971), 125–26.

Fig. 8.5: *Mary Throckmorton, Lady Scudamore*, Marcus Gheeraerts the Younger, 1615, National Portrait Gallery, London (NPG 64). Photo: National Portrait Gallery, by permission.

Vanitas is an unusual subject for a portrait because of the negative connotations associated with it. I think that the *vanitas* element to this painting was deliberately included by Elizabeth Vernon as social commentary. If one takes into account Elizabeth's banishment and her husband's imprisonment, both of which were a result of the queen's displeasure,[64] as well as the fact that her first cousin, the Earl of Essex, was on trial for treason in 1600, it is easy to see why Elizabeth would be dissatisfied with the political status quo. Therefore, it is quite possible that as a result of these injuries at the hand of the queen, Elizabeth chose the *vanitas* element to make a pointed negative reference to the queen's dominating ego and the fickle vanity of the court. The lack of a mirror in the portrait and her direct gaze that engages the viewer makes the audience part of the *vanitas* element, transferring the social context of the *vanitas* in the portrait to the audience. Nevertheless, this painting is not simply a reminder of the transitory nature of life, but also a portrait of a woman who was firmly entrenched in court life toward the end of Queen Elizabeth's reign.

Moving down the figure, one encounters a modest amount of pearl jewelry. The manner in which the pearls are worn in the Elizabeth Vernon portrait is similar to that depicted in established masque-dress portraits. Another point of interest is the fact that one of the jewels on the table greatly resembles another jewel that is depicted in a portrait that undoubtedly represents a lady in masque-costume: The flame-topped jewel on the dressing table resembles the one worn at the waist of the sitter in the 1606 portrait of Lucy Harrington in Ben Jonson's masque *Hymenaei* (fig. 8.3). The similarity of the jewels in the Elizabeth Vernon and Lucy Harrington portraits strengthens the connection to masque-costume in Elizabeth's portrait.

Elizabeth's jacket, too, is similar to Lucy Harrington's in many respects. Both are low-cut, with the opening at the front forming an inverted V; both have floral embroidery on a white ground, lace at the collar, and fringe at the lower edge. However, Elizabeth's jacket is of a different cut from the garments in other textual and visual representations of the embroidered jackets. First, the jackets are usually portrayed as quite fitted, requiring hip gussets to fit the wearer smoothly over the transition between waist and hip. The jacket in the Elizabeth Vernon portrait is clearly A-line in construction, with no apparent hip gussets.[65] The garment, as it is painted, does not fit the wearer—it does not appear to be large enough to close over the waist and hip area.[66] Another unusual feature of this jacket is the pink ribbon ties, specifically the

64 As Gerald Massey relates in *Secret Drama*, Southampton courted Elizabeth Vernon "with too much familiarity" and she soon became pregnant (58). Southampton and Elizabeth were "most anxious to get married," but the queen resolved that they should not (58). Her Majesty was bitterly opposed to the marriage, and Elizabeth Vernon was compelled to retire from court. The court chamberlain described the situation well: "Mistress Vernon is from the Court and lies at Essex House (at Wanstead, where the Earl of Essex was the fair Elizabeth's companion in disfavor). Some say she hath taken a *venue* under her girdle, and swells upon it; yet she complains not of *foul play*, but says my Lord of Southampton will justify it, and it is bruited underhand that he was lately here four days in great secret of purpose to marry her, and effected it accordingly" (67). Massey's footnote here states that "Mr. Chamberlain uses the word [venue] to signify a hit; the allusion is to being hit below the belt, and is reckoned a blow unfairly given." The lovers were married secretly in 1598, earning the queen's enmity. Her disapproval of the couple's secret marriage was so acute that she had Southampton arrested and sent to the Tower upon his return from an ambassadorial voyage to France and Italy.

65 It resembles to some degree the extant A-line embroidered jacket (V&A CIRC.541-1923).

66 This is most likely a mistake on the part of the artist; however, we have no way of knowing for sure.

row of pink bows running along the underside of the arm. Other portraits, such as that of Lady Dorothy Cary painted by William Larkin around 1615, contain jackets with ribbon ties up the front.[67] However, no other portrait displays the ribbon bows under the arm, adding a fantasy element to the garment. Typically, if a sleeve seam was left open, it was on the front of the arm, so that the wearer could free her arm from the sleeve with ease.

Another unusual feature of this jacket is the dagged hem, edged with a silver spangled fringe.[68] While such portraits as Marcus Gheeraerts' 1611 portrait of Frances Howard, Countess of Hertford, show skirts with dagged hems, none of the other images shows the jacket hem dagged. Newton, in her work on Renaissance theatre costume, makes specific reference to mummer's sleeves being dagged or "trimmed along their length by a serrated fringe."[69] A number of Inigo Jones' masque costumes clearly show dagged hems on various garment layers. In particular, both the Chloris costume from the 1631 masque *Chloris* as well as the Penthesileia and Candace costumes from the 1609 *Masque of Queens* clearly depict fanciful dagging around the hems of the outer layer of torso-covering garments. The use of dagging and the similarity of its placement on the body to the Jones drawings adds to the evidence for a masque context for the Elizabeth Vernon garment.

The fringe on Elizabeth Vernon's jacket and skirt hems is also noteworthy. As described above, glittery metallic fringe was a frequent feature of masque costumes. A number of portraits with clear masque associations, such as Gheeraerts' *Lady in Persian Dress*, clearly show the use of fringe.

The petticoat and transparent apron that Elizabeth wears in her portrait are unexceptional. In every portrait where the skirt can be seen, the petticoat is decorated in some fashion; usually embroidered as well as displaying metallic lace, fringe, spangles, or all of these. However, the shortened skirts of masque costumes are clearly depicted in most of the full-length masque-type portraits, including that of Elizabeth Vernon. The one item of interest concerning her skirts is the presence of lacing points at the waist area of the corset, tying the petticoat and corset layers together, under the apron waistband.[70] These points are rarely seen in women's clothing; they are usually associated with the joining of men's garments at the waist. The significance of this detail is unknown.

Other than Jonson's occasional descriptions, little is mentioned of the correct or ideal shoes for masque-dress. Newton specifically mentions a character's velvet mules.[71] Elizabeth Vernon is wearing an elegant pair of brown mules, decorated all over with pearls.

---

67 The portrait is now part of the Ranger's House collection and is reproduced in Julius Bryant, *London's Country House Collections* (London: Scala Books, 1993), 17.

68 Dagging was a decorative treatment made by cutting a fabric edge into points or other shapes.

69 Newton, *Renaissance Theatre Costume*, 186.

70 Lacing points, which were used to fasten garments, were short ribbons or strings with tips called aiglettes (which facilitate drawing the lacing through eyelet holes).

71 Newton, *Renaissance Theatre Costume*, 225.

Moving away from the figure of Elizabeth Vernon, we come to the other objects in the image. The ruff in itself is not noteworthy since ruffs were common items of dress for both genders. However, this portrait is perhaps unique in that a ruff is depicted, but the sitter is not wearing it. The loop-shaped object of gold, pearls, and jewels hanging from the curtain, beneath the ruff, is an interesting item.[72] By itself, in its limp, out-of-context arrangement, it is difficult to identify. However, after examining images of masque-dress, in particular the drawings of Inigo Jones, it is relatively easy to see that this is a masquer's headdress. Although the airy jeweled headdress does not appear to directly correspond with any particular Jones drawing, it does resemble to a great extent the layered pearl headdress in the British School portrait *Unknown Lady of the Spenser Family*; it also bears a resemblance to the piled Persian headdress in Gheeraerts' *Lady in Persian Dress* and to the headdress in a portrait of Mary Fitton painted in 1600 by an unknown artist.[73] In an undated but clearly later portrait[74] of Elizabeth Vernon, she is depicted wearing a pearl headdress, but no embroidered jacket.

The last noteworthy item in the Elizabeth Vernon portrait is what appears to be an ermine-lined mantle lying on some cushions beneath the ruff and pearl headdress. The combination of red velvet and ermine in a garment, particularly a cloak or mantle, is a clear statement of rank.[75] The inclusion of the classical mantle in its seventeenth-century incarnation completes the list of indicators of masque-dress; it also provides oblique validation for the sitter to be numbered among the elite of England and its court.

Although none of the above-mentioned points of intersection between masque-dress conventions and Elizabeth's portrait are proof of context in themselves, when combined as a whole within the frame of the portrait, the conclusion is inescapable: Elizabeth Vernon is wearing masque-dress, and this fact would have been immediately evident to a contemporary audience. It is no surprise that Elizabeth Vernon, although not mentioned by name in any of the court masques examined in the course of this paper, chose to be portrayed in the symbols of masque-dress.[76] Despite her drastic

---

72 It is difficult to imagine why these items would be hanging from the curtain, unless it was simply the way the artist chose to display them so that they would be recognizable to a contemporary viewer.

73 The *Unknown Lady of the Spenser Family* is pictured in Thomasina Beck, *Gardening with Silk and Gold: A History of Gardens in Embroidery* (Newton Abbot, Devon: David & Charles, 1997), 13; the Mary Fitton portrait appears in Jane Ashelford, *Dress in the Age of Elizabeth I* (New York: Holmes & Meier, 1988), pl. 4. Although neither of these portraits is masque-related, they do support the hypothesis that the pearl object in the Elizabeth Vernon portrait is a headdress.

74 The figure in this portrait is much older than that in the anomalous Elizabeth Vernon portrait and is wearing a style of clothing that does not come into fashion until after the embroidered jacket is no longer depicted.

75 In this period, those of the county rank would wear both red velvet and ermine on ritual court occasions, such as a coronation. This garment's inclusion in the portrait would have been a definite political statement, immediately understood by the contemporary viewer.

76 The absence of any reference to Elizabeth Vernon in the masque lists would be consistent with her apparent striking from court records after her fall from royal favor.

fall from royal favor, it was still important for her to be portrayed as a member of the social and political elite—the "masque set." To the seventeenth-century audience, a rendering of Elizabeth Vernon in masque-costume would have been a visual indicator for wealth, power, and social prestige, proof that she was a member of the "in crowd." In fact, by having herself portrayed as such, after the date of her banishment from court, she symbolically reclaimed her place as a star in the firmament of the English court—even as she made a rather bold and defiant political statement criticizing the vanity of the queen and her court, which was reinforced through her deliberate iconographic choices.

It is clear that the beautifully ornamented women's jacket was a fashionable item of clothing in early seventeenth-century England. This examination of this unusual article of apparel has also shown that the jacket's cultural context elevates it beyond the level of the purely sartorial and imbues it with considerable social significance.

Recent Books of Interest

The Bayeux Tapestry: Embroidering the Facts of History, edited by Pierre Bouet, Brian Levy, and François Neveux (Caen: Presses Universitaires de Caen, 2004). ISBN 2841332136. 426 pages, 219 illustrations (146 in color). Also available in French, ***La Tapisserie de Bayeux: l'art de broder l'histoire***, ISBN 2841331601.

This long-awaited volume of papers from the 1999 Colloquium at Cerisy-la-Salle provides a feast for Bayeux Tapestry scholars. The book is divided into sections titled "Historiography," "The Artefact as Textile," "Medieval Sources and Historical Narrative," "The Bayeux Tapestry as Documentary Evidence," and "The Work of Art." Shirley Ann Brown updates her 1988 bibliography and contributes a frank and lively critical essay on recent (1988–99) publications. The desperately needed results of the technical study of the embroidery carried out over only three months in 1982–83 are, as presented here, both exciting and frustrating. Colour photographs of the back of the embroidery are very welcome, but represent only a selection of the pictures taken in 1982–83. They shed light on the order the work was carried out (stem stitch outline before laid and couched filling); confirm that the inscription and figures were embroidered simultaneously at least in some parts of the Tapestry; and reveal that double stem, chain, double chain, and split stitches were part of the original repertoire (therefore chain stitch was not, as had been thought, confined to restorations). There is a little about many topics: stains from rust and candle wax, repairs, empty stitch holes, seams, insect infestation. The sixteenth-century backing cloth is given an essay in its own right.

MC&T readers will gravitate toward Olivier Renaudeau's essay on the costume in the Tapestry. I find much to argue with here, not least the statement "All the male figures in the Embroidery … wear the same tunic," which the author contradicts almost immediately with reference to "a second type of tunic." It is a fact of Tapestry commentary that different eyes see different things: Renaudeau's interpretation of the stem-stitched lines on tunic skirts as "triangular side-gussets," sometimes decorated, is interesting; his identification of Archbishop Stigand's archiepiscopal pallium conflicts with Barbara English's comment, on the scene of Harold's coronation, "Stigand had no pallium." (I have to side with Renaudeau here, though English's wide-ranging study of coronation regalia is fascinating.)

The contributors generally accept that the Tapestry was made under the patronage of Bishop Odo of Bayeux. Maylis Baylé ("The Bayeux Tapestry and Decoration in

North-Western Europe") accepts a Canterbury origin, while effectively placing the embroidery as a work of art in international context: English, Norse, and Norman. The general consensus points to a date sooner rather than later after 1066; not simply before Odo's imprisonment in 1082, but even before 1068, when William the Conqueror still hoped for reconciliation with the English (Pierre Bouet, "Is the Bayeux Tapestry Pro-English?"). Perhaps work was in progress before Eustace of Boulogne's revolt in the autumn of 1067. The suggestion that the rent which defaces the name commentators have read as E[usta]tius was both deliberate and early (François Neveux, "The Bayeux Tapestry as Original Source"), to eradicate a disgraced former ally from immortality in the Tapestry, is just one of the fascinating insights in this important book. Lavishly illustrated and reasonably priced, it is not to be missed. — *Gale R. Owen-Crocker, Editor*

Chaucer and Clothing: Clerical and Academic Costume in the General Prologue to the Canterbury Tales, by Laura F. Hodges (Cambridge: D. S. Brewer, 2005). ISBN 1843840332. 316 pages, 24 illustrations (8 in color).

Laura Hodges returns to examine the clothing mentioned in Chaucer's *General Prologue*, moving to the religious and academic pilgrims from the secular figures covered in her first book on this topic. Although Hodges' approach is wholly grounded in the literary tradition of costume rhetoric, which is concerned with what clothing signified to the medieval reader or listener, she turns to contemporary resources familiar to the historian of clothing or textiles to analyze and criticize common perceptions about the meaning of the clothing worn by Chaucer's pilgrims.

For example, she argues forcefully in the first two chapters against the traditional view of the clothing and rosary of the Prioress as overly luxurious. The Prioress' pleated veil, often described by scholars as "fluted" (a word not found in Chaucer), is placed into its proper context by comparison with contemporary accounts of acceptable clothing for religious women and depictions of nuns and personifications of the virtue of Prudence in art; her ample cloak and coral and glass rosary receive similar treatments. Hodges concludes that the medieval reader would not have seen the Prioress as lacking religious perfection by her clothing alone, and that the fact that her clothing and her actions are at odds makes her a more complex and interesting character. As another example of Hodges' approach, she argues that the Friar, in his clothing with its concealed knives and revealing cut, clearly represents lechery and a perverse interpretation of the religious statutes concerning dress. Particularly interesting from a textile researcher's standpoint is an examination of the types of woollen cloth, which is used to interpret Chaucer's choice of double worsted for the Friar's too-short clothing.

Hodges also treats clothing worn by the Clerk, the Monk, the Doctour of Phisik, the Summoner, the Pardoner, and the Parson. In all cases, her focus on the contemporary documentary and artistic evidence for the depictions and significance of clothing in the *Prologue* set this book apart from other purely literary studies and lend particular weight to her conclusions regarding how the medieval reader would have perceived Chaucer's religious pilgrims. — *Susan Carroll-Clark, Ontario, Canada*

Clothing Culture, 1350–1650, edited by Catherine Richardson (Aldershot, UK: Ashgate, 2004). ISBN 0754638421. 290 pages, 25 illustrations.

Although the title of this collection promises coverage of topics ranging from 1350 to 1650, all but two of the fifteen papers focus wholly or in large part on the 16th and 17th centuries, perhaps reflecting the editor's own specialty and the inclusion of papers from a 2003 conference on Renaissance studies as well as from the 2001 Clothing Culture conference in Canterbury that originally inspired the collection. As might be anticipated, essays about early modern England dominate the book, but well-placed studies of clothing topics from France, Italy, Russia, and Ireland add geographic breadth to the volume.

Among the best essays is one of those addressing the late medieval period: Joanna Crawford, analyzing the surprisingly flexible practices for bestowing livery in England, argues against the common impression of a "highly static image of medieval clothing culture." Readers interested in this period may also glean some useful tidbits from Sheila Sweetinburgh's analysis of charitable bequests of clothing, which draws on English wills from 1400–1540. Among the essays covering later periods, standouts include Ulrike Ilg's survey of 16th-century costume books and Tessa Storey's discussion of perception and reality of courtesans' wardrobes in Rome.

A sizable proportion of the essays rely on analysis of historical documents, such as wills, court records, and sumptuary laws; their concreteness helps offset the frustrating vagueness of several papers that provide extensive discussions of theory at the expense of any solid conclusions about clothing or its significance. A few papers, focusing on related study areas such as nudity and the body, include so little material on clothing as to appear misplaced in this collection. Richardson's introduction, both an overview and a defense of historical clothing study, offers a convenient summary of the development of the field; however, some unfortunate copyediting errors—notably here, but also throughout the book—impair the usefulness of the extensive bibliographic citations. — *Robin Netherton, Editor*

Glass Beads from Early Anglo-Saxon Graves, by Birte Brugmann (Oxford: Oxbow Books, 2004). ISBN 1842171046. 150 pages, 173 illustrations (113 in color).

This handsome monograph presents the results of a two-year research project covering over 32,000 beads from 106 inhumation sites, divided into nine regions and compared with datable finds from cemeteries in northwest Europe. The project's research questions concern the chronology and possible regional distribution of Anglo-Saxon beads; and the production sources, Anglo-Saxon or continental.

The majority of the beads in the sample were amber (56%), closely followed by glass (43%). Other materials, including metal and natural materials, such as amethyst, constituted only 1%. Glass beads are here categorised by shape (analysed in great detail), decoration, decorative patterns, and colour, all of which are illustrated by a generous selection of colour plates, clear diagrams, and precise descriptive terminology (such as "circumferential overlying crossing waves"). A few of the author's categories ("Traffic light," "Hourglass," "Candy") provide a lighter touch; and the possibility that a Bergh Apton woman made her own beads from green glass fragments, some of which were found in several graves at the cemetery, offers a welcome human perspective. However, this is not, basically, a book about people: It is about the chronology and distribution of artefacts, and it establishes an English terminology for glass beads which will be useful to anyone wishing to describe or discuss them.

Beads are the commonest of Anglo-Saxon grave-finds, yet probably the least exploited for research potential. Although the terms of the research project restricted its coverage, this book goes a considerable way toward remedying the situation. — G. R. O-C.

Medieval Fabrications: Dress, Textiles, Clothwork, and Other Cultural Imaginings, edited by E. Jane Burns (New York: Palgrave Macmillan, 2004). ISBN 1403961867 (hardback), 1403961875 (paperback). 280 pages, 25 illustrations.

In this fascinating and thought-provoking collection of essays, Burns has assembled scholarly voices from the fields of literature, history, art history, and cultural studies for the purposes of better understanding the role and importance of clothing and textiles in the Middle Ages. The interdisciplinary nature of this volume reflects the immense richness and variety inherent in the use of clothing and fashion as keys to comprehending the way medieval societies imagined themselves, as well as how individuals created social identities.

The essays take us from the eleventh century through to the early modern period and cover topics ranging from textile manufacture and importation practices to the analysis of literary and artistic representations of cloth and clothing. Kathryn Starkey, examining fifteenth-century bourgeois slippers decorated with an image from the Tristan tales, explores how courtly symbols of love were appropriated and adapted for consumption by a different social class. Sharon Kinoshita questions the modern assumption of a binary opposition between Christian and Muslim by examining the sericulture of Muslim Spain and how the international style of the twelfth and thirteenth centuries helped to produce a shared Mediterranean culture crossing religious barriers. As the title suggests, the volume focuses on the way in which the materiality of textiles extends into the abstract realm of representation. Andrea Denny-Brown analyzes the dress of Boethius's Philosophy, concluding that it both deepens her allegorical meaning and gives her a material dimension, while Roberta L. Krueger argues for a feminist reading of Griselda's request for a simple chemise as a sartorial sign of her virtue.

Medieval clothing, as Dyan Elliott reminds us, "was meant to mean," and this collection effectively elucidates many ways in which clothing accomplished this in the Middle Ages. — *Monica L. Wright, Middle Tennessee State University*

Northern Archaeological Textiles: NESAT VII: Textile Symposium in Edinburgh, 5th–7th May 1999, edited by Frances Pritchard and John Peter Wild (Oxford: Oxbow Books, 2005). ISBN 1842171623. 138 pages, 112 illustrations.

Since its inception in 1982, the North-European Symposium for Archaeological

Textiles has occupied a unique niche in scholarship, publishing new discoveries of archaeological textiles, revisiting older finds, and examining evidence of tools and manufacture. NESAT VII is the most physically attractive volume so far, a large-format hardback with text in two columns and a generous number of photographs and drawings. It contains twenty-four short papers, five of them in German, the rest in English. They discuss archaeological textiles ranging from the first to the seventeenth centuries, but mostly medieval, in Belgium, the Czech Republic, Denmark, France, Germany, Greenland, Ireland, the Netherlands, Poland, Spain, Sweden, and Switzerland; fleece types and weaving equipment; textile production; and dress fashions. Three papers are associated with a project to produce a wool sail for a reconstruction of an eleventh-century, Norwegian-built ocean-going ship which was sunk at Roskilde Fjord in Denmark. — G. R. O-C.

Was the Bayeux Tapestry Made in France? The Case for Saint-Florent of Saumur, by George Beech (New York: Palgrave Macmillan, 2005). ISBN 1403966702. 142 pages, 24 illustrations.

In this brief study, George Beech sketches the case that the Bayeux Tapestry was produced at the Loire valley abbey of Saint-Florent, and commissioned by William the Conqueror, who then paid the Angevin monastery with substantial land grants in Normandy and England. Beech's thesis is sensational, to say the least, but his execution has the curious effect of methodologically failing at his specific goal while succeeding to make a more general and significant point on the current state of Bayeux Tapestry scholarship.

Working through French charters, chronicles, and art, Beech stakes his claim on five ideas: Saint-Florent was a center for textile production in the late eleventh century; William the Conqueror knew and favored Saint-Florent and its abbot, William of Dol; regional art bears some iconic similarities to the Tapestry; the Tapestry emphasizes William's Breton campaign of 1064 in a way that connects to Abbot William's Breton family; and Baudri of Bourgueil's possible use of the Tapestry in his poem *Adelae comitissae* makes better sense if the Tapestry were produced at Saint-Florent. Regrettably, Beech never produces the material required to make his case compelling. Instead, to make these five points, he adduces, and at times quite questionably interprets, some very meager scraps of documentation (though he also stresses that more may be out there, waiting to be found). In the end, despite explicit attempts to preempt such objections, the evidence for the long-accepted theory of production at Canterbury, with William's half-brother Odo as patron, still remains more substantial and convincing.

The strongest argument here, though, derives from Beech's extended reading of the Tapestry's Breton campaign, and it is here that the book's relevance becomes apparent. None has adequately explained the presence of this long scene, and Beech quite rightly considers that there must be some connection to sources other than simply the English or Norman ones commonly cited in the largely Anglocentric Tapestry scholarship. In the late eleventh century, England, Normandy, and other regions of France underwent a massive cultural cross-fertilization, and the Tapestry no doubt was a product of this process. If Bayeux Tapestry scholars more rigorously follow Beech's call to catalog and assess relevant French documents and art, we stand a much better chance of cracking a few more of this famous textile's mysteries. — *Martin Foys, Hood College*

ALSO PUBLISHED

The Clothed Body in the Ancient World, edited by Liza Cleland, Mary Harlow, and Lloyd Llewellyn-Jones (Oxford: Oxbow Books, 2005). ISBN 1842171658. 192 pages, 46 illustrations.

King Harold II and The Bayeux Tapestry, edited by Gale R. Owen-Crocker (Woodbridge, UK: Boydell, 2005). ISBN 1843831244. 202 pages, 53 illustrations.

Index

Names of countries and English/Irish counties are those currently in use. Figures in italics refer to illustrations